# ROSE ELLIOT
## THE NEW
# VEGETARIAN
## COOKBOOK

# ROSE ELLIOT
## THE NEW
# VEGETARIAN
## COOKBOOK

DOUBLEDAY & COMPANY, INC.
GARDEN CITY, NEW YORK

# ACKNOWLEDGMENTS

Editor Moyra Fraser
Art Editor David Rowley
Photography by James Jackson
Photographic styling by Hilary Guy
Food prepared for photography by Valerie Eames and Janice Murfitt

First published in 1986 by Octopus Books Limited
59 Grosvenor Street, London W1
© Octopus Books Limited 1986

This 1987 edition published in the United States of America
by Doubleday & Company, Inc., 245 Park Avenue, New York
ISBN: 0-385-24153-4
Printed in Hong Kong

Library of Congress Cataloging-in-Publication Data

Elliot, Rose.
  The new vegetarian cookbook.

  Includes index.
  1. Vegetarian cookery.  I. Title.
TX837.E438  1987     641.5′636      87-529

# CONTENTS

Protein, Iron, Fiber and Calcium content are indicated per single serving of each recipe.

**PROTEIN**
Less than 3.9 grammes  ▲
More than 4 but less than 7.9 grammes  ▲▲
More than 8 grammes  ▲▲▲

**IRON**
Less than 2.4 milligrammes  ▲
More than 2.5 but less than 3.9 milligrammes  ▲▲
More than 4 milligrammes  ▲▲▲

**FIBER**
Less than 3.9 grammes  ▲
More than 4 but less than 6.9 grammes  ▲▲
More than 7 grammes  ▲▲▲
Not applicable  △

**CALCIUM**
Less than 109 milligrammes  ▲
More than 110 but less than 209 milligrammes  ▲▲
More than 210 milligrammes  ▲▲▲

**NOTES**
Standard spoon measurements are used in all recipes
All spoon measures are level

Fresh herbs are used unless otherwise stated. If unobtainable, use dry herbs instead but halve
the quantities stated.

# VEGETARIAN KNOW-HOW

Vegetarian food is colorful, healthy and full of flavor. It is prepared from such natural ingredients as fresh fruits and vegetables, nuts, grains, seeds and pulses and flavored with herbs and spices. Vegetarians also use milk, cheese and farm-raised eggs in cooking while stricter vegetarians, or vegans, do not use any animal produce at all. These simple ingredients form the basis of delicious meals, ranging from breakfasts and snacks to formal dinners. The menus and recipes throughout this book show just some of the possibilities – one of the joys of vegetarian cooking is the scope it gives for imagination and creativity!

The fresh, 'whole' ingredients used in vegetarian cooking ensure that this is a healthy way of eating, whether for the occasional meal or as a way of life. These foods can provide all the nutrients needed for good health, including the ones traditionally supplied by meat and fish; there are many healthy vegetarians (and children and grandchildren of vegetarians!) walking around to prove this! It's not difficult to create a vegetarian eating plan that's balanced and which supplies everything you need for health and vitality. It's helpful to know the best foods to choose and the richest sources of nourishment – that's what this chapter is all about!

*The fresh, whole ingredients used in vegetarian cooking ensure that this is a healthy style of eating. Hot Stuffed Avocados (left) is just one of the many colorful and appetizing dishes you will find in The New Vegetarian Cookbook (recipe on page 106).*

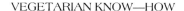

We're always being told that we should eat a 'good, balanced diet'. What this really means is a diet which supplies all the nutrients we need for health in roughly the right proportions. Here's a run-down on what those needs are, and how they can be supplied by a vegetarian diet.

### Protein

Protein is essential for healthy growth and repair of body cells; too little can result in stunted growth and general poor health. Contrary to what many people believe, getting enough protein on a vegetarian diet isn't usually a problem. Our need for protein is quite small; even a very active man only needs 3½ ounces protein a day, whereas most men would find 3 ounces sufficient. Women only need around 2 ounces, except when they're pregnant or breast-feeding, when their needs increase. Of course no foods consist of pure protein; they contain a proportion of protein, along with other nutrients. Cheese, for instance, contains around 25 per cent protein and almonds contain 20.5 per cent, while beef steak contains around 20 per cent, and eggs and oatmeal both contain around 12 per cent.

Protein is, however, quite a complicated substance, because it consists of about twenty-two parts, called amino acids. Of these eight are especially important, because our bodies cannot manufacture them in the same way that others are produced. So we need to eat protein which contains these eight, which are called the essential amino acids. Some foods, such as eggs and oatmeal, contain these in nearly the right proportions for our bodies to use straight-away. Other foods, particularly dry beans and lentils and most cereals, do not have them in such convenient proportions. But this doesn't matter, because during digestion the body mixes up all the amino acids from all the foods eaten at the same meal, and then puts them together again in the right proportions! So, even if a parti-

cular protein isn't exactly the right amino acid 'shape' for your body, you've probably eaten something else along with it – even potato or a green vegetable – that will be able to supply the extra element to make it up.

The main sources of protein for vegetarians are cheese, milk and milk products such as yoghurt; eggs; nuts, such as almonds, cashew nuts, hazelnuts, Brazil nuts, walnuts, pine nuts, pecans and peanuts; seeds, such as sunflower seeds, sesame seeds and pumpkin seeds; pulses, which means all kinds of dry peas, beans and lentils, including soybeans and flour, and milks made from these.

### Carbohydrates and Fiber

Carbohydrate is needed for energy and also for warmth. It is found in sugars and all foods containing sugar, such as honey, jam and fresh and dry fruit; also in starchy foods such as all types of cereals, bread, flour, pasta, potatoes and pulses (which are a source both of protein and carbohydrate).

In their natural state, most sources of carbohydrate also contain plentiful amounts of fiber. Fiber is the cellulose, woods and gums in grains, fruits and vegetables. It is not a nutrient, but it's vital to keep the digestive system functioning smoothly and healthily. (Many diseases of the civilized world, from constipation to cancer of the bowel, and diabetes to varicose veins, can be attributed to lack of fiber in the diet.) Fiber acts as a kind of rationing system, because it has to be chewed, and there's a limit to the amount of chewing anyone can do. This is why high-fiber diets can be helpful for slimmers. Fiber also prevents the sugars being absorbed into the bloodstream too quickly and thus avoids putting a strain on the body. (Straining the body's resources in this way has been linked with the development of diabetes.)

What all this really means is that, from the health point of view, you should take

your carbohydrates in as unrefined a form as possible. Choose whole grain cereals, brown rice, whole wheat bread, flour and pasta. Pulses and all fruits, vegetables, nuts and seeds are high in fiber. As these foods usually feature prominently in a vegetarian diet, a fiber shortage isn't usually a problem!

### Fats

Fats are needed for energy and warmth, and also for the absorption of the fat-soluble vitamins, A, D, E and K. Fats are found in nuts, seeds and also in avocados. They are also contained in milk, cheese, butter, cream and egg yolk and in vegetable oils, and margarine. These fats can be roughly divided, according to their chemical structure, into two groups: saturated fats and unsaturated fats. Animal and dairy fats come into the first category, while most vegetable oils and margarines come into the second group. The unsaturated fats are generally considered to be healthiest, although this is a complicated issue, and there are many experts who consider that the natural quality of butter makes it preferable to margarine, which is a processed food. What most experts do agree on is the need to reduce our overall fat intake. Very little fat is in fact needed for health and most people in developed countries eat too much. Calories from fat often make up about 40 per cent of the total calorie intake, whereas the ideal would be nearer 10 per cent! This is a very difficult level to reach, and would mean rather sparse, unattractive meals which we probably would not want to eat. But most people can cut their fat intake a little, with beneficial results.

It's helpful to look at a typical day's eating and notice where the fat is coming from. Some of it may be 'hidden' in things like cakes, chips, cookies and pastries; or it may be in foods like milk which do not appear to be very high in fat, but which may contribute a fair amount because of the quantity you consume during the day. Having seen where the fat is coming from, the next step is to reduce it where you'll miss it least! Personally, I prefer tea and coffee black, and it's no hardship to me to have a baked potato plain, and little or no butter on bread. But I do like French fries and pastry dishes sometimes, a good olive oil dressing on salads, and some cream or home-made ice cream occasionally. As a general rule, I find it easy to have a fatless or low-fat breakfast and lunch, and then I'm a bit more relaxed about my evening meal.

Your priorities and preferences may well be different from mine, and the great thing is to find a way of eating healthily that's practical and acceptable to you. For instance, many people find they can switch over to a skim or semi-skim milk in place of ordinary milk. It tastes different at first, but after the first few days they hardly notice, and after a couple of weeks, if they go back to ordinary milk they find it tastes too rich and sickly compared to skim milk. Other ways of cutting down on fat are to use skim milk yogurt and low or medium-fat cheeses; baking or broiling rather than frying food; cutting down on the amount of butter you

put on bread; avoiding the 'French fries-with-everything' trap by experimenting with other delicious ways of serving potatoes: boiled, with chopped herbs; baked, with a crunchy skin; or mashed to a smooth cream.

Some of the vegetarian sources of protein such as cheese, nuts and seeds are high in fat but are nevertheless important foods because they are concentrated sources of many essential nutrients and are used in small quantities. About ½ cup nuts or cheese is an average serving, along with cereals, fruit and vegetables which contain little or no fat. (Remember, too, that a vegetarian diet has the advantage of avoiding one major source of saturated fat: meat, and meat products such as salami and sausages.)

### Iron

Iron is needed for making blood and for carrying oxygen in the blood; lack of iron can cause anaemia. With a vegetarian diet, the intake of this mineral should be checked, though it is perfectly possible to get enough. The best vegetarian sources of iron are pulses (especially soybeans and lentils), soy flour, whole grain cereals

## INCREASING YOUR CALCIUM

Include the calcium-rich foods (milk, cheese, yogurt, broccoli, dry figs, sesame seeds and sesame spread) in your meals as often as you can; consider drinking Japanese bancha twig tea as a beverage instead of ordinary tea or coffee. A good way of boosting your calcium intake, if you drink milk and eat milk products, is to fortify milk (ordinary or liquid skim) by beating some powdered skim milk into it. Another way is to make your own bread and add 1 teaspoonful of calcium carbonate to each 4 cups of flour. You could also consider taking calcium tablets (but do remember to check with your doctor if you're pregnant).

(particularly whole wheat bread and millet, which contains the most iron of the grains), nuts and seeds, dark green vegetables and dry fruits (apricots, prunes and prune juice are particularly good sources). Brewer's yeast, molasses, wheat germ and egg yolk are also concentrated sources of iron.

A vegetarian or vegan diet, planned along the lines suggested on page 13, will meet the recommended iron levels. Within each group of foods, the choice is up to you. Your daily diet may consist of several slices of whole wheat bread, a serving of pulses, sprouted pulses or nuts, a couple of servings of cereals such as muesli and rice or pasta, a large baked potato, a little dry fruit and a serving of dark green leafy vegetables plus other fruit and vegetables during the day.

### Calcium

Calcium is needed for healthy bones, skin and teeth and for the function of the heart. The richest sources of calcium are milk, cheese and yoghurt, so it's not difficult for a lacto-vegetarian to obtain enough from these sources. Vegetarians who are not

## INCREASING YOUR IRON

Choose an iron-rich grain such as millet or whole wheat pasta in preference to rice; flaked millet is good added to muesli. Sprinkle wheat germ over your breakfast cereal, salads and fruit salads; add it to main courses, make it into muffins (see page 25) and use it to coat burgers, instead of bread crumbs. Concentrate on the pulses which are highest in iron such as lentils and soybeans, either cooked or sprouted. Have nibbles of almonds (preferably blanched), pumpkin seeds, and dry fruit. Add a little soy flour to your cooking where possible and take the suggested sup-

plement of brewer's yeast each day. You can also boost your iron level by taking some blackstrap molasses daily, off the spoon if you like the flavor, dissolved in milk, or 'diluted' in a little honey. Try drinking prune juice – it is much more palatable than it sounds, especially with a shot of soda water! This is one of the richest sources of iron and you can also moisten your breakfast cereal with it (it's good with muesli), or soak dry fruits in prune juice to make a compote. Bananas, raw spinach, water cress and baked potatoes are other useful sources of iron.

eating much dairy produce (just, say, one cup of milk or ¾ cup yogurt during the day), or vegans (who are not eating any), do need to be sure to include in their diet plenty of non-dairy sources of this mineral. Leafy green vegetables (especially broccoli and cabbage), dry figs and sesame seeds and sesame spread are foods high in calcium. Vegans would be well advised to use a calcium-enriched soy milk to drink and to make yogurt. Japanese bancha twig tea (available from health stores) is another very useful source of calcium. These foods, together with the grains, whole wheat bread, nuts, fruits, pulses and vegetables which make up the day's meals should ensure that needs are met.

### Phosphorus

This is needed, together with calcium, for the formation and good health of teeth and bones. It is present in many foods: milk, eggs, cereals, nuts, fruits and vegetables, so taking in enough of this mineral presents no problems for either vegans or vegetarians.

### Magnesium

Magnesium is needed for healthy bones and teeth, and also for drawing energy from carbohydrate foods. The best sources of magnesium for vegetarians and vegans are almonds, Brazil nuts, wheat germ, peanuts, soy flour, beans, millet and oatmeal. There is also some in dry and fresh fruit, in leafy green vegetables and in whole wheat bread. A balanced diet will therefore probably provide more than the recommended daily level. Heat does not damage magnesium, so fried, broiled and baked vegetables retain their full amount of magnesium; some may, however, be lost from boiled vegetables if you throw away the cooking water.

### Potassium and Sodium

Potassium and sodium together control the fluid balance throughout the organs and tissues of the body. The ratio of potassium to sodium is higher in the muscles, organs and soft tissues of the body, while sodium predominates in the blood plasma and fluids. The better these proportions are maintained, the better our health is likely to be. Both sodium and potassium occur naturally in foods, but we also add sodium to our diet in the form of salt. For this reason, and because the foods rich in potassium are fresh raw fruit and vegetables which do not figure prominently in many people's diet, most people have too much sodium and too little potassium. This means that gradually the proper sodium-potassium balance in their body breaks down and all vital organs, especially the liver and heart, can eventually suffer. A lack of potassium can contribute to tiredness, because it helps in the process of carrying oxygen to the cells.

A vegetarian diet containing fresh fruits and vegetables is usually high in potassium. There is also potassium in wheat germ, pulses and whole grains, so there shouldn't be a problem in getting enough of this mineral.

### B Vitamins

There are thirteen B vitamins and these are grouped together because they're interdependent. They tend to occur together in the same foods and, with the exception of B12, it's not advisable to take a supplement of an individual B vitamin, except under medical supervision, as this can upset the delicate balance.

The B vitamins are another nutrient which vegetarians need to check on because although they occur in many vegetarian foods, the amounts, with one notable exception, are not as concentrated as in some animal sources. The exception is brewer's yeast and also yeast extracts which are made from this. To be on the safe side, I recommend that vegetarians take 2 teaspoons of brewer's yeast (or the equivalent in yeast tablets) each day. If for any reason you are not eating whole wheat bread (which is also a major source of B vitamins), you can make up for this by taking an extra 2 teaspoons of yeast (or the equivalent in yeast tablets). Also base your diet on fruits, vegetables and one or two servings of other grains such as millet, together with regular servings of pulses and a little dairy produce (if you eat this). Best dietary sources of the individual vitamins are as follows:

**Vitamin B1 (Thiamin)** Thiamin is necessary for the release of energy from starches and sugars. A deficiency of this vitamin causes poor appetite and a general lack of well-being. The best sources of thiamin are brewer's yeast, yeast extract, wheat germ, fortified breakfast cereals, Brazil nuts, sunflower seeds and peanuts (raw and roasted, but raw ones contain more thiamin). Oatmeal, millet, brown rice, whole wheat bread, pulses and peas are also good sources, and green vegetables, dry fruits, milk, yogurt and cheese all supply useful amounts. A vegetarian or vegan diet which is planned along the lines suggested in this book should contain more than enough Vitamin B1 (thiamin) to meet the body's needs and so prevent any deficiency.

**Vitamin B2 (Riboflavin)** This vitamin is also needed for the release of energy from food and the absorption of iron. It is necessary for the proper functioning of the brain and resistance to infection. A lack of riboflavin can cause poor appetite and sores at the corners of the mouth and nose. Best sources are brewer's yeast, yeast extract and wheat germ; other good sources are eggs, cheese, milk and milk products, mushrooms, fortified breakfast cereals and chocolate. Millet, whole wheat bread and pasta, prunes, dark green leafy vegetables, peas and beans (dry and fresh), almonds, hazelnuts, sunflower seeds, pumpkin seeds, sesame seeds, walnuts and avocados also contain useful amounts. Other vegetables, oats, and also fresh and dry fruits all contribute to the day's total.

Again, a vegetarian diet planned along the lines suggested in this book should contain adequate amounts of riboflavin. Shortages could occur if you're eating very little dairy produce; vegans, or vegetarians who are only eating small quantities of milk and milk products, need to watch their intake of this vitamin. If you're using a soy milk in place of dairy milk, choose one that is fortified with riboflavin; take brewer's yeast, and make sure that you have one good serving of dark green leafy vegetables, each day. These foods, together with moderate use of whole grains, pulses, nuts, seeds and whole wheat bread, wheat germ (or extra yeast if you're allergic to these, see page 10) and yeast extract, should ensure your diet contains sufficient riboflavin.

**Nicotinic Acid** This has a function similar to riboflavin, and a lack can cause similar symptoms, and sometimes mouth ulcers. Again, it is found in brewer's yeast and yeast extract, wheat germ, whole wheat bread, whole grain cereals, especially millet, and whole wheat pasta, pulses, cheese, avocados, dry apricots, dates and figs, mushrooms, vegetables (especially dark green leafy vegetables and asparagus). Remember too, that it is also contained in almonds, cashew nuts, chestnuts, pine nuts, pecans, walnuts, and pumpkin seeds, and that sesame and sunflower seeds and peanuts are particularly rich in nicotinic acid. By including in your diet regular servings of the foods mentioned, and by taking brewer's yeast as suggested (see page 10), it is perfectly possible to get enough of this vitamin.

**Vitamin B6 (Pyridoxine)** This is needed by the body for breaking down and using protein and for making blood. Lack of B6 can result in irritability, depression, sore mouth, skin and scalp irritation, and may contribute to heart disease and diabetes. Best sources of B6 are brewer's yeast,

yeast extract and wheat germ, whole wheat bread, and whole grains, also fortified breakfast cereals, pulses and sprouted pulses. Nuts, especially chestnuts, Brazil nuts, hazelnuts, peanuts and walnuts are good sources, together with sunflower seeds, which are a particularly rich source. Dark green leafy vegetables, corn, cabbage, avocado and dry and fresh fruits, especially banana and pineapple, all contribute. There is also B6 in eggs, milk and milk products. A diet planned along the lines described on page 13 will meet the requirements for this vitamin. When vegetables are boiled, some of this vitamin is lost in the cooking water, so make sure that you strain off and use the water as stock. You can conserve it by steaming your vegetables or by using just enough water to enable it to be absorbed during cooking.

**Folic Acid** This nutrient works with B12 in the division of cells, and a deficiency may cause a form of anaemia. All foods except fats, sugar and spirits contain some folic acid, but for vegetarians, the richest sources are brewer's yeast, yeast extract and wheat germ. It is also contained in whole wheat bread and grains, most

vegetables (especially dark green leafy ones, asparagus and sprouted pulses), also fruits, especially oranges and bananas. Nuts, especially walnuts and almonds, and pumpkin seeds, are good sources, while cheese, milk and eggs also contribute.

Folic acid is sensitive to heat and light and 50-90 per cent of the folic acid in vegetables can be destroyed by cooking. So serve plenty of salads (if you like them); stir-fry or cook vegetables carefully for as short a time as possible in the smallest quantity of water, and keep the water for use in soups and sauces. Some brewer's yeast and wheat germ each day, together with the grains, fresh vegetables, pulses, fruits and nuts which make up a balanced vegetarian or vegan diet, will ensure sufficient amounts of this vitamin.

**Vitamin B12** This is needed for similar functions to B1, B2 and nicotinic acid, and also for bone marrow. Lack can cause pernicious anaemia. The major source of B12 for most people is meat and dairy produce; B12 is almost entirely absent from plants. So this is a vitamin which vegetarians, and especially vegans, need to watch. Vegetarians can get some B12 from eggs and dairy produce, and most yeast

---

## VEGETARIAN/VEGAN SOURCES OF VITAMIN B12

**Recommended daily requirements:**
Average man: 6µg (micrograms); average woman: 6µg; pregnant and breast-feeding women: 8µg; child 2-6µg; depending on age

| Food | Amount | µg of B12 |
|---|---|---|
| soy milk (fortified with B12) | 1 cup | 4.07* |
| egg | 1 | 0.39 |
| low-fat yogurt | 1 cup | 1.28 |
| low-fat milk | 1 cup plus 2 tablespoons | 3.0 |
| evaporated milk | 1 cup plus 2 tablespoons | 0.61 |
| hard cheese | ⅓ cup | 0.8 |
| fortified breakfast cereal | ⅓ cup | 0.5 |

* this varies between brands, so check the one you use

extracts. Some breakfast cereals and soy milks are fortified with this vitamin. If you are eating a balanced vegetarian diet which includes some milk, cheese and eggs, together with frequent use of fortified yeast extracts, you are probably getting enough, but you might like to check your intake using the following tables, and consider taking a vitamin supplement if your intake is on the low side.

### Vitamin C

This vitamin is important for resistance to infection and is needed for the absorption of iron, for tissue repair and normal growth. Vitamin C is present in many fresh fruits and vegetables, but it is easily lost through contact with air, heat and water. However, a normal vegetarian or vegan diet with its richness in fruit and vegetables, is unlikely to be lacking in vitamin C. A small glass (½ cup) of orange juice supplies daily needs, and raw cabbage, cauliflower, water cress and tomatoes are other good sources. Cooked cabbage and potatoes also contain useful amounts of this vitamin.

### Vitamin A

Vitamin A is essential for the proper functioning of the eyes and the mucous membranes throughout the body; it is also needed for growth and resistance to infection. Lack of vitamin A increases the risk of infections in the throat, eyes and skin, and also lowers resistance to bronchitis. Vitamin A is found in butter, eggs, cheese and fortified margarines, fortified skim milk and fortified evaporated milk. The body can make this vitamin from a substance called carotene which is found in carrots, apricots and dark green leafy vegetables. These are, therefore, excellent sources of vitamin A; ⅔ cup chopped carrots, for instance, will supply more than the day's requirements. A normal vegetarian or vegan diet is not likely to be short of this vitamin.

## VEGETARIAN/VEGAN SOURCES OF VITAMIN D

**Daily requirements:**
Average man: 2.5µg; average woman: 2.5µg; pregnant and breast-feeding woman: 10µg; child 1-4 years 10µg, 4+ years 2.5µg

| Food | Amount | µg Vitamin D |
| --- | --- | --- |
| butter | 2 tablespoons | 0.42 |
| margarine | 2 tablespoons | 2.24 |
| low-fat cottage cheese (not packed) | 1¼ cup | 0.06 |
| low-fat yogurt | 1 cup | 0.045 |
| low-fat milk | 1 cup plus 2 tablespoons | 0.11 |
| evaporated milk | 1 cup plus 2 tablespoons | 6.52 |
| hard cheese | ⅓ cup | 0.08 |
| egg | 1 | 0.75 |
| fortified breakfast cereal | ⅓ cup | 0.84 |

### Vitamin D

The body needs vitamin D in order to use calcium efficiently. This vitamin is present in few foods and with the exception of margarine and some breakfast cereals (which are fortified with vitamin D) these are all animal products. The richest source is cod liver oil which is obviously unsuitable for vegetarians. It is also present in eggs, butter, milk (including evaporated but not necessarily in skim milk – read the label), cheese, yogurt and cottage cheese. Vitamin D is also formed by the action of sunlight on the skin, but unless you live in a very sunny part of the world and do a lot of sunbathing, it's best not to rely on this source. People with dark skins cannot absorb vitamin D from sunshine, and so they can become deficient in this vitamin. Many experts recommend a daily vitamin D supplement for everyone, whether vegetarian or not, and I think this is sensible advice, especially for young children and elderly people. But if you are taking any general vitamin tablets, check whether these contain vitamin D before adding extra to your diet; and if you're taking a vitamin D supplement, be careful to measure the dose precisely as excessive vitamin D is toxic. Vegetarian and vegan sources of vitamin D are given above, and it is easy to check whether your normal diet is supplying enough to meet the recommended levels.

### Vitamin E

This vitamin improves general vitality and is important for the functioning of the heart. It may help to avoid hardening of the arteries and high blood pressure. It is also said to increase fertility, help prevent varicose veins and improve the body's ability to heal itself. (It is also a natural antioxidant. Its presence in unrefined oil helps prevent rancidity). The best sources of vitamin E are wheat germ and cold-pressed vegetable oils (see page 139), especially corn, safflower and wheat germ oil; it is also present in almonds, peanuts and Brazil nuts. Eggs, butter, cheese, whole wheat flour and bread, oats, rice and millet are quite good sources, as are apples, bananas, cantaloupe melon, orange and grapefruit. A vegetarian diet, with its regular use of whole grains, nuts and seeds, is unlikely to be short of this vitamin.

### Vitamin K

This is necessary for blood clotting and to prevent excessive loss of blood after injury. It can be manufactured by the intestinal bacteria, but this process is upset when these are damaged through taking antibiotics. Taking live yogurt afterwards will help encourage the intestinal bacteria to get back to normal. Vitamin K is found in leafy green vegetables, tomatoes, soybean oil, egg yolks and seaweed. A daily serving of leafy green vegetables will make sure that you have an adequate amount of this vitamin.

### Trace Elements

**Zinc** is a trace element which is vitally important in the formation of DNA and RDA (the hereditary material of all cells). A shortage of zinc is often indicated by white flecks on the finger nails, also skin problems such as eczema and acne. It is therefore very important to make sure your diet contains enough foods which provide this trace element. One of the richest sources for vegetarians is wheat germ, though it is not known how much of the zinc present is in a form which the body can use. Other good sources are brewer's yeast, whole wheat bread and other grains, nuts and seeds, especially pumpkin seeds. Pulses, cooked or sprouted; green leafy vegetables, especially spinach; also corn, peas, mushrooms, fresh asparagus and mango all contain zinc. Cheese, milk and yogurt can also supply useful amounts and a vegetarian diet containing some milk and cheese will probably meet the requirements. If you're vegan, you'd be wise to watch this trace element. Use a good quality soy milk which contains zinc, and make sure you're including regular daily servings of the foods mentioned above in your diet.

**Manganese** is another vitally important trace element. Best sources are whole wheat bread, wheat germ, almonds, Brazil nuts, cashew nuts, peanuts and walnuts. Dry figs, dates, peaches and apricots are also good sources, and brewer's yeast supplies some. Potatoes, bananas, fresh fruit and vegetables generally also contain manganese. A vegetarian or vegan diet planned along the lines suggested should not be deficient in this mineral.

**Iodine** is necessary for the proper functioning of the thyroid gland. The main sources are sea foods (including seaweeds and thus vegetarian jelling agents such as agar agar and gelozone, see page 139), sea salt and iodized table salt. So, for vegetarians and vegans, an excellent way of making sure you're getting enough of this trace element is to use sea salt or an iodized salt, to use agar agar or gelozone for making jellies, to add a little seaweed to stocks or to crumble or snip it over salads and vegetable stir-fries. Alternatively, you can take kelp (a kind of seaweed) tablets regularly.

## Planning Healthy Meals

If you've read this far and you're feeling a bit confused by all the dietary requirements and the various possible sources, I don't blame you! It can be simplified, though, if you break the foods down into a basic eating plan. If you eat according to this, you can be fairly sure of getting all your nutrients.

### Basic Eating Plan

Each day try to include the following:
**Group 1:** *Calcium-rich protein foods: at least one serving*
milk, cheese, yogurt, sesame seeds (and sesame spread and tahini)
**Group 2:** *Other protein foods; at least two servings*
eggs, nuts, seeds, pulses
**Group 3:** *Bread, cereals and potatoes: at least two or three servings*
whole wheat bread, whole wheat flour and products made from it, oats, brown rice, millet, barley and other grains, pasta, couscous, whole wheat crackers, potatoes
**Group 4:** *Fresh fruit and vegetables: at least one good serving, but the more the better*
all kinds, but especially a daily serving of dark green leafy vegetables if possible, and also carrots.
**In addition,** take some brewer's yeast plus yeast extracts, wheat germ and some dry fruits. Use of sea salt or an iodized table salt or regular use of seaweeds and seaweed jelling agents is also important, and take B12 and vitamin D supplements if needed (see pages 11-12).

Vegans, or vegetarians who do not wish to eat the dairy calcium-rich protein foods, need to find two other good sources of calcium each day in addition to the sesame seeds. These could include a good serving of broccoli, beet greens, spinach or kale, a tablespoonful of molasses, a serving of tofu (bean curd), a few dry figs, and drinking Japanese bancha twig tea. Alternatively, consider making your own bread and adding calcium carbonate, or taking a calcium supplement obtainable from health stores.

### Menu Planning

These basic foods make an excellent framework for planning meals, and you can adapt the plan according to your personal tastes and life-style. For instance, you might have one of your cereal servings at breakfast, in the form of breakfast cereal or muesli, with some milk, a sprinkling of wheat germ, and perhaps a few nuts and dry fruits; you might follow this with toast. For lunch you may choose a salad sandwich and a yoghurt, getting in a further serving of cereals (in the bread) and a calcium-rich protein serving (the yogurt). If you drink 1½-2 cups of milk during the day (on cereal or in tea and coffee) that, too, can count as a calcium-rich protein serving, as can Japanese bancha twig tea taken as a beverage throughout the day.

· VEGETARIAN KNOW—HOW ·

## A WEEK'S VEGETARIAN MENUS

Includes 1½-2 cups milk or fortified soy milk for drinks etc.
BREAKFASTS can be as given, or you may wish to have the same favorite one everyday.

| Breakfast | Lunch | Evening Meal |
|---|---|---|
| **SUNDAY** | | |
| *Banana Muesli | *Chilled Beet Soup with | *Crunchy Cabbage and |
| Whole wheat bread and | *Warm Herb Bread | Apple Salad |
| honey | *Tasty Nut Roast | Cheese |
| | *Pear and Ginger Pie | Fresh fruit |
| **MONDAY** | | |
| Hunza Apricots with | Salad sandwiches | *Cheese-topped Bell |
| Yoghurt | Dates and nuts | Peppers with carrots |
| Almonds | | and broccoli |
| | | *Blackberry Fool |
| **TUESDAY** | | |
| Oatmeal with raisins | *Greek Salad | *Spaghetti with Lentil |
| Whole wheat toast | Orange or apple | Bolognese Sauce |
| | | Fresh fruit |
| **WEDNESDAY** | | |
| Grated apple, yogurt and | Whole wheat pita bread | *Quick Pizza |
| wheat germ | filled with salad | *Lettuce and Fresh Herb |
| | Nuts and raisins | Salad |
| | | *Yogurt Knickerboker |
| | | Glory |
| **THURSDAY** | | |
| *Fruit Muesli | *Deep-dish Salad Bowl | *Vegetable Gratin |
| Banana or a few grapes | Piece of fresh fruit | *Crunchy Cabbage and |
| Nuts and raisins | | Apple Salad |
| | | *Apple and Raisin Compote |
| **FRIDAY** | | |
| Whole wheat cereal with | Baked potato with | *Stir-fried Vegetables |
| nuts and raisins | water cress and tomato | with Nutballs |
| Toast | | *Apricot Fool |
| **SATURDAY** | | |
| Fresh orange and | *Vegetable Soup with | *Garlic Mushrooms with |
| grapefruit segments | Nori | French Bread |
| *Wheat germ, Honey and | Pears | *Spinach Lasagne |
| Raisin Muffins | | Green Salad |
| | | *Lucky Dip Basket |

*see index for recipe page numbers.

Your evening meal could be an omelet and spinach, baked beans on toast, Tasty Nut Roast and vegetables or Spaghetti with Lentil Bolognese Sauce, followed by a piece of fresh fruit. The only thing you might be lacking with this scheme could be your dark green leafy vegetables (except with the omelet and spinach suggestion). So you could serve broccoli with the nut roast, or a salad made from water cress or shredded raw spinach with your baked beans or lentil Bolognese; or you might include these salad ingredients (and perhaps some grated carrot, too) with your lunch. There are plenty of possibilities. The important thing is to end up with meals which *you* like! Here is a suggestion for a week's menus, using recipes in this book.

## The Vegetarian Diet and Special needs

### Pregnancy

A vegetarian or vegan diet, planned along the lines suggested, will supply you with the basic nutrients you need for health and vitality. If you're improving your health in preparation for becoming pregnant in the future, it's best to use some form of contraception other than the pill, as this is known to affect the body's ability to metabolize vitamin B6, B2, B12 and folic acid, also zinc, copper and iron. Make sure your intake of vitamins D and B12 is adequate (see pages 11-12) – take supplements if necessary.

Carefully check your levels of the other B vitamins and be sure to take the daily dietary supplement of brewer's yeast or the equivalent in yeast tablets. Make sure you're getting enough vitamin E and iron, and include the zinc-rich foods, such as pumpkin seeds, fresh mango, corn, almonds, asparagus and sprouted pulses, in your menus as often as possible. Use sea-vegetables or seaweed-based jelling agents whenever you can (see pages 137-

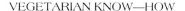
138) for iodine and other trace minerals, or take kelp tablets two or three times a week.

### Daily Requirements

During pregnancy and breastfeeding, your daily nutrient requirements increase considerably. More iron, folic acid, all the other B vitamins, and vitamins A, C, D and E are needed. Your calcium requirement also increases by around 50 per cent. An easy way to ensure you're getting enough of the very valuable and important B vitamins is to take an extra 3 teaspoons of brewer's yeast each day. This will then take care of the extra thiamin, riboflavin, nicotinic acid, B6 and folic acid needed during both pregnancy and lactation, while adding only 46 calories; this gives some useful iron, zinc and a little calcium and magnesium, too. A normal vegetarian diet provides enough vitamin E to allow for the extra requirement, though you could make sure by using cold-pressed corn oil (a rich source) for salad dressings. Both vegetarian and vegan diets are naturally rich in vitamins A and C, but you can make sure that you're taking in sufficient by having an extra orange or half cup of orange juice, a large banana, a piece of melon, or an extra serving of green vegetables.

The additional calcium requirement is most easily met by taking an extra 2 cups of skim milk or calcium-fortified soy milk, or a generous cup of yogurt, or ½ cup hard cheese, or by fortifying your ordinary day's supply of milk by beating 2 tablespoons powdered milk into it. If you take the additional brewer's yeast and the milk or soy milk, banana or orange, this will more than cover your increased phosphorus requirements, and contribute towards your magnesium. A few dates, a couple of dry figs, a few raisins and nuts, or a piece of whole wheat bread will easily make up the rest. Or you could cover your magnesium need

completely by having 2 extra tablespoons of wheat germ, which also contributes extra zinc; the extra milk or plant milk and the banana or orange juice supply zinc too. You will need to boost this level even more when you're breast-feeding, so try and include some other rich sources each day, such as pumpkin seeds, soy sprouts, Brazil nuts and, budget permitting, asparagus or fresh mango. These foods also increase both your iron intake and your protein, bringing them up to the recommended levels.

### Healthy Snacks

These extras can of course be added to the suggested meals, or they can be taken in the form of snacks, which is often more helpful when you're pregnant.

One of the best ways to take the brewer's yeast is as a soothing, sustaining drink. To make this, blend a cup of milk with two tablespoons yogurt, the yeast and a banana. The rest of the yogurt can be made into a kind of muesli with the wheat germ, some raisins, chopped dates or figs, a few pumpkin seeds or almonds, perhaps a chopped apple. If you feel like extra snacks during the day, try whole wheat toast and yeast extract, peanut butter or honey; nibble pumpkin seeds, raisins, dates, fresh peaches or mango. Another delicious and irresistible snack, if you feel like something sweet but healthy, is the frozen nutty carob bananas (see page 82); try coating them in wheat germ as well as the nuts suggested.

### Babies

A baby can be weaned on to a vegetarian diet quite easily. First of all, when the baby is 6 weeks old, you can give a little fresh, unsweetened orange or apple juice, diluted half-and-half with boiled, cooled water. Choose a pure juice without additives (except for vitamin C, in the case of apple juice). Give this fruit juice, from a teaspoon at first, in the middle of the morning or afternoon. As soon as the baby

gets used to taking it in this way, try giving it from a cup. Apart from this, continue with breast or bottle feeds in the normal way.

### Introducing Solids

Next, when the baby is 6 months old (or 4 months, if the baby no longer seems to be fully satisfied with milk, but not before this) you can give the first taste of solid food. Start with half a teaspoonful of a fruit or vegetable purée. Try puréed carrot, apple or pear, mashed ripe banana or avocado, very finely grated raw apple or pear, puréed ripe peach, mango or mashed potato. The first spoonfuls are really just to get the baby used to the taste and feel of solid food; they're not a real source of nourishment at this stage as the baby still needs milk feeds and the emotional satisfaction of sucking. Give this taste before one of the main feeds corresponding to breakfast, lunch or the evening meal, whichever is the most convenient, and follow with a milk feed as usual.

As the baby gets used to the flavor you can gradually increase the quantity so that, after a few weeks, your baby is having perhaps 2 tablespoonfuls of food at a time. This gradual increase is to enable the baby's digestive system to get used to coping with solid food. From 6 months onwards, a little crustless bread can be mashed into vegetable purées. For some babies, the bran in 100 per cent whole wheat bread may act as a laxative; if you find this to be the case, try an 81-85 per cent or wheatmeal type, preferably with added wheat germ for extra iron.

As the baby takes more solid food, the demand for milk will decrease. The baby will suck for a shorter time and, at around 8 months, eventually give up one milk feed entirely. You can then begin enriching the fruit and vegetable purées with vegetarian protein ingredients. Any of the following can be added: cooked lentils, mashed cooked beans, mashed drained tofu (bean curd), tahini, peanut butter, low-sodium yeast extract, wheat germ, brewer's yeast, finely grated nuts and seeds, cottage cheese, low-fat white cheeses such as quark, grated hard cheese, 'live' plain yogurt, egg yolk (stir into a hot vegetable purée, it will cook in the heat).

Once the baby is taking these solids happily, you can give an enriched vegetable purée as a main course, followed by a fruit purée or yogurt, or a cereal-based mixture as a 'dessert'. You can also begin introducing solids before the other main feeds of the day, so that, eventually, feeds which correspond to breakfast, lunch and the evening meal are composed entirely of solids. You will gradually be able to drop first one milk feed and then another, so that by the time the baby is around 9 months, the bedtime milk feed may be the only one left. Do not be in a hurry to wean the baby from the bliss of this; it may no longer be vital for nourishment, but it is important for the closeness to you and the emotional satisfaction which the sucking gives.

### Finger Foods

At this stage, particularly if the baby is teething, you can introduce some 'finger foods': a piece of apple, bread or rusk, but never leave a baby alone with food like this because of the danger of choking.

Quite soon you will find that the baby will quite easily and naturally eat a little of what you, as a family, are having. Just watch that the baby's portion isn't too highly seasoned, or salted. Try to avoid foods which contain preservatives, coloring and other additives, refined sugar, and those which are high in fat, such as pastry or deep-fried foods. Also watch the level of fiber which the baby is eating. As a vegetarian diet is naturally high in fiber, it's important for the baby to have some concentrated sources of nourishment each day, such as egg, cheese, yogurt, powdered nuts, yeast and yeast extract (low-sodium), and tahini.

### Tots and Teens

A vegetarian diet planned along the lines suggested can certainly meet the needs of growing children. It is important, however, to make sure that the children are getting enough nutrients. Deficiencies could result in listlessness, poor appetite, unhealthy skin, poor healing of cuts and broken bones, cracks and sores around the mouth, mouth ulcers and poor growth.

### HOW TO MEET THE NUTRITIONAL NEEDS OF CHILDREN

| 7-8-year-old child — quantities gradually increasing to | 15-17-year-old boy or girl |
| --- | --- |
| 2 cup milk or soybean milk or equivalent in cheese, yogurt etc | 2 cup milk or soybean milk or equivalent in cheese, yogurt etc |
| 1/3 cup vitamin-enriched breakfast cereal or the equivalent described below | Good serving fortified breakfast cereal or 1/2 cup rolled oats (as oatmeal or in muesli base) |
| 2 good slices of whole wheat bread | at least 4 good slices whole wheat bread |
| 1/3 cup of orange juice or a medium-sized orange | 1/2 cup of orange juice or 1 orange |
| 1 serving whole grain cereal such as brown rice, whole wheat pasta, or potato or more whole wheat bread | 1 serving whole grain cereal such as brown rice, whole wheat pasta, or potato or more whole wheat bread |
| a few nuts and/or pumpkin seeds, especially almonds and peanuts | a few nuts and/or pumpkin seeds, especially almonds and peanuts |
| 2 servings of protein foods: choose from more nuts or peanut butter, cheese, eggs, and cooked pulses such as lentils, kidney beans, baked beans | 2 servings of protein foods: choose from more nuts or peanut butter, cheese, eggs, and cooked pulses such as lentils, kidney beans, baked beans |
| 1 teaspoon brewer's yeast or equivalent in yeast pills | 1 heaped teaspoon brewer's yeast or equivalent in yeast pills |
| 1 teaspoon wheat germ | 1 heaped teaspoon wheat germ |
| 1 serving dry fruit | 1 serving dry fruit |
| 1 serving leafy green vegetables | 1 serving leafy green vegetables |
| vitamin D and B12 supplements | vitamin D and B12 supplements |
| use of iodized salt | use of iodized salt |
| frequent use of yeast extract | frequent use of yeast extract |
| plus other fresh fruits and vegetables as desired | plus other fresh fruits and vegetables as desired |

PLUS fruits, vegetables, dairy produce, as required
PLUS B12, vitamin D and iodine supplement as necessary

The easiest way to meet the calcium needs of children and a good percentage of B vitamins, too, is to see that they drink 2 cups of milk a day. If they are vegan (and therefore not eating any dairy produce) they should be sure to drink a soy milk which is fortified with calcium and riboflavin. Milk (or soy milk) can of course be taken in forms other than as a straight drink. Serve as yogurt (flavored and lightly sweetened if necessary), on breakfast cereals, as popsicles, frothy milk shakes, home-made ice cream or puddings, cheese sauce, cottage cheese (perhaps as a snack, in celery sticks or as a dip with carrot strips), and cheese (perhaps in sandwiches or in cubes, with apple).

Fortified breakfast cereals can be a good idea because of the B vitamins and iron which they contain. Other important foods for children are whole wheat bread and whole grain cereals such as brown rice, pulses, Brazil nuts, almonds, peanuts and peanut butter, sesame seeds and sesame spread, sunflower seeds, pumpkin seeds, dry fruit, leafy green vegetables (if possible!), raw or cooked carrots, eggs, yeast extract and wheat germ. Also important are potatoes, bananas, mushrooms, peas and lima beans. Baked beans are a nutritious food, especially if they're served on whole wheat toast. As with adults, brewer's yeast is an excellent source of nutrients and children should be encouraged to take some (or some yeast tablets) each day. Teenage girls can sometimes be short of iron, so it's important for them to concentrate on the iron-rich foods described on page 9. In addition, vitamin B12 and vitamin D supplements are recommended for all children (see page 16).

### Slimming on a Vegetarian Diet
A vegetarian diet is not necessarily more nor less 'slimming' than a meat one. It depends which foods you choose to eat! There are many approaches to slimming, but the key to success is to find the one which suits you and your life-style, and which you can keep to, with slight adaptations, once you have reached your desired weight.

When counting calories, aim for between 1,000 and 1,500 a day, as this is a proven way of losing weight steadily. However, there are also other approaches which work (by naturally limiting your calorie intake without the need for calculations). One way is to eat normal meals but to cut down on the amount of fat and sugar you are eating. Stop putting sugar in tea and coffee – this becomes much easier after the first few days – and change ordinary milk for skim milk. Be very sparing in the amount of butter or margarine you use in cooking or at the table, while increasing your intake of fresh fruit and vegetables.

Another way of losing weight without counting calories is to eat only fruit for breakfast. For lunch have more fruit or a bowl of home-made vegetable soup, a salad or a baked potato (with only a little butter or margarine). In the evening prepare a small portion of a protein-rich main course with plenty of lightly-cooked vegetables (but no potatoes) followed by an apple, orange or pear. Have sunflower seeds for 'nibbles' if you're hungry, and take a double dose of brewer's yeast tablets each day, to make up for the B vitamins which you might be lacking through not eating many cereal foods. On the whole, I think it's a mistake to eat 'slimmers'' foods when you're slimming; these immediately make you feel deprived and give the feeling that slimming is something apart from normal eating. I think it's much better to eat small portions of normal foods, backed up with plenty of fresh vegetables. Then when you reach your desired weight, you can just increase the amount of these normal foods. Make sure you keep slim by keeping breakfast and lunch very simple (as a general rule) but be more relaxed about the evening meal. Do take a bit more exercise, weigh yourself regularly (or try on a slim-fitting pair of pants!) and get rid of the odd extra pound or two while it's a relatively easy job and not a major campaign!

### Later in Life
As we get older we need fewer calories (unless we're still very active), but we still need protein for the repair of cells and tissues. It's also important to continue to get sufficient vitamins, especially vitamins A and C to fight infection, the B vitamins for the nervous system and general health, and vitamin D for healthy bones. Many older people are short of vitamin D, especially if they are not getting out into the sunshine very often. So check your vitamin D level against the table on page 12 and take a supplement if necessary, or take an all-round vitamin tablet which includes this vitamin.

Nutrients need to be in a form that's easy to eat. Concentrated sources of protein, minerals and vitamins such as brewer's yeast, yeast extract, tahini, wheat germ and nuts are particularly valuable. Milk is an important and useful food because it's nourishing and easy to eat together with cheese and eggs. Try fortifying your milk as described on page 9, for extra calcium. Eat the concentrated foods with fruits, vegetables and whole wheat bread to make sure you're getting enough fiber. If you find it difficult to chew salads, make warming vegetable soups such as those on pages 43-46; sprinkle these with grated cheese or finely-grated nuts or sunflower seeds. Have some unsweetened fruit juice each day to make up your vitamin C. A baked potato makes a nourishing meal which is both easy to make and eat.

Nitritional values of foods throughout this chapter taken from *The Composition of Foods*, R. A. McCance and E. M. Widdowson, and *Nutrition Almanac*, Nutrition Search, Inc.

# BREAKFASTS AND BRUNCHES

Few aromas can compare with the delicious early morning fragrances of toast and freshly-brewed coffee. Breakfast can be a delightful meal, especially a vegetarian breakfast! If you stop to think about it, you'll probably find that you often eat a vegetarian-style breakfast anyway. So if you want to change over to the vegetarian way of eating, this can be a good meal to start with. There are plenty of foods to choose from, and you may find, as many people do, that 'going vegetarian' at breakfast actually means they eat in a more varied and interesting way than before.

You can choose from the whole range of cereals, including muesli mixes, granola and cereal dishes such as oatmeal. These can be sweetened with dry fruits, honey, maple syrup or dark brown moist sugar and topped with different kinds of nuts, chopped or grated, sunflower or pumpkin seeds and wheat germ. Or you can feast on any kind of fresh fruit, either on its own (what could be nicer than a ripe peach, or bowl of fresh cherries?) or served with creamy yogurt. Make a compote of mixed fruits and honey, or mix the original real muesli, with fresh fruit, oats and nuts. If 'just a piece of toast' is more your line, you can try the recipe on page 20 for home-made bread or make oatcakes, whole wheat, date and cinnamon scones or wheat germ, raisin and honey muffins, for a change.

*A delicious feast to start the day. Left to right: warm slices of Quick and Easy Bread; Mango Compote; Banana Muesli (recipes on pages 20-21).*

## A SIMPLE BREAKFAST
*Serves 4*

*Banana Muesli*

*Quick and Easy Bread*

*Mango Compote*

## BANANA MUESLI

The oats give this muesli a natural creaminess, and this is increased if you can leave them to soak overnight in the water. If you also soak the sunflower seeds, they will begin to germinate, adding extra health-giving enzymes to put a spring into your step!

**Ingredients**
*1⅓ cup rolled oats*
*⅔ cup sunflower seeds*
*1¾ cup water*
*2 tablespoons honey*
*2 large bananas, peeled and sliced*
*½ pound black grapes, halved and seeded*
*grated peel of 1 large well-scrubbed orange and 1 large well-scrubbed lemon*
*⅓ cup sliced almonds, toasted*

Put the rolled oats and sunflower seeds into a bowl with the water; leave to soak overnight if possible. Mix well until creamy, and add the honey, bananas, grapes and orange and lemon peel, stirring so that the fruit is thoroughly incorporated. Spoon into a large serving bowl or four small ones and sprinkle with toasted sliced almonds.

**Protein** ▲▲      **Iron** ▲▲
**Fiber** ▲▲      **Calcium** ▲

## QUICK AND EASY BREAD

This is a quick bread to make, and adding the ascorbic acid speeds it up even more because the ascorbic acid helps to accelerate fermentation. The finished bread has a light, moist, open texture.

You do need to use real 100 per cent whole wheat flour for this recipe as it doesn't work properly with other types of flour. For a wholesome, country look you can sprinkle the loaves with whole wheat grains (from health stores) before baking them.

**Ingredients**
*4 cup 100 per cent whole wheat flour*
*2 level teaspoons salt*
*2 packets quick acting instant dry yeast*
*25 mg tablet ascorbic acid (vitamin C) (optional)*
*1 tablespoon honey or molasses*
*about 1½ cup tepid water*

Grease two 8×5×3½ inch bread pans thoroughly with butter. Put the flour, salt and yeast into a large bowl. Crush the ascorbic acid tablet, then mix it with the honey or molasses and the water; stir well, then add this to the flour. Mix well to make a dough that is just too soft to knead. Divide the dough in half and place one half in each pan. Cover the pans loosely with oiled plastic wrap and leave in a warm place – or on the kitchen work top – until the dough has risen by one-third. This will take 30-45 minutes, depending on the temperature. Fifteen minutes or so before the dough is ready, heat the oven to 450°. Bake the bread for 35 minutes. Turn the loaves out of their pans and put them on a wire rack to cool.
Makes two 1 pound loaves.

**Protein** ▲      **Iron** ▲
**Fiber** ▲      **Calcium** ▲

## MANGO COMPOTE

Mangoes are a particularly good source of zinc and make a delicious breakfast treat.

**Ingredients**
*4 large ripe mangoes, halved, peeled and pits removed*
*⅔ cup water*

Cut the mango flesh into large even-sized pieces. Put half a cupful of these into the food processor or blender with the water and blend until very smooth. Put the remaining mango into a glass serving bowl. Add the puréed mango, which provides a thick sauce, stir well to coat evenly. Serve chilled.

**Protein** ▲      **Iron** ▲
**Fiber** ▲      **Calcium** ▲

### QUICK START IDEAS
★ flaked millet covered with grape, raisin or prune juice and soaked overnight, with sliced banana added next day. This breakfast would be very high in iron
★ sliced ripe peaches or nectarines or orange segments, or halved and seeded grapes with thick plain yogurt
★ couscous soaked as described for flaked millet
★ sliced banana in fresh orange juice
★ raisins in coconut cream: put some raisins into a bowl, cover with boiling water and add 2 tablespoons creamed coconut cut into small pieces or grated. Stir until the creamed coconut has completely dissolved. Serve warm or cold, with a sprinkling of cinnamon, chopped nuts or wheat germ
★ fresh strawberris or cherries, when in season

## BREAKFAST EXTRAS
### Serves 4

*Hunza Apricots with
Thick Yogurt*

*Basic Muesli Mix*

*Dry Fruit Compote*

*Oatmeal*

*Homemade Yogurt*

*Breakfast Pancakes*

## HUNZA APRICOTS WITH THICK YOGURT

These are whole wild apricots which are dried without preservatives and are therefore brown in color instead of orange. They have a wonderful flavor and a natural sweetness – really delicious!

**Ingredients**
*1½ cup Hunza apricots, washed
water to cover*
**To serve**
*1 cup thick plain yogurt, Greek or
homemade (see page 22)*

Put the apricots into a medium-sized saucepan and cover generously with water. Leave to soak for a couple of hours if possible (or, even better, overnight). Then simmer the fruit over a gentle heat, un-covered, until the fruit is very tender and the liquid has reduced to a syrup. Serve hot or cold, with the yogurt.

**Protein** ▲▲    **Iron** ▲▲
**Fiber** ▲▲▲    **Calcium** ▲▲

## BASIC MUESLI MIX

If you like homemade muesli, it can save time to make up a bulk supply of mixture. Here is a basic recipe; you can vary the ingredients according to taste.

**Ingredients**
*2⅔ cup rolled oats
⅔ cup raisins
1⅓ cup mixed chopped Brazil nuts and
sunflower seeds*

Put all the ingredients into a bowl and mix together. Store in an airtight jar or plastic container. To use, simply add milk or water to the required amount. You can eat it as it is, or add other ingredients to your taste: see HINTS FOR HEALTH AND FLAVOR.
Makes 7-8 servings

**Protein** ▲▲    **Iron** ▲
**Fiber** ▲▲    **Calcium** ▲

## DRY FRUIT COMPOTE

This compote is made from the dry fruit mixture which you can buy at health stores; alternatively, you could buy your favorite fruits separately and make your own mix.

Serve it hot or cold; I think it is best cold, with some thick Greek yogurt and a sprinkling of grated hazelnuts or toasted sliced almonds. Or try some 'spiced yogurt'. Stir a little honey and a pinch of cinnamon into thick, plain yogurt.

## HINTS FOR HEALTH AND FLAVOR

Dry fruits such as raisins, dates and chopped dry apricots, wheat germ, nuts and seeds, either whole, chopped or grated, make delicious additions to a bowl of breakfast cereal or muesli and are an excellent source of many valuable nutrients. They can be stored in small containers or jars (such as clean coffee jars) ready for use at breakfast time. Pumpkin seeds are an excellent source of iron and zinc; almonds, too, are rich in iron.

The dry fruits, with their natural sweetness, can be used as a healthy sugar replacement, or add sliced sweet fresh fruit, such as banana, ripe pear or grapes; honey, too, makes a delicious sweetener for some cereals. If you want to add sugar, try the really dark brown molasses sugar which contains some iron and other trace elements (unlike other sugars).

As a change fom cow's milk, try soybean milk, or make your own delicious nut milk, by blending a generous ⅓ cup cashew nuts or almonds with ⅔ cup water.

**Ingredients**
*1¼ cup mixed dry fruit such as apricots
peaches, pears and prunes
piece of pared orange or lemon peel*

Put the dry fruit and orange or lemon peel into a medium-sized saucepan and cover generously with water. Leave to soak for a couple of hours if possible (or, even better, overnight). Simmer the fruit over a gentle heat, uncovered, until the fruit is tender and the liquid syrupy.

**Protein** ▲▲    **Iron** ▲▲
**Fiber** ▲▲▲    **Calcium** ▲▲

## OATMEAL

A bowl of steaming hot oatmeal makes a delicious, and very healthy, start to the day.

**Ingredients**
*⅔ cup rolled oats*
*1¼ cup water*
*pinch of salt*

Put the oats and water into a saucepan with the salt. Stir over a medium heat for about 2 minutes, until the oatmeal is thickened and smooth. If the oatmeal is too thick, add more water. Serve immediately with the topping of your choice: see TOPPINGS FOR OATMEAL.

**Protein** ▲▲          **Iron** ▲
**Fiber** ▲▲          **Calcium** ▲

## HOMEMADE YOGURT

Yogurt is easy to make at home. Make sure that the yogurt you use for the 'starter' is really 'live': read the label carefully, or go to the health store.

**Ingredients**
*2½ cup fresh skim milk*
*4 tablespoons powdered skim milk*
*1 tablespoon plain live yogurt*

Put the milk into a saucepan and bring to the boil, then remove from the heat and cool to tepid. Then put in the powdered skim milk and yogurt, and beat to make sure it's all well blended. Scald a bowl or jar with boiling water to sterilize and warm it, then pour in the yogurt mixture. Cover the container with a piece of foil, then wrap it in a towel, to help keep the heat in.

## HOT AND APPETIZING

From the health point of view, an uncooked, low-fat breakfast based on fruits and/or cereals, or oatmeal, is best, but there are times when something hot and appetizing may be just what you would like for a change. Here are some ideas:

★ mushrooms lightly fried in a little butter or margarine and served on whole wheat toast
★ peeled, sliced tomatoes on whole wheat toast, broiled, with or without a sprinkling of sunflower seeds or grated hazelnuts; or the toast can first be spread with sesame spread or peanut butter
★ sliced avocado on whole wheat toast, warmed through under the broil
★ baked potato with sour cream and grated cheese
★ parsley potato cakes with mushrooms and broiled tomatoes
★ omelet
★ boiled, poached or scrambled eggs with whole wheat toast
★ whole wheat toast topped with grated cheese, melted under the broil
★ baked beans on toast

Place the mixture in a warm (but not too hot) place. Then leave the yogurt undisturbed for 5-8 hours, until it has set. If you then put it into the refrigerator, it will firm up even more. Save a tablespoon of this batch of yogurt to start off your next one, and you can go on making yogurt in this way for a while. You will find that the next few batches will get thicker and better each time, but after a while you may get a batch that's a bit on the 'thin' side, and then you'll need to buy a new carton to start you off again.

**Protein** ▲▲          **Iron** ▲
**Fiber** △          **Calcium** ▲▲▲

### TOPPINGS FOR OATMEAL
★ maple syrup
★ dark brown moist sugar
★ molasses
★ a little cream
★ chopped or grated nuts
★ sliced banana
★ raisins or chopped dates
★ sprinkling of cinnamon, ground ginger or grated nutmeg
★ thick Greek yogurt

## BREAKFAST PANCAKES

**Ingredients**
**For the pancakes**
*1 cup whole wheat flour*
*½ teaspoon salt*
*2 eggs*
*1¼ cup skim milk*
*2 tablespoons melted butter or margarine*
*extra butter for frying*

Put all the ingredients into a good processor or blender and blend until smooth; or put the flour and salt into a bowl, mix in the egg, then gradually beat in the milk and melted butter. Heat 1 tablespoon butter in a small skillet and when it sizzles, pour off the excess, so that the skillet is just lightly greased. Keep the skillet over a high heat, then pour in two tablespoons of butter, and tip the skillet so that the butter runs all over the base. Cook the pancake until it is set on top and golden brown underneath, then flip the pancake over and cook the other side. Serve at once.

**Protein** ▲          **Iron** ▲
**Fiber** ▲          **Calcium** ▲

## FRUIT MUESLI

This refreshing recipe is based on the original muesli, a light fruit dish, invented by Dr. Bircher-Benner in Zurich at the end of the last century. Dr. Bircher-Benner used sweetened condensed milk (because cow's milk was not considered safe in those days) and you could use this if you prefer, instead of the yogurt and honey.

**Ingredients**
*6 tablespoons thick plain yogurt*
*6 tablespoons rolled oats*
*6 medium-sized ripe pears, chopped*
*6 tablespoons chopped or grated hazelnuts or almonds*
*honey to taste*

Put the yogurt into a bowl and mix until smooth. Add the oats and chopped pears and stir well. If the mixture seems too stiff, stir in a little water. Add honey to taste, then spoon into a serving bowl and sprinkle the nuts on top.

***Protein*** ▲▲      ***Iron*** ▲
***Fiber*** ▲▲      ***Calcium*** ▲▲

## CREAMY POTATO BAKE

This creamy potato dish is wonderful for a special treat once in a while, especially when served as the 'main course' of the meal, as in this brunch menu.

**Ingredients**
*2 tablespoons butter or margarine*
*1½ pounds potatoes, peeled and sliced as thinly as possible*
*salt and freshly ground black pepper*
*a little freshly grated nutmeg (optional)*
*1 garlic clove, crushed*
*4-6 tablespoons heavy cream*

Preheat the oven to 325°. Grease a shallow casserole generously with half the butter or margarine. Put the potato slices into a colander and rinse well under cold water; drain and pat dry on paper towels. Arrange the potato slices in the prepared casserole in layers, putting a seasoning of salt, pepper and grated nutmeg (if using) and a touch of crushed garlic between each layer. Spoon the cream evenly over the top and dot with the rest of the butter. Bake, uncovered, for 1½-2 hours, or until the potatoes are cooked, with a golden brown crust on top of the dish.

***Protein*** ▲      ***Iron*** ▲
***Fiber*** ▲      ***Calcium*** ▲

## BROILED BASIL TOMATOES

These tomatoes can be broiled, or cooked in the oven with the potato bake.

**Ingredients**
*6 medium-sized tomatoes, halved across*
*salt and freshly ground black pepper*
*1 tablespoon butter or margarine*
*2 teaspoons chopped fresh basil*

Put the tomatoes, cut side up, in a lightly greased shallow casserole. Sprinkle with salt and pepper. Divide the butter or margarine between the tomatoes, putting a small piece on top of each, and finally scatter a little chopped basil on top. The tomatoes may be broiled for 10-15 minutes, until soft but still holding their shape; or bake them in the top of the oven with the potato bake, as described, for about 15-20 minutes.

***Protein*** ▲      ***Iron*** ▲
***Fiber*** ▲      ***Calcium*** ▲

## OATCAKES

Homemade oatcakes are delicious and easy to make. Make sure the oatmeal is really fresh, with no hint of a stale smell.

**Ingredients**
*2⅔ cup oatmeal*
*1 teaspoon salt*
*1 tablespoon butter or margarine*
*scant 1 cup tepid water*
*extra oatmeal for rolling*

Preheat the oven to 350°. Put the oatmeal and salt into a bowl and rub in the butter or margarine. Add the water, mix, then leave for 5-10 minutes for the oatmeal to absorb the water. Gather the mixture together and put it on a board that has been sprinkled with oatmeal. Roll out the mixture to a depth of about ⅛ inch, using plenty of oatmeal to prevent sticking. Then cut into rounds using a 3 inch round cookie cutter. Place these on an ungreased cookie sheet and bake for 15 minutes, then turn the oatcakes over and bake for a further 5 minutes. Cool on a wire rack.
Makes 20-22

***Protein*** ▲▲      ***Iron*** ▲
***Fiber*** ▲      ***Calcium*** ▲

### REFRESHING SUMMER BRUNCH
*Serves 4*

*Orange and Grapefruit Refresher with Mint Sherbet*

*Fruit Feast*

*Wheat germ
Honey and Raisin Muffins*

This light, refreshing brunch with the emphasis on fruit makes a perfect start to the day, especially if you're feeling jaded, with that 'morning after' feeling. And if you've been celebrating, and want to continue the festive feeling, Buck's Fizz – one part freshly squeezed orange juice with two parts non-vintage Champagne – makes the ideal accompaniment, along with clear China or herb tea, or black decaffeinated coffee. The mint sherbet for the grapefruit and orange refresher needs to be made the night before, and it's also helpful to measure out the ingredients for the muffins and put them into a bowl ready for mixing. The rest of the meal can be put together quite quickly in the morning.

## ORANGE AND GRAPEFRUIT REFRESHER WITH MINT SHERBET

**Ingredients**
*2 large grapefruits*
*2 large oranges*
*a little honey*
**For the mint sherbet**
*2 tablespoons honey*
*⅔ cup water*
*2 tablespoons finely chopped mint*

**To serve**
*4 sprigs of mint*

First make the sherbet. Mix together the honey, water and mint, then pour into a shallow container and freeze until the mixture is half solid. Break up the mixture with a fork, then freeze until firm.

With a small, serrated knife, and holding the fruit over a bowl, cut all the skin and pith from the grapefruits and oranges. Cut the segments from between the pieces of skin. Sweeten with honey to taste, then divide the fruit between four bowls. Put a spoonful of sherbet on each, decorate with mint, and serve immediately.

Protein    Iron
Fiber    Calcium

## FRUIT FEAST

**Ingredients**
*3 ripe peaches, pits removed and flesh sliced*
*3 sweet apples, cored and diced*
*½ pound black or green grapes, halved and seeded*
*½ pound strawberries, hulled and halved or quartered*
*⅔ cup orange juice*
**For the topping**
*1 cup low-fat soft white cheese*
*⅔ cup milk*
*1 teaspoon honey*
**To finish**
*⅓ cup sliced almonds, toasted*

Put all the fruit into a large bowl, add the orange juice and mix gently. Spoon this mixture on to a large flat serving plate. Put the soft white cheese into a bowl and mix

*Left to right: Wheat germ, Honey and Raisin Muffins; Orange and Grapefruit Refresher with Mint Sherbet; Fruit Feast with a creamy, honey topping.*

with a fork until creamy, then gradually blend in the milk and honey to make a thick, smooth consistency. Spoon this over so that some of the fruits show prettily round the edges, then sprinkle the almonds on top. Serve with the warm muffins.

Protein    Iron
Fiber     Calcium

## WHEAT GERM, HONEY AND RAISIN MUFFINS

These muffins contain the goodness of wheat germ and raisins and are quick and easy to make. They're delicious served warm from the oven with the fruit feast salad, or as a healthy snack.

**Ingredients**
*2 cup wheat germ*
*2 teaspoons baking powder*
*pinch of salt*
*½ cup raisins*
*4 tablespoons honey*
*½ stick butter or margarine, melted*
*2 small eggs*
*about 6 tablespoons milk*

Preheat the oven to 350°. Grease a muffin pan with butter. Put the wheat germ, baking powder, salt and raisins into a bowl, then add the honey, butter or margarine and eggs. Mix until blended, then stir in enough milk to make a fairly soft mixture which drops heavily from the spoon when you shake it. Put heaped tablespoons of the mixture into the muffin pan, dividing the mixture between twelve sections. Bake for 15-20 minutes, until the muffins have puffed up and feel firm to a light touch. Serve warm.
Makes 12

Protein      Iron
Fiber     Calcium

## SIMPLE AND DELICIOUS
### Serves 4

*Chilled Tomatoes and Horseradish*

*Breakfast Risotto*

*Lettuce and Fresh Herb Salad*
*(see page 66)*

*Date and Cinnamon Scones*

---

## CHILLED TOMATOES AND HORSERADISH

**Ingredients**
*1 pound tomatoes, peeled and sliced*
*salt and freshly ground black pepper*
*1 tablespoon horseradish*
*3 tablespoons sour cream or thick Greek yogurt*
*chopped parsley*

Divide the tomatoes between four individual bowls; sprinkle with a little salt and pepper and chill for one hour. Mix together the horseradish and cream. Spoon the horseradish mixture over the tomatoes, then sprinkle with chopped parsley. Serve at once.

*Variation:* for an alternative topping, try mixing equal quantities of mayonnaise and lightly-whipped cream with chopped chives and a pinch of paprika. Or, for a pretty color contrast, top with a spoonful of the Avocado Cream on page 123.

**Protein** ▲          **Iron** ▲
**Fiber** ▲          **Calcium** ▲

*Left to right: Chilled Tomatoes with Horseradish: Lettuce and Fresh Herb Salad; Breakfast Risotto; Date and Cinnamon scones.*

---

## BREAKFAST RISOTTO

**Ingredients**
*½ stick butter or margarine*
*1 onion, peeled and chopped*
*2-3 garlic cloves, crushed*
*1⅓ cup brown rice*
*2½ cup water*
*2 teaspoons vegetarian bouillon powder*
*salt and freshly ground black pepper*
*¾ pound button mushrooms, washed and sliced*
*chopped parsley*

Melt half the butter or margarine in a medium-sized saucepan with a heavy base, then put in the onion and fry for 10 minutes, until soft. Add the garlic and rice, stir for 1-2 minutes, then pour in the water and add the bouillon powder and a teaspoon of salt. Bring to the boil, then turn the heat down, cover the saucepan tightly and leave the rice to cook very gently for 45 minutes. When the rice is nearly cooked, fry the mushrooms quickly in the rest of the butter for 2-3 minutes. Add the mushrooms to the cooked rice, stirring gently with a fork. Check seasoning. Serve in a shallow, warmed casserole with some parsley sprinkled on top. The rice will keep warm in a covered casserole in a low oven, but add the parsley just before serving.

*Variation:* Artichoke risotto makes a delicious variation. To make this, cut the leaves and hairy choke from 3 globe artichokes. Slice the bases and fry them with the onion, then continue as above.

**Protein** ▲▲          **Iron** ▲▲
**Fiber** ▲▲          **Calcium** ▲

## DATE AND CINNAMON SCONES

**Ingredients**
*2 scant cup 100 per cent whole wheat flour*
*4 teaspoons baking powder*
*2 teaspoons cinnamon*
*pinch of salt*
*½ stick butter or margarine*
*½ cup dark brown moist sugar*
*½ cup dates, chopped*

¾ *cup milk and water mixed*
*extra flour for rolling*

Preheat the oven to 425°. Sift the flour, baking powder, cinnamon and salt into a bowl, adding the bran left in the sieve, too. Rub in the fat, then add the sugar, dates and milk. Mix to a dough, then turn it out on to a floured surface and knead gently for a minute or two; the consistency will be sticky and soft. Place the dough on a lightly floured surface and roll or pat out to a thickness of ¾ inch. Cut into six circles using a 2 inch round cookie cutter. Put the scones on a cookie sheet and bake for 10-15 minutes, until risen and firm. Cool on a wire rack. Serve warm.
Makes 10-12 scones

*Variation:* these scones can be varied by using other spices, dry fruits, nuts and seeds. Try raisin and ginger scones, replacing the cinnamon with ground ginger and the dates with raisins.

**Protein** ▲▲          **Iron** ▲▲
**Fiber** ▲▲          **Calcium** ▲

### HINTS FOR HEALTH BEVERAGES
From the health point of view, it's best to choose brands of tea and coffee which are low in caffeine. Try Ceylon and China teas, or some of the many varieties of herb teas which you can get at health stores. The Japanese bancha twig tea is low in caffeine but rich in calcium. It's possible, too, to buy excellent decaffeinated coffee of all kinds: beans, ground and instant.

# LIGHT LUNCHES

Lunch is one of the most versatile meals; it can be a filling sandwich snatched at an office desk, a special meal for one or two friends, or something quick and filling for the family at the weekend! So, in this section, I've given a wide range of recipes and menu suggestions for appealing and well-balanced meals to cover all these occasions.

Many of the soups and salads can be packed and taken to work or school; however, for children (and grown-ups!) who prefer a more conventional lunch box, there are ideas and recipes for delicious sandwiches, as well as a week of lunch box menus.

If you prefer to have your main meal in the middle of the day, these lunch-time suggestions would be equally suitable for light evening meals.

*Left: Simple salad bowls for light, nourishing lunches. Clockwise from the left: Carrot, Banana and Pecan Salad; Cracked-wheat Salad; Deep-dish Salad Bowl; Kidney Bean Salad; Cheese Dip with Carrot and Celery Sticks (recipes on pages 32-33).*

## Salad Lunches

A crisp salad makes a delicious and refreshing light lunch. It's also very healthy, because it contains enzymes and vitamins which are normally destroyed by cooking. It can be quickly made from whatever mixture of fresh vegetables and fruits you have to hand. Some crisp celery, a crunchy apple and some grated cheese, for instance, or some grated carrot mixed with home-sprouted beans served on lettuce. All kinds of fresh fruits and vegetables can be used; the traditional salad vegetables, of course, but also root vegetable such as rutabagas, turnips and raw beets. Green vegetables which are normally served cooked, such as Brussels sprouts, spinach, Chinese cabbage and broccoli are excellent to use raw. Both fresh and dry fruits, too, make pleasant additions, especially sweet apples, orange segments, raisins, muscats or white raisins and snipped dry apricots or peaches. The mixture can be as simple or elaborate as you like.

Salads need not be served just as summer meals, there's always some vegetable or fruit in season that can be used and winter salads, like the Colorful Cabbage Salad on page 41, or the Chicory, Orange and Water Cress Salad on page 33, can be among the most delicious.

If you're making lunch for one or two people, you may find you need only a few leaves of lettuce, or half a bell pepper, one or two scallions, a stick of celery or part of a cabbage to make a salad. The rest will keep perfectly for up to a week, unwashed, in the bottom of the refrigerator.

## Salad Dressings

The purpose of a salad dressing is to make the salad look and taste more delicious and also to put a light coating around the fresh ingredients to protect them from the air. Like soufflés, the making of salad dressings has acquired a mystique which is quite unjustified! All salad dressings, even mayonnaise, are just simple mixtures, and anyone can make them as long as they have the right ingredients. The very simplest dressing is just fresh lemon juice, orange juice or well-seasoned tomato juice with perhaps a few chopped fresh herbs if they're available. This kind of dressing is also ideal if you're trying to slim. Plain yogurt also makes a low-calorie dressing stirred into a salad mixture to coat the ingredients. Another simple salad dressing is sour cream which you just spoon from the carton on to the salad or mix with a little crushed garlic first. This one isn't quite so slimming but it makes a tangy, creamy dressing for a special occasion.

### Good Ingredients

A French dressing (or vinaigrette) is nearly as simple. The most important thing is to make sure that you have the best ingredients. You need a really fine-quality olive or cold pressed oil, a good cider or wine vinegar, sea salt and freshly ground black pepper (for more details about these, see Vegetarian Pantry, pages 129-139). Then all you have to do is to mix your ingredients together, either in a small bowl or jar or directly in the bowl with the salad.

### Clever Dressing

A salad made from firm vegetables and fruits can be coated with dressing in advance, but one made from leafy green vegetables or tomatoes needs to be dressed at the last minute. One way to do this is to mix the dressing in a salad bowl; cross a pair of salad servers on top of the dressing and put in the green salad on top of these, so that the salad is ready in the bowl but raised above the dressing. Then you can use the servers to toss the salad into the dressing just before you serve it.

---

## HOMEGROWN BEAN SPROUTS

Bean sprouts are extremely rich in minerals and vitamins. They make a delicious and healthy addition to any diet. These bean sprouts are different from the type sold in the supermarket, because the shoot is shorter and still has the bean attached, giving a pleasant crunchy texture. To grow them, all you need is a jar, a piece of cheesecloth to go over the top and a rubber band. The little round green mung beans are usually used for sprouting, but most types, with the exception of kidney beans, can be sprouted. Whole lentils, chick peas and soybeans are especially good, and so are alfalfa, and sunflower seeds.

### Sprouting Know-How

To sprout the beans, grains or seeds, put two heaped tablespoons in the jar, cover with cold water and leave to soak for 8-12 hours. Fasten the piece of cheesecloth over the top of the jar with the rubber band, then drain off the water through the cheesecloth. Fill the jar with fresh cold water, swish it around and pour it out again. All this can be done without removing the cheesecloth, which prevents the beans or seeds from falling out of the jar. The rinsing has to be repeated twice a day; do not leave the beans or seeds soaking in the water, or they'll rot. They will soon start to produce little shoots and are ready for eating in 2-4 days. They can be used in salads and sandwiches, or in stir-fries; they can be stored in the refrigerator for several days. If you like home-sprouted beans, you may like to buy a special sprouter (see page 141) so that you can have three batches of sprouts growing at the same time.

*Protein* ▲ ▲          *Iron* ▲
*Fiber* ▲              *Calcium* ▲

## FRENCH DRESSING (VINAIGRETTE)

**Ingredients**
*1 tablespoon Dijon mustard*
*½ teaspoon sugar or honey*
*½ teaspoon salt*
*1 tablespoon red or white wine vinegar*
*4 tablespoons olive oil or cold pressed sunflower oil*

Put the mustard, sugar and salt into a small bowl; mix together and add the vinegar. Then, beating all the time with a fork, gradually add the oil, to make a thick mixture.

*Variation:* for a mint vinaigrette, add 1 tablespoon finely chopped fresh mint. Other fresh herbs can also be used: tarragon, basil, dill and chives are especially good. If you like the flavor of garlic, add a large crushed garlic clove to the mixture before mixing in the oil.
  Poppy seeds, toasted sesame seeds and mustard seeds also make interesting additions to French dressing.

| | | | |
|---|---|---|---|
| **Protein** ▲ | | **Iron** ▲ | |
| **Fiber** △ | | **Calcium** ▲ | |

## MAYONNAISE

Although a jar of good mayonnaise is useful to keep in the refrigerator, nothing can equal the flavor of homemade.

**Ingredients**
*2 large egg yolks*
*¼ teaspoon each, salt and mustard powder*
*freshly ground black pepper*
*2 teaspoons wine vinegar*
*2 teaspoons lemon juice*
*a generous ¾ cup cold pressed sunflower oil*

### HEALTHY LUNCHES

Lunch can be a very healthy meal if you base it on fresh fruit or vegetables in the form of a salad or vegetable soup and cut down on the amount of fat you add in the form of dressings, cheese, butter or oil. For a more filling meal, serve the soup or salad with whole wheat bread or a baked potato, but again, avoid too much butter. (Potatoes can be topped with yogurt for example).

This can be made in a blender or food processor, or by hand. If you're using a *blender or food processor*, break the egg straight into the blender or bowl, and add the salt, mustard, pepper, vinegar and lemon juice. Blend for a minute at medium speed until these ingredients are well mixed, then turn the speed up to high and gradually add the oil, in a very thin trickle through the opening in the top. When you have added about half the oil, you will find that the mayonnaise has begun to thicken. Continue adding the oil more quickly in a thin stream until the desired consistency is reached.
  To make the mayonnaise *by hand*, put the egg yolks, salt, mustard, pepper, vinegar and lemon juice into a bowl and beat for a minute or two until well blended. Then add the oil, a drop at a time, beating well after each addition. When you have added about half the oil, the mixture will thicken and begin to look like mayonnaise. At this point you can add the oil a little more quickly, still beating hard. Continue adding oil until the mixture is thick and creamy.
  Taste the mixture and adjust the seasoning if necessary. If the mayonnaise is too thick you can thin it by beating in a teaspoon or two of boiling water.

| | | | |
|---|---|---|---|
| **Protein** ▲ | | **Iron** ▲ | |
| **Fiber** △ | | **Calcium** ▲ | |

## TOMATO DRESSING

**Ingredients**
*2 large tomatoes, peeled and quartered*
*1-2 tablespoons olive oil, optional*
*½ teaspoon mild paprika pepper*
*3-4 drops Tabasco*
*salt and freshly ground black pepper*
*few drops of lemon juice or wine vinegar, optional*

If you want a completely smooth dressing, remove the seeds from the tomatoes: I prefer to leave them in. Then put the tomatoes into a blender or food processor with the olive oil if you're using this, the paprika pepper and Tabasco and blend until fairly smooth. Season with salt, pepper and add a little lemon juice or wine vinegar to taste if necessary. Stir again before serving.

| | | | |
|---|---|---|---|
| **Protein** ▲ | | **Iron** ▲ | |
| **Fiber** ▲ | | **Calcium** ▲ | |

## CREAMY MUSTARD DRESSING

**Ingredients**
*1 tablespoon Dijon mustard*
*⅔ cup light cream*
*1-2 teaspoons honey*
*salt and freshly ground black pepper*
*a few chopped herbs when available, optional*

Put the mustard into a small bowl and stir in the cream to make a smooth mixture. Then add honey, salt and pepper to taste, and add the herbs if you're using them. Stir again before serving.

| | | | |
|---|---|---|---|
| **Protein** ▲ | | **Iron** ▲ | |
| **Fiber** △ | | **Calcium** ▲ | |

3

LIGHT LUNCHES 

Put the corn into a strainer and rinse under hot water to defrost, then place in a bowl with the kidney beans, celery, grated carrot, chopped onion, oil, vinegar and seasoning. Mix well. Arrange the lettuce leaves in two bowls, spoon the kidney bean mixture on top and sprinkle with chopped parsley. If you're making this for 1 person, the remaining mixture will keep well overnight in the refrigerator.

*Variation:* Omit the kidney beans and use the same quantity of chick peas.

**Protein** ▲  **Iron** ▲
**Fiber** ▲▲▲  **Calcium** ▲

---

## DEEP-DISH SALAD BOWL

The joy of this salad is that the ingredients are arranged in layers in one large or two individual deep bowls and topped with a creamy dressing, so everything gets pleasantly mixed together as you plunge in your fork and eat the salad.

**Ingredients**
*4 lettuce leaves, shredded*
*½ cup cold cooked potato, diced*
*4 tablespoons mayonnaise or sour cream, or a mixture of both*
*salt and freshly ground black pepper*
*1 cup bean sprouts, preferably homegrown*
*1 tablespoon olive oil*
*1 tablespoon wine vinegar*
*2 tomatoes, chopped*
*4 inches cucumber, cubed*
*2 tablespoons raisins*
*1 large carrot, finely grated*
*1 raw beet, peeled and finely grated*
**To garnish**
*a little salad cress or water cress*

Put the shredded lettuce in the bottom of two deep dishes or soup bowls. Mix the

potato with half the mayonnaise, sour cream or mayonnaise/sour cream mixture; season, then spoon into the bowls on top of the lettuce. Mix the bean sprouts with the oil, vinegar and some salt and pepper to taste. Put these on top of the potatoes, followed by the tomatoes, cucumber, raisins, grated carrot and beet, piling the mixture up attractively. Spoon the remaining mayonnaise, sour cream or mayonnaise/sour cream mixture on top of the beet and sprinkle with some salad cress or water cress. Serve immediately.

This salad is quick to make if you save some cooked potato from a previous meal; this will keep in a covered bowl in the refrigerator for a day or two. Grated carrot and beet will also keep for 24 hours in the refrigerator (although there will be a small loss of vitamins). Other ingredients can be used in this salad: try it with shredded cabbage in place of the lettuce and diced celery instead of cucumber, or use raw vegetables of your choice.

**Protein** ▲▲▲  **Iron** ▲▲▲
**Fiber** ▲▲▲  **Calcium** ▲▲

---

## CHEESE DIP WITH CARROT AND CELERY STICKS

**Ingredients**
*¼ cup butter or margarine*
*generous 1 cup grated vegetarian Cheddar-type cheese*
*6 tablespoons milk*
*3-4 drops Tabasco*
*salt and freshly ground black pepper*
*1 celery, cleaned and trimmed*
*4-6 carrots, scraped*
**To garnish**
*mint sprig*

Beat the butter or margarine until soft, then gradually add the cheese and milk, beating until smooth; or blend these ingredients

---

## LIGHT AND EASY SALADS

### ONE

*Kidney Bean Salad*

*Deep-dish Salad Bowl*

*Cheese Dip with Carrot and Celery Sticks*

*Carrot, Banana and Pecan Salad*

*Cracked-wheat Salad*

Quantities for these easy salad lunches are given for 2 people unless otherwise stated; the amounts can easily be doubled for 4, or halved for 1 person according to the occasion. Alternatively, make the whole amount of the salad of your choice and keep half in the refrigerator, covered with plastic wrap.

---

## KIDNEY BEAN SALAD

**Ingredients**
*¼ cup frozen corn kernels*
*½ cup dry kidney beans, cooked and drained (see page 131), or 2 cups canned kidney beans, drained and rinsed under the faucet*
*1 large stick of celery, finely diced*
*1 large carrot, scraped and coarsely grated*
*1 scallion, chopped, or 2 teaspoons finely chopped onion*
*1 tablespoon olive oil*
*1 tablespoon wine vinegar*
*salt and freshly ground black pepper*
**To serve**
*4 crisp lettuce leaves*
*chopped parsley*

32

in the blender or food processor. Add the Tabasco and salt and pepper to taste. Cut the celery and carrots into strips about ¼ inch wide and 2 inches long. Spoon the cheese dip into a small serving bowl. Garnish with a sprig of mint. Arrange the carrot and celery sticks neatly around the dip.

**Protein** ▲▲▲          **Iron** ▲▲
**Fiber** ▲▲▲          **Calcium** ▲▲▲

## CARROT, BANANA AND PECAN SALAD

This is a delicious combination of flavors and textures and is popular with people who do not like the usual salad mixtures. The pecans give a delicious flavor but you can omit these and use walnuts or chopped almonds, if you prefer. For an alternative dressing, try using mayonnaise, either alone or mixed half and half with plain yogurt. For a slimmer's version, simply toss the salad in a little orange juice to preserve the color of the banana.

### Ingredients
*2 bananas, peeled and sliced*
*1 large carrot, coarsely grated*
*3 tablespoons sour cream or thick plain yogurt*
*1 tablespoon unsweetened shredded coconut*
*½ bunch water cress*
*¼ cup pecans, chopped*

Mix together the bananas, carrot, sour cream and coconut. Spoon the mixture into the center of one large or two individual bowls, then arrange the water cress round the edge. Sprinkle the nuts on top of the banana mixture.

**Protein** ▲▲          **Iron** ▲
**Fiber** ▲▲▲          **Calcium** ▲▲

## CRACKED-WHEAT SALAD

This is a substantial Middle Eastern salad based on wheat which has been cracked and steamed. This wheat, called bulgur or burghul wheat, can be bought at health stores.

There is a large quantity of parsley and mint in the salad; they are used rather like a vegetable, and the more you put in the better. In the winter, when it's difficult to get fresh herbs, try using chopped water cress instead. Cracked-wheat salad makes a useful addition to a supper buffet along with other contrasting salads, such as a tomato salad and a cucumber and yogurt salad.

### Ingredients
*¾ cup bulgur wheat*
*1¼ cup boiling water*
*2 tablespoons lemon juice*
*1 tablespoon olive oil*
*4 tablespoons chopped parsley*
*4 tablespoons chopped scallion*
*2 tablespoons chopped mint*
*2 tomatoes, peeled and finely chopped*
*salt and freshly ground black pepper*
*4 lettuce leaves*
### To garnish
*lemon slices*
*tomato slices*

Put the wheat into a bowl and cover with boiling water. Leave for 10-15 minutes, until the wheat has absorbed all the water and puffed up. Add the lemon juice, oil, chopped parsley, scallion, mint and tomato. Mix well and season to taste. Put two lettuce leaves on two serving plates or in one large bowl, then spoon the salad mixture into the lettuce leaves. Garnish with the lemon and tomato slices.

**Protein** ▲▲          **Iron** ▲▲▲
**Fiber** ▲▲▲          **Calcium** ▲▲

## LIGHT AND EASY SALADS

### TWO

*Endive, Orange and Water Cress Salad*

*Cheese, Tomato and Bell Pepper Salad with Honey and Mustard Dressing*

*Greek Salad*

*Stuffed Avocado Salad*

*Mixed Root Salad*

## ENDIVE, ORANGE AND WATER CRESS SALAD

### Ingredients
*2 heads of chicory, washed*
*½ bunch water cress*
*2 small oranges, peeled and cut into slices*
### For the dressing
*½ cup blue or Roquefort cheese*
*4 tablespoons sour cream*

Arrange the endive leaves and sprigs of water cress alternately in a circle with the leaf tips pointing outwards, like the spokes of a wheel, on a large serving plate or two individual plates. Put the orange slices in the center, also in a circular pattern. Make the dressing by mixing together the cheese and sour cream. Pour the dressing into the center of the salad over the orange.

**Protein** ▲▲          **Iron** ▲
**Fiber** ▲▲          **Calcium** ▲▲

## CHEESE, TOMATO AND BELL PEPPER SALAD WITH HONEY AND MUSTARD DRESSING

A pleasant combination of flavors and textures with a creamy, tangy dressing, this salad also makes a good first course.

**Ingredients**
*4-6 lettuce leaves*
*4 tomatoes, peeled and sliced*
*1 cup vegetarian Cheddar-type cheese, finely diced*
*½ red bell pepper, seeded and finely diced*
*½ green bell pepper, seeded and finely diced*
*½ yellow bell pepper, seeded and finely diced, or 1 carrot, scraped and finely diced*

**For the dressing**
*½ teaspoon mustard powder*
*1 tablespoon honey*
*2 tablespoons wine vinegar*
*2 tablespoons olive oil*
*salt and freshly ground black pepper*

Arrange the lettuce on four individual serving plates or in one large bowl. Place the tomatoes in a circle on top of the lettuce, and the cheese in a pile in the center. Arrange the bell peppers or bell peppers and carrot around the plate or bowl. To make the dressing, blend the mustard powder with the honey until smooth, then gradually add the vinegar, then the oil. Season to taste, mix well. Serve separately in a small jug.
Serves 4

Protein ▲▲▲    Iron ▲
Fiber ▲    Calcium ▲▲▲

*Colorful and appetizing main-meal salads. Clockwise from the top: Stuffed Avocado Salad; Cheese, Tomato and Bell Pepper Salad with Honey and Mustard Dressing; Greek Salad ; Endive , Orange and Water Cress Salad (recipe page 33).*

· LIGHT LUNCHES ·

## GREEK SALAD

### Ingredients
1 medium-sized onion, peeled and sliced
1 tablespoon olive oil
1 tablespoon wine vinegar
salt and freshly gound black pepper
4 tomatoes, thinly sliced
½ cucumber, peeled and diced
10-12 black olives (optional)
1 cup feta cheese or other white, crumbly cheese, diced
### To garnish
chopped parsley (optional)

Put the onion into a bowl with the oil, vinegar and a little salt and pepper; mix well, then leave to stand for 30-60 minutes, if possible, to allow onion to soften slightly. Stir occasionally. Add the tomatoes, cucumber, olives and cheese, mixing gently to distribute all the ingredients. Serve sprinkled with chopped parsley.

**Protein** ▲▲▲  **Iron** ▲
**Fiber** ▲▲  **Calcium** ▲▲▲

## STUFFED AVOCADO SALAD

### Ingredients
1 large ripe avocado, halved and pit removed
1 tablespoon lemon juice
2 tomatoes, peeled and chopped
2 scallions, chopped
½ small green bell pepper, seeded and finely chopped
½ cup vegetarian Cheddar-type cheese, grated
salt and freshly ground black pepper
### To serve
4 lettuce leaves
few sprigs water cress
1 carrot, scraped and cut into matchsticks

Using a teaspoon, scoop out the avocado flesh, being careful not to damage the skin which will be needed for serving the salad. Dice the flesh and place in a bowl with the lemon juice, tomatoes, scallion, green bell pepper and cheese. Season to taste. Spoon the mixture into the avocado skins. Arrange the stuffed avocados on the lettuce leaves and garnish with water cress and carrot sticks.

**Protein** ▲▲▲  **Iron** ▲▲
**Fiber** ▲▲  **Calcium** ▲▲▲

## MIXED ROOT SALAD

### Ingredients
1 medium-sized ripe avocado, halved, peeled and pit removed
2 tablespoons lemon juice
3 tablespoons mayonnaise
3 tablespoons thick plain yogurt
1 tablespoon wine vinegar
salt and freshly ground black pepper
1 small raw beet, peeled and grated
1 large carrot, scraped and grated
½ cup rutabaga, peeled and grated
½ cup celeriac, peeled and grated
½ cup parsnip, peeled and grated
orange juice

Brush the avocado halves all over with lemon juice, then place each, flat side down, in the center of a large individual plate. Mix together the mayonnaise, yogurt and vinegar; season to taste, then spoon this mixture over the top of the avocados and smooth it with a knife to completely cover the avocados. Keeping grated root vegetables separate, moisten each with a little orange juice, then arrange all round the avocados and serve immediately.

**Protein** ▲▲  **Iron** ▲
**Fiber** ▲▲▲  **Calcium** ▲▲

## A Vegetarian Lunch Box

For many people – schoolchildren as well as workers – lunch during the week means a packed meal. If the canteen at work or school isn't switched on to new eating ideas, a packed lunch can be the most satisfactory solution both for us vegetarians and also from the health point of view.

Sometimes, I know, people wonder whether they're missing out nutritionally if they have packed lunch every day. But a well-planned packed meal can be just as nourishing as a cooked meal and it can also be delicious. A Thermos of one of the soups on pages 43-46, or the salads on pages 32-35, transported in a plastic container, make excellent lunches and are a pleasant change from sandwiches. Even easier are wedges of hard-cooked egg or cubes of vegetarian Cheddar-type cheese with salad and fruit, or a crunchy apple with some nuts and raisins and perhaps a carton of yogurt.

Vegetarian sandwiches can also be attractive, and these are often appreciated by children, who need something which is easy to eat with their fingers. If they're eating their packed lunch at school, they also like to take something which does not look too different from what all their friends are having! It's important always to use whole wheat bread, because of the valuable fiber and other nutrients which it contains. Now that there are so many different types available it's usually possible to find one which even the most fussy child will eat. Spread the bread very thinly with butter or margarine, to reduce the fat content of the sandwiches, or, if you're using a spread, put this straight on to the bread.

For a sustaining packed meal, make sure that you have included in the lunch box a concentrated source of protein such as nuts, a nut or seed spread, cheese or egg. Add some salad (such as a tomato or a scraped carrot) and fresh or dry fruit.

Many children like to round off their lunch with something sweet, so include

dates, a few nuts and raisins in a twist of plastic wrap, some of the fruit and nut mixes you can get at health stores, a sandwich with one of the sweet filling suggestions, a wholefood crunchy bar or a piece of one of the whole wheat bakes on pages 38-40. Don't give whole nuts to children under five or six because of the risk of choking; instead, mix ground almonds to a smooth paste with honey and use this to

stuff dates – this makes a delicious treat for adults too!

Hot and cold drinks (see page 38) can be packed in a colorful children's unbreakable Thermos which you can buy, often with a matching plastic lunch box. A Thermos is also ideal for transporting soup, if your child likes this idea. Do take care, though, not to make soup or any hot drinks too hot when giving them to children.

## SANDWICH SUGGESTIONS

**Appetizing Ideas**
*Sesame spread or vegetable pâté with any of the following:*
*Grated carrot*
*Sliced cucumber*
*Sliced tomato*
*Bean sprouts or home-sprouted lentils, mung beans, alfalfa or soybeans*
*Finely shredded lettuce*
*Sliced onions*

*Yeast extract and either cress, sliced tomato (with or without sliced onions), shredded lettuce, or sliced cucumber*

*Grated carrot blended with mayonnaise and raisins*

*Grated cheese with grated carrot*

*Sliced or grated cheese and either sliced tomato, shredded lettuce, sliced cucumber, chutney, chopped dates or date spread*

*Curd or cottage cheese with either chopped fresh herbs, sliced cucumber, raisins or chopped dates, shredded lettuce, grated carrot, or water cress*

*Pita bread filled with crisp salad*

*Peanut butter with finely grated carrot*
*Peanut butter with sliced cucumber*

*Mashed hard-cooked egg blended with a little milk or mayonnaise*
*Mashed hard-cooked egg with cress*

*Herb or garlic butter with tomato slices or cucumber*

**Sweet ideas**
*Sesame spread and honey*
*Sesame spread with either sliced banana or grated sweet apple, with or without raisins, chopped dates or unsweetened shredded coconut*

*Date spread with sliced bananas and walnuts or chopped almonds*

*Cottage or curd cheese with sliced banana or chopped dates or raisins or candied ginger*

*Sliced banana with finely grated walnuts, almonds or sunflower seeds and honey*

*Honey and finely grated sunflower or pumpkin seeds*

*Honey mixed with finely grated nuts*

*Peanut butter beaten together with curd cheese and sliced banana*
*Peanut butter with grated sweet apple*

· LIGHT LUNCHES ·

## SCHOOL LUNCH BOX

### MONDAY
Egg and cress sandwiches
Tangerine
*Little Brown Sugar Chocolate Buns, or
Nuts and Raisins
### TUESDAY
Curd cheese and grated carrot sandwiches
Small bunch of sweet grapes
Sunflower seeds and raisins
*Brown Sugar Flapjacks, or
piece of *Old-fashioned Fruit Cake
### WEDNESDAY
*Date spread or peanut butter and
cucumber sandwiches
Carrot sticks
*Date Squares, or
*Crunchy Carob Biscuits
### THURSDAY
Yeast extract or
*Date Spread sandwiches
Cubes of vegetarian Cheddar-type cheese
Apple
*Honey Parkin, or Dates stuffed with
Brazil nuts
### FRIDAY
Vegetable Pâté and
Cucumber sandwiches
Piece of celery
Banana
*Gingerbread Men or
*Whole Wheat Jam Tarts
Nuts and Raisins
*Recipes on pages 37-41

## DATE CHEWS

### Ingredients
1¼ cup cooking dates (not sugar coated)
½ stick butter
1 cup Graham cracker-type cookie crumbs –
read the packet to make sure you get a type
which does not contain animal fat

4 ounces sweet chocolate or carob bar,
melted

First prepare an 8 inch square pan by lining it with a piece of greased wax paper. Chop the dates roughly and put them into a saucepan with the butter. Heat gently until the butter has melted and the dates have softened, stirring several times. Remove from the heat. Add the cookie crumbs to the date mixture and stir well. Spoon this mixture into the prepared pan and spread it over the base, pushing it well into the corners and pressing it down well. Put into the refrigerator for 1 hour to chill, then spread the melted chocolate or carob evenly over the top and leave to set. Cut into squares while still in the pan, remove carefully and serve.
Makes 16 squares

Protein ▲   Iron ▲
Fiber ▲   Calcium ▲

## GINGERBREAD MEN

### Ingredients
2 tablespoons butter
generous ¼ cup dark brown moist sugar
1 tablespoon blackstrap molasses
2 tablespoons molasses
scant 1 cup fine 100% whole wheat flour
½ teaspoon baking soda
½ teaspoon ground ginger

Preheat the oven to 350°. Grease a large cookie sheet. Put the butter, sugar and molasses into a small saucepan and heat gently until melted. Remove from the heat and allow to cool to tepid. Sift the flour into a bowl with the soda and ginger, adding the bran left behind in the sieve too. Add the melted ingredients to the flour mixture and stir to make a pliable dough. Roll it out about ¼ inch thick and cut into gingerbread men shapes. Bake for about 10 minutes.

Allow to cool a little on the cookie sheet before removing.

Protein ▲   Iron ▲
Fiber ▲   Calcium ▲

## DATE SPREAD

### Ingredients
scant ½ cup dates (not sugar-coated)
5 tablespoons water

Chop the dates and remove any pits. Put the fruit into a saucepan with the water and heat gently, stirring often, for about 5 minutes, until the dates have softened. Beat with a wooden spoon to make a fairly smooth consistency. Makes about ½ cup.

Protein ▲   Iron ▲
Fiber ▲   Calcium ▲

## BROWN SUGAR FLAPJACKS

### Ingredients
1½ sticks butter or margarine
2 cups dark brown moist sugar
3 cups rolled oats

Preheat oven to 350°. Grease a 7×11 inch jelly roll pan. Put the butter or margarine and sugar into a large saucepan and heat gently until melted, then remove from the heat and stir in the oats. Mix well, then spread the mixture into the pan and press down evenly. Bake for 20 minutes, until brown all over. Mark into fingers while still hot, then leave in the pan until cold. The flapjacks become crisp as they cool and keep well in an airtight container. Makes about 20.

Protein ▲   Iron ▲
Fiber ▲   Calcium ▲

· LIGHT LUNCHES ·

## DRINKS TO PACK

*A Thermos of homemade soup
(not too hot for a child)*

*Cold milk*

*Hot carob or cocoa for
cold weather*

*Homemade Milk Shake (recipe page 80)*

*Real fruit juice in a Thermos or carton*

## LIGHT LUNCH BOX IDEAS

*A carton of thick plain yogurt and some
fresh fruit, a few nuts and raisins*

*Halved avocado with dressing packed
separately*

*Carton of cottage cheese with carrot,
celery and cucumber sticks, strips
of bell pepper, sprigs of cauliflower*

*Cold nut roast with pickles and salad*

*Piece of cold tart or pie with salad*

*Pieces of celery, apple and cheese*

*Shredded lettuce, grated carrot, sliced
cucumber and grated cheese, kidney beans
or soy sprouts in pita bread*

*Nut Burger (recipe page 95) in
soft whole wheat bun, with chutney,
sliced tomato or sliced onion*

*Whole wheat pita bread filled
with Greek Salad or
Kidney Bean Salad (recipes page 32)*

## DATE SQUARES

A sweet date filling sandwiched in a crumbly, "oaty" pastry.

**Ingredients**
*1 cup self-rising 100 per cent whole
wheat flour
1¼ cup rolled oats
1 stick butter or margarine
½ cup dark brown moist sugar*
**For the filling**
*generous 1 cup cooking dates (not
sugar-coated)
5 tablespoons water
½ teaspoon vanilla*

Preheat the oven to 350°. Grease an 8 inch square pan. First prepare the filling: chop the dates roughly, removing any pits or hard bits of stalk. Put them into a small saucepan with the water and heat gently for about 10 minutes, stirring often, until the fruit has softened. Add the vanilla, then beat the dates with a wooden spoon to make a thick purée. Set aside to cool. Put the flour and oats into a bowl; add the butter, rubbing it in with your fingertips until the mixture looks like bread crumbs. Mix in the sugar. Press half the mixture into the greased pan, then spread the cooled date mixture on top. Sprinkle the rest of the flour and oat mixture over the date mixture and press down with the back of a spoon. Bake for 30 minutes. Mark into squares, then leave to cool in the pan.
Makes 16 squares

*Protein* ▲          *Iron* ▲
*Fiber* ▲          *Calcium* ▲

*Clockwise from top left: Old-fashioned Fruit
Cake; Brown Sugar Flapjacks; Crunchy
Carob Cookies; Whole Wheat Jam Tarts;
Little Brown Sugar Chocolate Buns; Honey
Parkin (recipes on pages 40-41).*

LIGHT LUNCHES

## WHOLE WHEAT JAM TARTS

These are unfailingly popular with the children I know.

**Ingredients**
*1 cup 100 per cent whole wheat flour*
*½ stick butter or margarine*
*6 teaspoons cold water*
**For the filling**
*4 heaped tablespoons jam or jelly*
*(preferably reduced-sugar)*

Preheat the oven to 375°. Grease a shallow muffin pan. Put the flour into a bowl; add the butter, then rub it in with your fingertips until the mixture looks like bread crumbs. Add the water, pressing the mixture together to form a dough. Roll the pastry out carefully on a lightly floured surface, then cut out 12 circles using a 2½ inch cookie cutter. Press a pastry circle lightly into each cavity in the pan, then put a heaped teaspoonful of jam or jelly on to each. Bake the jam tarts near the top of the oven for about 10 minutes, until the pastry is lightly browned. Cool the tarts in the pan before removing.
Makes 12

**Protein** ▲          **Iron** ▲
**Fiber** ▲          **Calcium** ▲

## CRUNCHY CAROB COOKIES

Children love these light, crunchy cookies.

**Ingredients**
*generous 1 cup self-rising 85 per cent whole wheat flour*
*2 tablespoons carob powder*
*1 stick butter or margarine*
*½ cup dark brown moist sugar*
*1 tablespoon milk*

Preheat the oven to 375°. Grease a cookie sheet. Sift the flour and carob powder. Cream the butter or margarine and sugar until light, then add the flour mixture. Mix to a dough, adding a little milk if necessary to make a firm consistency. Form into 24 small balls, flatten and place on the cookie sheet. Bake for 10 minutes. Cool on a wire rack.
Makes 24

**Protein** ▲          **Iron** ▲
**Fiber** ▲          **Calcium** ▲

## LITTLE BROWN SUGAR CHOCOLATE BUNS

A variation is to use carob powder instead of cocoa, and a carob bar instead of chocolate. Carob powder and carob bars are both available from health stores.

**Ingredients**
*1½ cup self-rising 85 per cent whole wheat flour*
*1 tablespoon cocoa powder*
*1 stick soft butter or margarine*
*1 cup dark brown moist sugar*
*2 eggs*
*a few drops of vanilla*
*12 paper cupcake cases*
**For the topping**
*4 ounces sweet chocolate, melted*

Preheat the oven to 375°. Sift the flour and cocoa into a bowl, then add the butter or margarine, sugar, eggs and vanilla and beat well with a wooden spoon or with a hand electric mixer, until all the ingredients are well blended; the mixture should be thick and slightly shiny looking. Drop a good heaped teaspoonful of mixture into each paper cupcake case, then either put the cases into the sections of a deep muffin pan or stand them on a cookie sheet. Bake for 15-20 minutes until the cakes have risen and feel firm to a light touch. Remove them from the oven and leave to cool on a wire rack. When the cakes are cool, spread a little melted chocolate on top of each one.
Makes 12

**Protein** ▲          **Iron** ▲
**Fiber** ▲          **Calcium** ▲

## HONEY PARKIN

Sticky Honey Parkin is a traditional English tea-time treat. It gets stickier if wrapped in aluminum foil and stored in an airtight container for 2-7 days.

**Ingredients**
*1 cup 100 per cent whole wheat flour*
*2 teaspoons baking powder*
*2 teaspoons ground ginger*
*1⅓ cup oatmeal*
*½ cup dark brown moist sugar*
*⅓ cup blackstrap or regular molasses*
*⅓ cup honey*
*1 stick butter or margarine*
*¾ cup milk*

Preheat the oven to 350°. Line an 8 inch square pan with greased wax paper. Sift the flour, baking powder and ginger into a bowl, adding the leftover bran from the sieve and also the oatmeal. Put the sugar, molasses, honey, butter or margarine into a saucepan and heat gently until melted. Cool until you can comfortably put your hand against the pan, then add the milk. Add to the dry ingredients, mixing well, then pour the mixture into the prepared pan. Bake for 50-60 minutes, until firm to the touch. Lift the parkin out of the pan and put on a wire rack to cool, then cut into pieces.
Makes 12-16 pieces

**Protein** ▲          **Iron** ▲
**Fiber** ▲          **Calcium** ▲

· LIGHT LUNCHES ·

## OLD-FASHIONED FRUIT CAKE

This cake is best fresh, but will keep for 7-10 days if wrapped in wax paper and aluminum foil and kept in an airtight container.

**Ingredients**
*3 cup 85 or 100 per cent whole wheat flour*
*1 teaspoon mixed spice*
*1½ sticks butter or margarine*
*1½ cup dark brown moist sugar*
*1¼ cup mixed dry fruit, including candied peel, washed and dried thoroughly on paper towels.*
*½ cup candied cherries, rinsed and halved grated peel of 1 well-scrubbed orange*
*½ cup ground almonds*
*½ cup milk*
*2 tablespoons vinegar*
*¾ teaspoon baking soda*

Preheat the oven to 300°. Grease an 8 inch cake pan and line with a double layer of greased wax paper. Sift the flour and spice into a bowl, adding the bran from the sieve, too, if you're using 100 per cent whole wheat flour. Rub the fat into the flour with your fingers until the mixture resembles bread crumbs, then add the sugar, dry fruit, cherries, orange peel and ground almonds. Warm half the milk in a small saucepan and add the vinegar. Dissolve the soda in the rest of the milk, then add to the milk and vinegar mixture. Quickly stir this into the flour and fruit, mixing well so that everything is combined.

Spoon the mixture into the prepared cake pan. Bake for 2-2½ hours, until a cake tester inserted into the center of the cake comes out clean. Leave the cake in the pan to cool, then strip off the wax paper. Wrap in fresh wax paper and foil if you are going to store it.

**Protein** ▲   **Iron** ▲
**Fiber** ▲▲   **Calcium** ▲

---

### FAMILY FOOD
*Serves 4*

### ONE

*Colorful Cabbage Salad*

*Baked Potatoes with Chives*

*Bananas with Ginger Cream*

## COLORFUL CABBAGE SALAD

Red cabbage can also be used in this recipe either totally replacing the white cabbage or mixing it half and half. For an extra creamy dressing beat 2 tablespoons of thick plain yogurt into the oil and vinegar.

**Ingredients**
*¾ pound white cabbage, washed and shredded*
*2 carrots, scraped and coarsely grated*
*2 tomatoes, peeled and chopped*
*2 celery sticks, diced*
*1 red bell pepper, seeded and finely chopped*
*4 scallions, chopped*
*2 tablespoons olive oil*
*2 tablespoons red wine vinegar*
*4 tablespoons raisins (optional)*
*salt and freshly ground black pepper*
**To garnish**
*¾ cup roasted cashew nuts (optional)*

Put all the ingredients into a bowl and mix together well. Garnish with the roasted cashew nuts, if using.

**Protein** ▲▲   **Iron** ▲
**Fiber** ▲▲   **Calcium** ▲

---

## BAKED POTATOES WITH CHIVES

**Ingredients**
*4×8-10 ounce potatoes, scrubbed*
*4 tablespoons sour cream*
*4 teaspoons chopped chives*

Preheat the oven to 450°. Using a sharp knife, cut a cross in the top of each potato. Place the potatoes in a roasting pan and bake for 1-1¼ hours, until the potatoes feel soft when squeezed. Open the cross shape on top of the potatoes by squeezing the sides of the potatoes gently. Mix together the sour cream and chives and spoon into the cross openings before serving the baked potatoes.

**Protein** ▲▲   **Iron** ▲
**Fiber** ▲▲▲   **Calcium** ▲

---

## BANANAS WITH GINGER AND CREAM

This is a quick, simple dessert that's popular with all the family. Other ripe fresh fruits such as pears can be used.

**Ingredients**
*4 ripe bananas, peeled and sliced*
*2 tablespoons lemon juice*
*4 tablespoons chopped candied ginger*
*⅔ cup light cream*

Put the bananas into a bowl and add the lemon juice, turning the bananas gently so that they all get coated with the lemon juice. Divide the bananas between four individual serving bowls, sprinkle with the chopped ginger and serve with the cream.

**Protein** ▲   **Iron** ▲
**Fiber** ▲   **Calcium** ▲

## TWO

*Hummus with Pita Bread*

*Chunky Salad, or*

*Cauliflower and Apple Salad*

*Date Squares (recipe page 38)*

## HUMMUS

**Ingredients**
*1½ cup dry chick peas (garbanzos), soaked and cooked as described on page 131, or 2 cans (about 3½ cup) chick peas (garbanzos)*
*2 garlic cloves, crushed*
*4 teaspoons sesame paste (tahini)*
*2 tablespoons olive oil*
*2 tablespoons lemon juice*
*salt and freshly ground black pepper*
**To serve**
*extra olive oil*
*paprika*
*slices of lemon*
*black olives, optional*

Drain the chick peas (garbanzos), reserving the liquid. Put them into a food processor or blender with ½ cup of the reserved liquid, the garlic, sesame paste, olive oil and lemon juice. Blend until smooth. Season, then spoon into a serving bowl. Pour a little olive oil over the top, then sprinkle with paprika and garnish with lemon slices and olives. Serve with warm Pita bread cut in half or into pieces.

| **Protein** ▲▲▲ | **Iron** ▲▲ |
| **Fiber** ▲▲▲ | **Calcium** ▲ |

## CHUNKY SALAD

**Ingredients**
*1 large lettuce with a firm heart, such as Iceberg, or 2 small lettuces with firm hearts, such as cos or Romaine*
*4 firm tomatoes, washed and cut into quarters or smaller*
*½ cucumber, washed and cut into chunky pieces*
*8 scallions, chopped*

Cut the lettuce into chunky pieces, then wash these carefully under running water, keeping the pieces as intact as possible. Shake well. Put the lettuce chunks into a bowl with the tomatoes, cucumber and scallions.

| **Protein** ▲ | **Iron** ▲▲ |
| **Fiber** ▲▲ | **Calcium** ▲▲ |

## CAULIFLOWER AND APPLE SALAD

**Ingredients**
*¾ pound cauliflower cut into florets*
*1 sweet apple, washed, cored and diced*
*2 tomatoes, washed and chopped*
*2 carrots, scraped and coarsely grated*
*bunches of water cress, shredded*
*1-2 tablespoons lemon juice*
*scant ½ cup raisins*
*2 tablespoons olive oil (optional)*
*salt and freshly ground black pepper*

Mix together all the salad ingredients adding olive oil if you're using it. Season with salt and pepper. (The cauliflower florets may be lightly cooked in boiling, salted water for 2-3 minutes, if wished).

| **Protein** ▲▲ | **Iron** ▲ |
| **Fiber** ▲▲ | **Calcium** ▲ |

## SATISFYING SOUPS
*Serves 4*

### ONE

*Easy Tomato Soup*

*Garlic Bread*

*Mixed grapes*

---

## EASY TOMATO SOUP

**Ingredients**
*2 tablespoons olive oil*
*1 onion, chopped*
*¾ pound potatoes, peeled and diced*
*1 pound fresh tomatoes, peeled and sliced,*
*and 2 cup canned tomatoes*
*4½ cup light vegetable stock*
*salt and freshly ground black pepper*
*2 tablespoons chopped basil or parsley*
*(optional)*

Heat the oil in a large saucepan and add the onion. Fry for 5 minutes, then put in the potatoes and tomatoes and continue to cook over a low heat for 10 minutes, stirring occasionally. Add the water or stock and bring to the boil. Cover and simmer for 15-20 minutes, until the potatoes are soft. Blend the soup until smooth. Reheat gently. Serve in heated bowls with chopped fresh basil or parsley sprinkled on top.

*Protein* ▲          *Iron* ▲
*Fiber* ▲▲▲      *Calcium* ▲

*Just right for a weekend snack; a crisp combination of raw fruit and vegetables with a creamy dip and warm wedges of bread. Clockwise from bottom left: Cauliflower and Apple Salad; Hummus; Pita bread (recipes on page 42).*

*Homemade soup makes a warming and economical meal at any time of the day. Clockwise from top left: Leek and Potato Soup; Roasted Hazelnut Soup with Red Pepper Cream (recipes on page 46); Garlic Bread; Easy Tomato Soup; Vegetable Soup with Nori (recipes on pages 43-45).*

---

## GARLIC BREAD

**Ingredients**
*French bread, white or whole wheat*
*3-4 garlic cloves, crushed*
*1 stick butter, softened*

Preheat the oven to 400°. Make slices in the French bread 1 inch apart, cutting almost through but ensuring that the slices are still joined at the base. Make the garlic butter and spread this on both sides of each slice of bread. Push the slices together to re-form the bread, then wrap it in aluminum foil; place on a baking sheet and bake for about 20 minutes.

**Protein** ▲▲▲          **Iron** ▲▲
**Fiber** ▲▲          **Calcium** ▲

---

### TWO

*Vegetable Soup with Nori*

*Apples and celery sticks*

---

## VEGETABLE SOUP WITH NORI

This is a delicious soup which can be varied according to whatever vegetables are available. It is good made with leeks instead of the zucchini. I think the sprinkling of nori (which is a kind of seaweed, see page 138) gives the soup a tangy, salty flavor and it's full of minerals and vitamins. But this idea doesn't appeal to everyone (even in my family!) so leave it out – or sprinkle it on and don't tell them what they're eating until after the meal!

**Ingredients**
*2 tablespoons olive oil*
*2 onions, peeled and chopped*
*4 celery sticks, diced*
*½ pound carrots, scraped and diced*
*¾ pound zucchini, trimmed and diced*
*½ pound Chinese cabbage,*
*shredded*
*4 garlic cloves, crushed*
*2 teaspoons vegetarian bouillon powder*
*4½ cup water*
*salt and freshly ground black pepper*
**Optional garnish**
*2-4 sheets of nori, crisped over a flame or under a broiler, then crumbled, or as described on page 138*

Heat the olive oil in a large saucepan and add the onions, celery and carrots. Fry gently for 5 minutes, without letting the vegetables brown, then add the zucchini, cabbage and garlic. Stir, and fry gently for a further 5 minutes. Add the bouillon powder, cook for 2-3 minutes more, then stir in the water. Bring up to the boil, then let the soup simmer for about 10 minutes, until the vegetables are just tender. You can serve the soup as it is, but I think it's better if you blend two cupfuls, then stir these back into the soup. This has the effect of slightly thickening the soup. Season to taste. Serve the soup in bowls, and sprinkle with the nori, if you're using this, or serve the nori separately in a small bowl for people to sprinkle over the top of their soup if they like.

**Protein** ▲▲▲          **Iron** ▲
**Fiber** ▲▲▲          **Calcium** ▲▲

· LIGHT LUNCHES ·

## THREE

*Leek and Potato Soup*

*Pears and Curd Cheese*

## FOUR

*Roasted Hazelnut Soup
with Bell Pepper Cream*

*Quick Whole Wheat Rolls*

*Mixed grapes*

---

## LEEK AND POTATO SOUP

**Ingredients**
*2 tablespoons butter or margarine*
*¾ pound trimmed leeks, washed and
sliced*
*1½ pounds potatoes, peeled and diced*
*3 teaspoons vegetarian bouillon powder*
*salt and freshly ground black pepper*
*4½ cup water*

Melt the butter in a large saucepan, then
add the leeks and potatoes and fry these
very gently, covering the pan, for 10
minutes, stirring often. Sprinkle the
bouillon powder and a little salt and pepper
over the potatoes and leeks, stir, then continue to cook gently, still covered, for a
further 10 minutes, stirring often. It doesn't
matter if the vegetables brown slightly, but
don't let them get too brown. Add the
water, stir, then simmer for 5-10 minutes,
until the vegetables are cooked. Check the
seasoning, then serve.

**Protein** ▲          **Iron** ▲
**Fiber** ▲          **Calcium** ▲

---

## PEARS AND CURD CHEESE

Arrange curd cheese and sliced ripe pears
on individual plates. Sprinkle some
chopped fresh walnuts or hazelnuts on top
of the curd cheese, if you like.

---

## ROASTED HAZELNUT SOUP
## WITH BELL PEPPER CREAM

**Ingredients**
*1 cup hazelnuts, roasted under the broiler
and skins removed*
*1 onion, peeled and chopped*
*2 tablespoons butter*
*1 pound potatoes, peeled and diced*
*1 garlic clove, crushed*
*salt and freshly ground black pepper*
*4½ cup water*
*2 teaspoons vegetarian bouillon powder*
*1 tablespoon lemon juice*
**For the Bell Pepper Cream**
*1 small red bell pepper*
*⅔ cup whipping cream*
*salt and freshly ground black pepper*

Grate the hazelnuts as finely as possible in a
food processor, nut grinder or clean electric
coffee grinder. Leave on one side. Fry the
onion in the butter for 5 minutes, letting it
brown lightly, then add the potato, garlic
and a little salt and pepper and cook gently,
covering the pan, for a further 5-10
minutes. Put in the water and bouillon
powder, bring to the boil, then leave to
simmer gently for 10-15 minutes, until the
potatoes and onion are cooked. Blend the
soup and stir in the grated hazelnuts, lemon
juice and seasoning to taste.

To make the bell pepper cream, put the
bell pepper under a hot broiler until the
outer skin has become charred all over.
Rinse the bell pepper under the cold faucet
and remove the stalk, seeds and outer skin,
which should come off easily. Mash the bell
pepper finely. Whip the cream until just
forming peaks, then beat in enough of the
bell pepper to color the cream pink, and
add seasoning to taste.
    Serve the soup in individual bowls, with a
spoonful of the bell pepper cream on top of
each.

**Protein** ▲ ▲ ▲          **Iron** ▲
**Fiber** ▲ ▲          **Calcium** ▲

---

## QUICK WHOLE WHEAT ROLLS

**Ingredients**
*⅔ cup milk*
*⅔ cup water*
*½ stick butter or margarine*
*2 cup whole wheat flour*
*2 cup unbleached white flour*
*1 teaspoon each, salt and sugar*
*¼ ounce packet of quick acting dry yeast*

Heat together the milk, water and butter
gently until the butter has melted. Cool to
tepid. Put the flours into a large bowl with
the salt, sugar and yeast; add the milk
mixture. Mix to a dough, then knead for 5
minutes. Put the dough into a clean, lightly-
oiled bowl, cover with plastic wrap, and
leave in a warm place for about 1 hour, until
doubled in bulk. Preheat the oven to 425°.
Knock back the dough with your fist, then
knead it again for 1-2 minutes. Shape into
8-10 rolls, place well apart on a floured
baking sheet. Cover and leave in a warm
place for 15-20 minutes. Bake for 15-20
minutes. Serve warm.

**Protein** ▲          **Iron** ▲
**Fiber** ▲          **Calcium** ▲

3

· LIGHT LUNCHES ·

**SUMMER SPECIAL**
*Serves 4*

*Grapefruit and Avocado Salad with Minty Dressing*

*Tomatoes stuffed with Almonds*

*Mango Sherbet with Honey and Cardamom Sauce*

## GRAPEFRUIT AND AVOCADO SALAD WITH MINTY DRESSING

**Ingredients**
*2 avocados, halved, peeled and pits removed*
*2 grapefruits*
*2 oranges*
*½ teaspoon sugar*
*2 tablespoons olive oil*
*1 tablespoon chopped mint*
*salt and freshly ground black pepper*
*6-10 lettuce leaves, washed and torn into bite-sized pieces, or 2 heads of curly endive, washed*

Cut the avocados into thin slices. Spread the slices out on a plate. Holding a grapefruit over the plate (so that the juice will go over the avocado slices), peel it with a sharp knife. Do this with a sawing action, cutting round the fruit down to the flesh and removing all the white pith. Then cut each segment of fruit away from the inner white skin. When all the segments have been removed from the grapefruit, squeeze the remaining juice from the skin over the avocados. Repeat this with the other grapefruit and the oranges, putting the segments on a separate plate. Turn the avocado slices

in the juice, then drain off any excess juice into a small bowl, adding the sugar, olive oil, mint and seasoning to make a dressing. To assemble the dish, cover four plates with lettuce or endive, then arrange segments of grapefruit, orange and avocado on top, dividing them between the plates. Give the dressing a quick stir, then spoon a little over each salad and serve the salads immediately.

Protein ▲            Iron ▲
Fiber ▲              Calcium ▲

## TOMATOES STUFFED WITH ALMONDS

**Ingredients**
*6 beefsteak tomatoes, weighing about 8 ounces each*
*salt and freshly ground black pepper*
*1½ cup curd cheese*
*1½ cup sliced almonds*
*grated peel of 1 well-scrubbed lemon*
*1 tablespoon chopped basil or parsley*
**To serve**
*1 Chinese cabbage, finely shredded*
*1 tablespoon butter or margarine*

Preheat the oven to 375°. Cut the tops off the tomatoes and, if necessary, slice a small piece off the base of each so that they stand upright. Using a teaspoon, scoop out the seeds and pulp but leave the flesh around the sides of the tomatoes. Sprinkle the inside of each tomato with a little salt and turn each upside down on a plate to drain. Meanwhile, mix together the curd cheese, almonds, lemon peel, basil or parsley and season the mixture with some salt and pepper to taste.

Place the tomatoes on a baking sheet; fill each with some of the curd cheese and almond mixture. Bake for 10-15 minutes, until the tomatoes are just tender and the tops lightly browned. Just before they are

ready, heat the butter or margarine in a large saucepan, add the Chinese cabbage and stir-fry for 1-2 minutes, until beginning to become tender. Serve at once with the tomatoes.

Protein ▲▲▲          Iron ▲▲▲
Fiber ▲▲▲            Calcium ▲▲▲

## MANGO SHERBET WITH HONEY AND CARDAMOM SAUCE

**Ingredients**
*2 large ripe mangoes, halved, peeled and pits removed and flesh cut into even-sized chunks*
*2 egg whites*
**For the sauce**
*1 teaspoon cardamom pods*
*3 tablespoons honey*
*3 tablespoons orange juice*
**To decorate**
*a few pistachio nuts, shelled and chopped*

Blend the mango flesh which should make about 2½ cup of purée. Put this into a plastic container and freeze until firm round the edges. Beat the egg whites until stiff. Add the cold mango purée to the egg whites a little at a time, continuing to beat. Put this mixture back into the freezer and freeze until firm. Meanwhile make the sauce. Crush the cardamom pods and remove the black seeds. Crush the seeds as finely as you can. Then mix with the honey and orange juice. Cover and leave for at least 30 minutes for the flavors to blend. Just before serving, strain the sauce. Remove the sherbet from the freezer 30 minutes before it is required. Serve in individual bowls with the sauce and a few pistachio nuts sprinkled on top.

Protein ▲            Iron ▲
Fiber ▲              Calcium ▲

LIGHT LUNCHES ·

## WARM-WEATHER LUNCH
### Serves 4

*Chilled Cucumber Soup with Dill and Radishes*

*Spinach Roulade with Mushroom and Sour Cream Filling*

*Fresh Tomato Sauce*

*Baby carrots and zucchini with fresh herbs*

*Strawberries with Cointreau, or*

*Blueberry Bombe with cream*

This warm-weather lunch, full of the flavors of summer, begins with a simple, refreshing, chilled cucumber soup that can be prepared ahead. Although the roulade needs to be cooked just before eating, it only takes 10-15 minutes to bake and the basic preparation can be done beforehand ready for beating and adding the egg whites. The strawberries can be prepared in advance, and the blueberry meringue ice cream (if you're using this dessert), can be served straight from the freezer.

*A refreshing menu for a warm summer day. Clockwise from the left: Grapefruit and Avocado Salad with Minty Dressing; Tomatoes Stuffed with Almonds; Mango Sherbet with Honey and Cardamom Sauce (recipes on previous page).*

## CHILLED CUCUMBER SOUP WITH DILL AND RADISHES

**Ingredients**
*1 cucumber, peeled and cut into rough chunks*
*2 cup thick plain yogurt*
*2 tablespoons heavy cream*
*8 sprigs of mint*
*2-3 teaspoons wine vinegar*
*salt and freshly ground black pepper*
**To garnish**
*8 thin slices of radish*
*4 feathery dill leaves or mint leaves*

Put the cucumber into a blender with the yogurt, cream and mint and blend until smooth. Add enough wine vinegar to sharpen the flavor, and salt and freshly ground black pepper to taste. Chill. Serve in chilled bowls garnished with the radish slices and dill or mint leaves.

| **Protein** ▲▲ | **Iron** ▲ |
| **Fiber** ▲ | **Calcium** ▲▲▲ |

## FRESH TOMATO SAUCE

**Ingredients**
*1 onion, peeled and chopped*
*1 tablespoon butter or margarine*
*1 pound tomatoes, peeled and chopped, or 2 cup canned tomatoes*
*1 garlic clove, crushed*
*salt and freshly ground black pepper*

Fry the onion gently in the butter for 10 minutes until tender but not browned. Add the tomatoes and garlic and blend in a food processor or blender. Heat gently and season to taste before serving.

| **Protein** ▲ | **Iron** ▲ |
| **Fiber** ▲ | **Calcium** ▲ |

· LIGHT LUNCHES ·

## SPINACH ROULADE WITH MUSHROOM AND SOUR CREAM FILLING

Like an appetizing jelly roll, this looks impressive and is always popular.

**Ingredients**
*2 pounds fresh spinach or 1 pound chopped frozen spinach*
*1 tablespoon butter or margarine*
*salt and freshly ground black pepper*
*4 eggs, separated*
*a little grated Parmesan cheese*
**For the filling**
*2 cup button mushrooms, wiped and sliced*
*1 tablespoon butter or margarine*
*1¼ cup sour cream*
*grated nutmeg*
**To garnish**
*water cress sprigs*

Cook the fresh spinach in a saucepan without water for about 10 minutes, until the spinach is tender, then drain thoroughly and chop. Cook frozen spinach according to instructions on the packet, drain well. Add the butter or margarine, a little salt and pepper and the egg yolks and mix thoroughly.

Line a shallow 7×11 inch jelly roll pan with greased wax paper to cover the base of the pan and extend 2 inches up each side. Sprinkle with Parmesan cheese. Preheat the oven to 400°. Beat the egg whites until stiff but not dry and fold them into the spinach mixture. Pour the mixture into the prepared pan and bake for 10-15 minutes, until the roulade is risen and springy to touch.

While the roulade is cooking, make the filling. Heat the butter in a saucepan and fry the mushrooms quickly over a high heat (this keeps them dry) for 2-3 minutes. Then add the sour cream, a little salt, pepper and

grated nutmeg and heat gently, just to warm through the cream. Don't let it boil.

Have ready a large piece of wax paper dusted with Parmesan cheese and turn the roulade out on to this; strip off the first wax paper. Spread the filling over the roulade, then roll it up like a jelly roll and slide it on to a warmed serving plate. Return to the oven for 5 minutes to heat through. Serve immediately garnished with water cress sprigs.

**Protein** ▲▲▲    **Iron** ▲▲▲
**Fiber** ▲▲▲    **Calcium** ▲▲▲

## STRAWBERRIES WITH COINTREAU

**Ingredients**
*1½ pounds small ripe strawberries, hulled and washed*
*2-3 tablespoons fruit sugar*
*3 tablespoons Cointreau or other orange liqueur*
*thin strips of peel from 1 large, well-scrubbed orange*
**To serve**
*thick Greek yogurt (optional)*

Put the strawberries into a bowl and sprinkle with the fruit sugar and Cointreau. Add the orange peel, stir gently, then cover the strawberries and leave to soak for 1 hour. Serve on individual plates, with the liqueur liquid spooned over the strawberries.

**Protein** ▲    **Iron** ▲
**Fiber** ▲    **Calcium** ▲

## BLUEBERRY BOMBE

This is a useful ice cream because it can be used straight from the freezer, without

thawing. For this recipe the meringues are made with less sugar than usual.

Make sure that the serving plate you use is not a metal one. The acidity of the blueberries combined with the metal would discolor the mixture.

**Ingredients**
*3 egg whites*
*scant 1 cup brown sugar*
*1 pound fresh or frozen blueberries*
*fruit sugar*
*1¼ cup whipping cream*

Preheat the oven to 225°. Line a large baking sheet with wax paper; brush with oil. Beat the egg whites until very stiff, then beat in half the sugar and fold in the rest. Put spoonfuls of the mixture on to the baking sheet, then bake the meringues for 2-3 hours, until dried out and crisp. Meanwhile, prepare the blueberry purée. Put the blueberries into a saucepan and cook gently, without adding water, for about 10 minutes, until the juices run and the blueberries are tender. Blend, then sieve the blueberries. Sweeten the purée to taste. Leave to cool.

To complete the mixture beat the cream until standing in soft peaks, adding a little sugar to taste. Break the meringues into rough pieces, not too small, and fold these into the cream, together with the blueberry purée, to create a ripple effect. Spoon the mixture into a serving bowl and freeze until firm.

**Protein** ▲▲    **Iron** ▲
**Fiber** ▲    **Calcium** ▲

*Simple but sumptuous for eating al fresco. Clockwise from top left: Chilled Cucumber Soup with Dill and Radishes; Strawberries with Cointreau; Spinach Roulade with Mushroom and Sour Cream Filling; Baby carrots and zucchini with fresh herbs; Whole wheat rolls; Fresh Tomato Sauce (recipes on pages 49-50).*

# QUICK MAIN MEALS

▲

Whe you begin to prepare vegetarian meals one of the main problems is deciding what to eat for the main meal of the day. Many people find that when meat, fish and poultry are 'off the menu' they have difficulty in deciding what to put in their place. Yet, if you think about it, you probably already have several favorite main dishes which are vegetarian; these may include an appetizing quiche, pizza, or stuffed baked potatoes. If you concentrate on these familiar dishes, gradually adding new ones to your range, you should not find the transition too difficult.

Another thing which often puzzles new vegetarians is how to plan a balanced meal without meat. The easiest way to overcome this problem is to decide on a vegetarian protein dish (containing eggs, cheese, pulses or nuts) and think of this as the 'meat', then plan around it in the usual way. All the menus and recipes in this section were tried out on my own family and friends and met with their approval so I hope you'll enjoy them too.

▲

*Left: Quick, tasty concoctions for weekend family meals. Clockwise from the top: Creamy Coleslaw; Vegetarian Gratin; Couscous with Spiced Vegetable Stew; Apple and Raisin Compote (recipes on pages 54-55).*

A FAMILY WEEKEND
*Serves 4*

*SATURDAY LUNCH*

*Couscous with Spiced Vegetable Stew*

*Cucumber, Fennel
and Radish Salad*

## COUSCOUS WITH SPICED VEGETABLE STEW

Couscous is a pre-cooked grain, so it only needs to be soaked then heated through. The easiest way to do this is to put the couscous into a steamer above the pan of stew.

**Ingredients**
*1½ cup couscous
½ teaspoon salt dissolved in 3 cup
warm water
2 tablespoons olive oil
2 tablespoons chopped parsley*
**For the Spiced Vegetable Stew**
*2 tablespoons olive oil
2 onions, peeled and chopped
1 pound carrots, scraped and cut into
even-sized slices
2 teaspoons each cinnamon, ground cumin
and ground coriander
¾ cup raisins
1½ cup dry chick peas (garbanzos), soaked,
cooked until tender then drained, or 2 cans
(about 3½ cup) chick peas (garbanzos),
drained, or 1 pound frozen lima beans, peas
or corn
3¾ cup water
4 tablespoons tomato paste
salt and freshly ground black pepper*
**To garnish**
*lemon wedges*

Place the couscous in a bowl. Add the water and set aside. Heat the oil in a large saucepan or the saucepan part of the steamer. Add the onion and carrots and fry gently for 10 minutes. Add the spices and cook for 2-3 minutes, stirring. Put in the raisins and the chick peas, beans, peas or corn, the water and tomato paste. Bring to the boil, then turn the heat down so that the stew just simmers. By this time the couscous will have absorbed the water. Put it into the top part of the steamer, a metal colander or strainer, breaking it up a little with your fingers as you do so. Place over the stew, cover and steam for 25-30 minutes. Season to taste. Stir the olive oil and parsley into the couscous and serve with the stew. Garnish with lemon wedges.

*Protein* ▲▲▲    *Iron* ▲▲▲
*Fiber* ▲▲▲    *Calcium* ▲▲

## CUCUMBER, FENNEL AND RADISH SALAD

**Ingredients**
*2 fennel bulbs
1 cucumber, peeled and cubed
1 bunch of radishes, trimmed and sliced
into circles
1 tablespoon lemon juice
4 tablespoons thick plain yogurt
salt and freshly ground black pepper*

Remove any leaves from the fennel and reserve these for decoration. Trim, wash and slice the fennel then put into a bowl with the cucumber and radishes, reserving a few circles for decoration. Add the lemon juice and yogurt; mix well and season with salt and pepper. Spoon mixture into a serving bowl and decorate with the reserved fennel and radish circles.

*Protein* ▲    *Iron* ▲
*Fiber* ▲    *Calcium* ▲

SATURDAY EVENING

*Vegetable Gratin*

*Creamy Coleslaw
(recipe page 96)*

*Bean Sprout and Bell Pepper Salad*

*Apple and Raisin Compote*

## VEGETABLE GRATIN

**Ingredients**
*1½ pounds parsnips, peeled and sliced
1 large onion, peeled and sliced
½ pound carrots, scraped and sliced
½ pound zucchini, sliced
6 ounces cauliflower florets
2 cup grated vegetarian Cheddar-type
cheese
salt and freshly ground black pepper*

Preheat the oven to 400°. Boil the parsnips and onion in 1 inch water for 5-7 minutes, until nearly tender. In a separate saucepan boil or steam the carrots, zucchini and cauliflower for about 5 minutes, until nearly tender. Grease a large shallow casserole. Put half the onion mixture in a layer in the base, sprinkle with a third of the cheese, the carrots, zucchini and cauliflower. Sprinkle with another third of the cheese and a little seasoning. Cover with the remaining onion mixture and the cheese. Bake for 30 minutes until the top is golden.

*Protein* ▲▲▲    *Iron* ▲▲
*Fiber* ▲▲▲    *Calcium* ▲▲▲

## BEAN SPROUT AND BELL PEPPER SALAD

**Ingredients**
*generous 2 cup bean sprouts, washed*
*1 red bell pepper, seeded and chopped*
*1 small onion, peeled and sliced*
*1 large carrot, scraped and coarsely grated*
**For the dressing**
*1 teaspoonful sugar*
*2 teaspoons Dijon mustard*
*1 tablespoon wine vinegar*
*1 tablespoon soy sauce*
*2 tablespoons olive oil*
*salt and freshly ground black pepper*

Put all the vegetables into a bowl. To make the dressing, mix together the first four ingredients then gradually beat in the oil. Toss into the vegetable mixture before serving.

**Protein** ▲          **Iron** ▲
**Fiber** ▲          **Calcium** ▲

## APPLE AND RAISIN COMPOTE

**Ingredients**
*1½ pounds apples, peeled, cored*
*and sliced*
*2 tablespoons honey*
*1 small, well-scrubbed orange*
*pinch of ground cloves*
*¼ cup raisins*
**To serve**
*thick Greek yogurt*

Put the apples into a heavy-based saucepan with the honey, orange peel and juice, ground cloves and raisins. Heat gently for about 10 minutes, until the apples are tender. Serve hot or cold, with the yogurt.

**Protein** ▲          **Iron** ▲▲
**Fiber** ▲▲          **Calcium** ▲▲

---

## SUNDAY LUNCH

*Chilled Beet Soup with Warm Herb Bread*

*Tasty Nut Roast*

*Gravy (recipe page 116)*

*Roast potatoes*

*Buttered cabbage*

*Carrots and leeks*

*Pear and Ginger Pie*

---

## WARM HERB BREAD

**Ingredients**
*1 whole wheat French bread*
*1 stick butter, softened*
*2 tablespoons chopped mixed herbs*

Preheat the oven to 400°. Make slices in the bread 1 inch apart, cutting almost through so that the slices are still joined at the base. Beat the butter with the herbs until soft. Spread the herb butter on both sides of each slice of bread. Push the slices together to re-form the loaf, then wrap it in aluminum foil. Place on a baking sheet and bake for about 20-25 minutes.

**Protein** ▲▲▲          **Iron** ▲▲
**Fiber** ▲▲▲          **Calcium** ▲

---

## CHILLED BEET SOUP

I think this soup tastes particularly delicious when it's chilled, but it is also very good served hot. Use ready-cooked beets or, if you can't get them, buy raw beets and cook them at home. (Don't use beets that have been preserved in vinegar.) To do this, choose even-sized beets. If they still have their leaves attached, cut these off leaving about 4 inches of stem (this prevents the color draining away in young, fresh beets). Put the beets into a saucepan, cover with cold water, bring to the boil, and boil gently for 1-2 hours, or until tender. Slip off the skins with your fingers. Dice the beets and use as described below.

**Ingredients**
*1 onion, peeled and chopped*
*1¼ cup peeled and diced potato*
*1 tablespoon olive oil*
*1 pound cooked beets, peeled and diced*
*2½ pints water*
*salt and freshly ground black pepper*
*a little grated lemon peel*
*1 tablespoon lemon juice*
**To serve**
*3 tablespoons sour or light cream (optional)*

Fry the onion and potato in the oil in a large saucepan for 10 minutes, until they become soft, but not brown. Then add the beets and water. Bring to the boil, then turn the heat down and let the soup simmer for 15-20 minutes, until the vegetables are soft. Blend the soup, then return it to the saucepan. Season to taste, adding lemon peel and juice if necessary to sharpen the flavor. Reheat, then serve in bowls, with a swirl of cream, if wished.

**Protein** ▲          **Iron** ▲
**Fiber** ▲▲▲          **Calcium** ▲

· QUICK MAIN MEALS ·

· QUICK MAIN MEALS ·

## TASTY NUT ROAST

*½ stick butter or margarine*
*2 large onions, peeled and finely chopped*
*1 cup cashew nuts, grated, or*
*1 cup peanuts, grated*
*1 cup hazelnuts or almonds, grated*
*2 cup soft whole wheat bread crumbs*
*1 tablespoon chopped mixed herbs*
*1-2 teaspoons yeast extract*
*salt and freshly ground black pepper*
**Optional garnish**
*sprigs of parsley*

Preheat the oven to 350°. Grease an 8 inch square pan or shallow casserole. Melt the butter in a large saucepan and fry the onions gently for 10 minutes, until tender. Then add the nuts, bread crumbs, herbs, yeast extract and salt and pepper to taste. Press into the prepared pan or casserole and smooth the top. Bake for 35-40 minutes.

Ease the nut roast out of the pan or casserole; cut it into wedges and serve these on individual plates or arrange them on a warmed serving plate with the vegetables and garnished with sprigs of parsley if wished.

**Protein** ▲▲▲     **Iron** ▲▲▲
**Fiber** ▲▲▲     **Calcium** ▲▲

## GRAVY

Make the gravy with sherry as described on page 116, using half the quantity.

*An impressive menu to serve for Sunday lunch. Left to right: Tasty Nut Roast; roast potatoes, carrot and leeks; buttered cabbage; Pear and Ginger Pie; Chilled Beet Soup with Warm Herb Bread (recipes on pages 55-57).*

## PEAR AND GINGER PIE

This is a pleasant change from the classic apple pie, but you could replace the pears with the same quantity of tart apples.

**Ingredients**
*2 cup 85 or 100 per cent*
*whole wheat flour*
*1 stick butter or margarine*
*3 tablespoons cold water*
**For the filling**
*1 teaspoon ground ginger*
*1½ pounds ripe sweet pears, peeled, cored and sliced*
*2 tablespoons dark brown moist sugar*
**To finish**
*milk to glaze*

If you're following this menu, the pie can be cooked at the top of the oven, with the nut roast, but if you are cooking it on its own, preheat the temperature to 400°. Sift the flour into a bowl, adding the bran left behind in the sieve, too. Rub in the butter with your fingertips until the mixture looks like bread crumbs, then mix in the water to make a dough. Roll out half of the pastry on a floured surface and use to line an 8-9 inch pie pan. Sprinkle the ginger over the pastry, making sure that it's well distributed, then put the pears on top of the pastry and sprinkle with the sugar.

Roll out the rest of the pastry and use it to make a top for the pie. Trim the pastry and crimp the edges of the pie with a fork. Make two or three holes for steam to escape and brush with milk. Bake for about 30 minutes, until the pastry is crisp and lightly browned.

If the pears make a great deal of liquid, simply pour this off after you have cut the first slice of pie.

**Protein** ▲▲     **Iron** ▲
**Fiber** ▲▲▲     **Calcium** ▲

*AFTERNOON COFFEE*

*Whole Wheat Victoria Layer Cake*

*Walnut Bread*

## WHOLE WHEAT VICTORIA LAYER CAKE

Follow the instructions for the basic cake on page 84, but use 1½ sticks each of butter or margarine, 1 cup sugar and 1½ cup flour, and 3 eggs, and bake the cake in two 7 inch layer pans. Fill the cake with jam or jelly and sprinkle with superfine sugar.

**Protein** ▲          **Iron** ▲
**Fiber** ▲             **Calcium** ▲

## WALNUT BREAD

**Ingredients**
*scant 1 cup dates*
*1½ cup whole wheat flour*
*3 teaspoons baking poweder*
*¾ cup walnuts, chopped*
*½ teaspoon vanilla*

Preheat the oven to 350°. Grease an 8×5×3½ inch bread pan and line with greased wax paper. Simmer the dates with 1¼ cup water until reduced to a purée. Cool. Sift the flour and baking powder into a bowl. Add the walnuts, vanilla and date mixture. Stir well. Spoon into the prepared pan, and bake for 50-60 minutes. Cool before serving.

**Protein** ▲          **Iron** ▲
**Fiber** ▲             **Calcium** ▲

*SUNDAY EVENING*

*Spinach Gnocchi*

*Crunchy Cabbage and Apple Salad*

*Apricot Fool*

*Crunchy Cookies*

## SPINACH GNOCCHI

**Ingredients**
*1½ pounds fresh spinach, cooked, drained and chopped or 1 pound packet frozen chopped spinach, defrosted*
*1 cup soft white cheese made from skim milk*
*¾ cup curd cheese*
*¾ cup grated Parmesan cheese*
*2 egg yolks*
*salt and freshly ground pepper*
*freshly grated nutmeg*
**To finish and serve**
*wheat germ*
*a little butter or margarine*
*grated Parmesan cheese*
*fresh basil*

Purée the spinach in a blender or food processor. Put the purée back into the saucepan and dry off over the heat for a minute or two. Remove from the heat. Put the skim milk cheese, curd cheese, Parmesan cheese and egg yolks into a bowl and mix together, then add the puréed spinach. Season with salt, pepper and nutmeg. With wet hands, roll heaped teaspoonfuls of the mixture in wheat germ. Half-fill a large saucepan with lightly salted

water and bring to the boil. Drop six or eight of the gnocchi into the water and let them simmer very gently for about 4-5 minutes. When cooked they will float to the surface of the water. Make sure the water does not go beyond simmering point, and remove the gnocchi as soon as they are ready, or they may fall apart. Drain them well, then put them on to a warmed serving plate, dot with a little butter or margarine and keep them warm in a low oven while you cook another batch. Sprinkle with grated Parmesan cheese, garnish and serve immediately.

*Protein ▲▲▲*          *Iron ▲▲▲*
*Fiber ▲▲▲*            *Calcium ▲▲▲*

## CRUNCHY CABBAGE AND APPLE SALAD

**Ingredients**
*1 pound white cabbage, finely shredded*
*2 apples, cored and diced*
*2 cooked beets, peeled and diced*
*2 celery sticks, chopped*
*6 scallions, sliced*
*a few drops of lemon juice*
*salt and freshly ground black pepper*
**To serve**
*a few leaves of radicchio, washed*

Put all the salad ingredients into a bowl and mix together. Season with a little salt and pepper. Place the radicchio in a deep serving bowl and spoon the cabbage salad into the leaves.

*Protein ▲▲*           *Iron ▲*
*Fiber ▲▲▲*            *Calcium ▲▲*

*Delicious gnocchi provides a taste of Italy for a late evening meal. Clockwise from the left: Crunchy Cabbage and Apple Salad; Apricot Fool; Spinach Gnocchi (recipes on pages 58-60).*

## APRICOT FOOL

**Ingredients**
*1 cup dry apricots, covered with boiling water, soaked overnight, then simmered for 20-30 minutes until tender*
*1 cup thick Greek yogurt*
*honey or fruit sugar to taste*
*a few toasted sliced almonds*

Purée the apricots in a food processor or blender. Mix with the yogurt. Sweeten to taste with honey or fruit sugar. Spoon into individual glasses or bowls; chill. Sprinkle with toasted almonds before serving.

**Protein** ▲▲  **Iron** ▲
**Fiber** ▲▲▲  **Calcium** ▲▲

## CRUNCHY COOKIES

**Ingredients**
*1 stick butter or margarine*
*generous ½ cup soft brown sugar*
*1 egg*
*few drops of vanilla or almond flavoring*
*1 cup self-rising 81 or 85 per cent whole wheat flour*
*sliced almonds for coating*

Preheat the oven to 350°. Grease one or two large cookie sheets. Cream the butter or margarine with the sugar, then beat in the egg and flavoring. Add the flour and mix gently until combined. Roll heaped tea-spoonfuls of the mixture in sliced almonds, then place them on the cookie sheets, allowing space for spreading, and flatten them slightly. Bake for 15 minutes, until golden. Carefully remove with a flat knife. Makes 20-24

**Protein** ▲  **Iron** ▲
**Fiber** ▲  **Calcium** ▲

### FAMILY SUPPER
#### Serves 4

*Stir-fried Vegetables with Nutballs*

*Stuffed Melon Halves,
or Fresh fruit*

## STIR-FRIED VEGETABLES WITH NUTBALLS

**Ingredients**
**For the nutballs**
*1 onion, peeled, chopped and fried*
*1 cup grated cashew nuts*
*1 cup grated raw cauliflower*
*1 cup fresh whole wheat bread crumbs*
*2 tablespoons chopped parsley*
*1 teaspoon mixed dry herbs*
*2 eggs*
*salt and freshly ground black pepper*
**For the vegetables**
*2 tablespoons oil*
*1 onion, peeled and chopped*
*1 garlic clove, crushed*
*piece of fresh ginger about the size of a walnut, peeled and finely grated*
*2 pounds prepared vegetables, shredded; white cabbage, carrots, zucchini, leeks, broccoli, cauliflower (as available)*
*salt and freshly ground black pepper*
*soy sauce*

First prepare the nutballs: simply mix everything together and form into balls about the size of walnuts. Half-fill a large saucepan with salted water and bring to the boil. Drop the nutballs into this, cover and cook very gently for 4-5 minutes: the nut-balls are ready when they float to the sur-face of the water. Keep the water at a gentle

simmer, or the nutballs may fall apart. Remove them with a slotted spoon when they're ready and keep them warm while you cook the stir-fried vegetables. To do this, heat the oil in a large saucepan or wok and fry the onion, garlic and ginger for 5 minutes, then put in the vegetables and stir-fry for 2-3 minutes. Season with salt, pepper and soy sauce to taste and serve at once, with the nutballs.

**Protein** ▲▲▲  **Iron** ▲▲
**Fiber** ▲▲▲  **Calcium** ▲▲▲

## STUFFED MELON HALVES

Choose small round melons for these, allowing half for each person; little cantalope melons are ideal.

**Ingredients**
*2 small round melons*
*½ pound strawberries, hulled and cut into even-sized pieces if necessary, or black grapes, halved and seeds removed*
*a little honey*

Cut the melons in half width-wise and remove the seeds. Carefully scoop out the flesh, keeping the skins intact. Use a melon-baller if you have one, or use a spoon and then cut the pieces into even-sized portions. Put the melon into a bowl with the strawberries or grapes and mix gently, adding a little honey to taste if necessary. Spoon the mixture into the melon skins, taking care not to damage the fruit and pile it up attractively.

*Variation:* for another, completely differ-ent way of serving melons, try them halved and filled with ice cream (see page 82).

**Protein** ▲  **Iron** ▲
**Fiber** ▲  **Calcium** ▲

## TAGLIATELLE VERDE WITH MUSHROOMS AND SOUR CREAM

When you're pressed for time, there's nothing to beat pasta for an easy meal. This is a beautifully quick pasta dish with a wonderful, creamy mushroom sauce, which can be cooked while the pasta is boiling.

**Ingredients**
*½-¾ pound tagliatelle verde*
**For the sauce**
*1 onion, peeled and chopped*
*2 tablespoons butter or margarine*
*1 garlic clove, crushed*
*¾ pound button mushrooms, wiped and sliced*
*1¼ cup sour cream*
*salt and freshly ground black pepper*
*freshly grated nutmeg*
**To garnish**
*flat-leafed parsley or water cress sprigs*

First make the sauce: fry the onion gently in 1 tablespoon of the butter or margarine for about 10 minutes until softened. Then add the garlic and mushrooms and cook quickly for 2-3 minutes. Add the sour cream, season with salt, pepper and nutmeg, then remove from the heat. Half-fill a large saucepan with water and bring to the boil, then add the tagliatelle. Stir once, then leave the tagliatelle to cook, uncovered, for 10-15 minutes, until a piece feels tender but not soggy then you bite it. Drain immediately into a colander, then tip back into the still-hot saucepan, add the rest of the butter or margarine and some salt and pepper. Stir for 1 minute until the butter has melted. Quickly re-heat the sauce, then tip the tagliatelle into a hot serving bowl. Pour the sauce over the top and serve at once garnished with flat-leafed parsley or water cress sprigs.

*Protein* ▲▲▲　　*Iron* ▲
*Fiber* ▲▲▲　　*Calcium* ▲

## SPAGHETTI WITH LENTIL BOLOGNESE SAUCE

**Ingredients**
*½-¾ pound spaghetti*
*1 tablespoon butter or margarine*
*freshly ground black pepper*
**For the sauce**
*1¼ cup cooked whole green lentils (see page 131) or 2 cans (about 1¾ cup) lentils*
*2 onions, chopped*
*2 tablespoons oil*
*2 garlic cloves, crushed*
*2 celery stick, chopped*
*2 carrots, finely diced*
*2 tablespoons tomato paste*
*salt and freshly ground black pepper*
**To serve**
*grated Parmesan cheese*

First, start to prepare the sauce: drain the lentils, keeping the liquid. Fry the onions in the oil for 5 minutes, then add the garlic, celery and carrots. Simmer covered for 15 minutes, until tender. Stir in the lentils, tomato paste, seasoning and a little of the reserve liquid to make a thick, soft consistency. Simmer for about 10 minutes, adding more liquid if necessary. Half-fill a large saucepan with water, add a teaspoon of salt and bring to the boil. Add the spaghetti and simmer for about 10 minutes, until just tender. Drain the spaghetti, then return to the saucepan with the butter or margarine and pepper. Make sure the spaghetti is hot, then turn it out on to a hot serving plate and pour the sauce on top. Hand round grated cheese separately.

*Protein* ▲▲▲　　*Iron* ▲▲▲
*Fiber* ▲▲▲　　*Calcium* ▲

## ENDIVE, WALNUT AND WATER CRESS SALAD

**Ingredients**
*1 garlic clove, crushed*
*salt and freshly ground black pepper*
*1 tablespoon wine vinegar*
*3 tablespoons olive oil*
*4 heads of endive, washed*
*1 large bunch water cress*
*½ cup walnuts, roughly chopped*

Put the garlic into a salad bowl with some salt and pepper and the wine vinegar. Mix together, then add the oil. Break the endive into even-sized pieces and add these to the bowl, together with the water cress and walnuts. Toss the salad gently with salad servers so that everything gets evenly coated with the dressing. Check the seasoning and serve immediately.

*Protein* ▲　　*Iron* ▲
*Fiber* ▲　　*Calcium* ▲

THREE

*Pasta Shells with Red Lentil and Tomato Sauce*

*Broiled Basil Tomatoes (recipe page 23)*

## PASTA SHELLS WITH RED LENTIL AND TOMATO SAUCE

### Ingredients
*½-¾ pound pasta shells*
*1 tablespoon butter or margarine*
**For the sauce**
*1 large onion, peeled and chopped*
*2 tablespoons oil*
*2 garlic cloves, crushed*
*½ teaspoon cinnamon*
*1½ cup red lentils, washed*
*2 cup canned tomatoes*
*2 cup water*
*salt and freshly ground black pepper*

First start to prepare the sauce. Fry the onion in the oil for 10 minutes, then add the garlic, cinnamon, lentils, tomatoes and water and bring to the boil. Simmer gently for about 20 minutes, until the lentils are tender. Season. Cook the pasta shells as described in the previous recipe. Serve with the red lentil sauce.

**Protein** ▲▲▲     **Iron** ▲▲▲
**Fiber** ▲▲▲     **Calcium** ▲▲▲

**From the left: Broiled Basil Tomatoes (recipe on page 23); Pasta Shells with Red Lentil and Tomato Sauce; Tagliatelle Verde with Mushrooms and Sour Cream; Lettuce and Fresh Herb Salad (recipe on page 66); Spaghetti with Lentil Bolognese Sauce (recipes on pages 61-62).**

## HEARTY CASSEROLES
*Serves 4*

### ONE

*Chili Vegetarian-Style*

*Brown Rice*

*Shredded Spinach with Mushrooms*

## CHILI VEGETARIAN-STYLE

**Ingredients**
*1 onion, peeled and chopped*
*1 green bell pepper, seeded and chopped*
*1 tablespoon olive oil*
*1 garlic clove, crushed*
*2 cup canned tomatoes*
*¾ cup dry kidney beans or use*
*2 cans (about 3 cup) kidney beans*
*1 cup cooked green lentils (page 131)*
*1 teaspoon mild paprika*
*½-1 teaspoon chili powder*
*salt, sugar and freshly ground black pepper*

If using dry kidney beans, soak for 6-8 hours then drain; cover with fresh water, boil hard for 10 minutes, then simmer gently for 1¼-1½ hours, until tender.

Fry the onion and bell pepper in the oil in a large saucepan for 10 minutes, then add the garlic and tomatoes. Drain the kidney beans and the lentils, reserving the liquid, and add the beans and lentils to the tomato mixture. Flavor with the paprika and chili powder, salt, sugar and pepper to taste. Simmer for 10-15 minutes, season and serve with the rice.

**Protein** ▲ ▲ ▲     **Iron** ▲ ▲ ▲
**Fiber** ▲ ▲ ▲     **Calcium** ▲ ▲

## BROWN RICE

There are two ways of cooking brown rice. You can half-fill a large saucepan with salted water, bring to the boil, add the rice and let it boil for 20-30 minutes, until tender, then drain. Or you can put 1 measure of rice into a saucepan with 2 measures of cold water and some salt; bring to the boil, then turn the heat down, cover the pan and cook very gently for 40-45 minutes, until the rice is tender and all the water has been absorbed. In either case, allow 1¼ cup rice (and 2½ cup water for the absorption method) for 4 people. Add a knob of butter or margarine and some freshly ground black pepper to the cooked rice.

**Protein** ▲ ▲          **Iron** ▲
**Fiber** ▲          **Calcium** ▲

## SHREDDED SPINACH WITH MUSHROOMS

**Ingredients**
*1 tablespoon Dijon mustard*
*1 tablespoon wine vinegar*
*1 garlic clove, crushed*
*½ teaspoon salt*
*3 tablespoons olive oil*
*1 pound tender spinach leaves, washed and finely shredded*
*generous 1 cup button mushrooms, wiped and sliced*

Put the mustard, vinegar, garlic and salt into a bowl. Gradually stir in the oil to make a thick dressing, then add the spinach and mushrooms and stir gently, until all the ingredients are well coated.

**Protein** ▲          **Iron** ▲
**Fiber** ▲ ▲ ▲          **Calcium** ▲

---

**TWO**

*All-season Vegetable Casserole with Whole Wheat Dumplings*

*Ripe grapes, or Creamy Chocolate Layer*

---

## ALL-SEASON VEGETABLE CASSEROLE WITH WHOLE WHEAT DUMPLINGS

**Ingredients**
*1 tablespoon olive oil*
*2 onions, peeled and chopped*
*2 celery sticks, sliced*
*½ pound carrots, scraped and sliced*
*½ pound parsnips, scraped and diced*
*2 garlic cloves, crushed*
*2 tablespoons 100 per cent whole wheat self-rising flour*
*2½ cup water*
*2 teaspoons yeast extract*
*1 tablespoon vegetarian bouillon powder*
*3 tablespoons soy sauce*
*4 medium potatoes, peeled and halved*
*½ cup pearled barley*
*1 pound button mushrooms, wiped and sliced*
*salt and freshly ground black pepper*
**For the dumplings**
*generous 1 cup 100 per cent whole wheat flour*
*1½ teaspoons baking powder*
*½ teaspoon salt*
*generous ½ stick hard butter, grated*
*1 teaspoon yeast extract*
*water to mix*

Preheat the oven to 350°. Heat the oil in a large saucepan, fry the onions, celery, carrots and parsnips for 10 minutes, stirring occasionally. Stir in the garlic, flour, water, yeast extract, bouillon powder and soy sauce. Add the potatoes, barley and mushrooms. Bring to the boil, then transfer to a large casserole and bake the vegetables and sauce for 1 hour.

About half an hour before the casserole is ready, prepare the dumplings. Half-fill a large saucepan with water and bring to the boil. Put the flour, baking powder, salt and butter into a bowl and mix well together. Then add the yeast extract and enough water to make a soft dough. Form into eight even-sized balls. Simmer the dumplings for about 20 minutes, until puffed up. Drain the dumplings and serve with the casserole.

**Protein** ▲ ▲ ▲          **Iron** ▲ ▲ ▲
**Fiber** ▲ ▲ ▲          **Calcium** ▲ ▲ ▲

## CREAMY CHOCOLATE LAYER

**Ingredients**
*generous 1 cup whole wheat bread crumbs*
*½ cup brown sugar*
*2 tablespoons cocoa (or carob) powder*
*2 teaspoons instant coffee powder*
*1½ cup whipping cream*
*grated chocolate (or carob) bar to decorate*

Mix together the bread crumbs, sugar, cocoa (or carob) powder and instant coffee powder. Whip the cream until it's standing in soft peaks. Layer the bread crumb mixture with the cream in glass bowls. Grate a little chocolate (or carob) bar on top. Chill.

**Protein** ▲          **Iron** ▲
**Fiber** ▲          **Calcium** ▲

*Clockwise from the left: Shredded Spinach with Mushrooms; All-season Vegetable Casserole with Whole Wheat Dumplings; Chili Vegetarian-Style with Brown Rice (pages 63-64).*

· QUICK MAIN MEALS ·

· QUICK MAIN MEALS ·

## PIZZA SUPPER
### Serves 4

*Quick Pizza*

*Lettuce and Fresh Herb Salad, or*

*Fennel and Water Cress Salad with Orange Dressing*

*Yogurt Knickerbocker Glory, or*

*Mocha Maple Ice Cream with Almond Shortbread*

## QUICK PIZZA

**Ingredients**
*2 cup self-rising 85 or 100 per cent whole wheat flour*
*2 teaspoons baking powder*
*½ teaspoon salt*
*½ stick butter or margarine*
*8-9 tablespoons water*
**For the topping**
*2 onions, peeled and chopped*
*2 tablespoons oil*
*2 tablespoons tomato paste*
*1-2 teaspoons oregano or mixed herbs*
*salt, sugar and freshly ground black pepper*
*generous 1 cup button mushrooms, sliced, or 8-10 black olives, or a small green bell pepper, seeded, chopped and fried*
*¾ cup grated cheese*
**To garnish**
*radish slices*
*parsley sprigs*

Preheat the oven to 425°. Brush a large baking sheet or a 12 inch round pizza pan with oil. Sift the flour and baking powder into a bowl, tipping in the residue of bran which will be left in the sieve if you're using 100 per cent whole wheat flour. Add the salt, rub the butter into the flour with your fingertips, then pour in the water and mix to a pliable dough. Either divide the dough in half and roll out into two 8 inch circles, or make one large circle to fit the pizza pan. Put the dough on the baking sheet or plate, prick all over. Bake for 10 minutes. Meanwhile prepare the topping. Fry the onion in the oil for 10 minutes, then remove from the heat and add the tomato paste, herbs and salt, sugar and pepper to taste. Spread this mixture on top of the pizza base, top with the mushrooms, olives or green bell pepper and sprinkle with grated cheese. Bake for 15-20 minutes. Garnish with radish slices and parsley sprigs before serving.

**Protein** ▲▲▲    **Iron** ▲▲▲
**Fiber** ▲▲▲    **Calcium** ▲▲

## LETTUCE AND FRESH HERB SALAD

**Ingredients**
*1 tablespoon Dijon mustard*
*½ teaspoon sugar*
*1 tablespoon red wine vinegar*
*3 tablespoons olive oil*
*salt and freshly ground black pepper*
*½ small cucumber, peeled and thinly sliced*
*1 small hearty lettuce, shredded*
*2 tablespoons chopped mixed herbs*

Mix together the mustard, sugar, red wine vinegar and oil. Season, add the cucumber, lettuce and herbs just before serving.

**Protein** ▲    **Iron** ▲
**Fiber** ▲    **Calcium** ▲

*Clockwise from top left: Fennel and Water Cress Salad with Orange Dressing; Yogurt Knickerbocker Glory; Lettuce and Fresh Herb Salad; Quick Pizza (recipes on pages 66-68).*

## QUICK MAIN MEALS ·

# FENNEL AND WATER CRESS SALAD WITH ORANGE DRESSING

**Ingredients**
*1 large fennel bulb, washed, trimmed
and sliced
1 bunch of water cress*
**For the dressing**
*3 well-scrubbed oranges
2 teaspoons honey
2 teaspoons Dijon mustard
4 tablespoons olive oil
salt and freshly ground black pepper*

First make the dressing: put the peel of 1 orange into a large bowl with the honey, mustard, 4 tablespoons orange juice and olive oil and mix together well, adding a little seasoning to taste. Put the fennel and water cress into a bowl. Peel the remaining two oranges. Cut the orange flesh into pieces and add to the fennel and water cress. Just before you want to serve the salad, pour in the dressing and mix the salad gently. Garnish with fennel tops.

**Protein** ▲          **Iron** ▲
**Fiber** ▲          **Calcium** ▲

# YOGURT KNICKERBOCKER GLORY

**Ingredients**
*1 generous cup thick Greek yogurt
1½ cup raspberry yogurt, preferably
made with real fruit and sweetened with
dark brown moist sugar
2 large bananas, peeled and sliced
½ cup chopped hazelnuts*

Layer the plain yogurt, raspberry yogurt and banana attractively in four deep glasses, putting some of the banana slices down the sides of the glasses. Sprinkle the chopped nuts on top. Chill.

**Protein** ▲ ▲ ▲          **Iron** ▲
**Fiber** ▲          **Calcium** ▲ ▲ ▲

# MOCHA MAPLE ICE CREAM

**Ingredients**
*1¼ cup whipping cream
2 tablespoons real maple syrup
1 tablespoon good-quality instant coffee,
dissolved in 2 tablespoons hot water
1 cup cashew nuts, roughly chopped
¾ cup raisins*

Whip the cream. Stir in the maple syrup, coffee, nuts and raisins. Turn into a container and freeze until firm. Remove from the freezer 30 minutes before serving.

**Protein** ▲ ▲          **Iron** ▲
**Fiber** ▲          **Calcium** ▲

# ALMOND SHORTBREAD

**Ingredients**
*1½ sticks soft butter or margarine
scant ½ cup soft brown sugar
1½ cup 81 or 85 per cent
whole wheat flour
½ cup brown rice flour
scant ½ cup ground almonds*

Preheat the oven to 300°. Grease a 7×11 inch jelly roll pan. Cream the butter and sugar, then beat in the rest of the ingredients. Press the mixture into the pan, prick the top and bake for about 1 hour or until pale golden. Cool slightly, then cut into fingers.

**Protein** ▲          **Iron** ▲
**Fiber** ▲          **Calcium** ▲

## FAMILY FAVORITES
### Serves 4

## ONE

*Cheese Fritters with Parsley Sauce*

*Oven French Fries*

*Lightly cooked broccoli*

*Broiled tomatoes*

*Fruit salad*

# CHEESE FRITTERS

These are a firm family favorite, the vegetarian equivalent, I think, of fish fingers! They're a bit fiddly to make, but freeze excellently and can be fried from frozen, so it's worth making up a double quantity if you like them.

**Ingredients**
*3 cup milk
1 small onion, peeled and stuck with 3-4
cloves
1 bay leaf
1 cup semolina or cream of wheat
1 cup grated vegetarian Cheddar-type
cheese
½ teaspoon dry mustard
salt and freshly ground black pepper*
**To coat**
*1 large egg, beaten
dry bread crumbs
oil for shallow frying*
**To garnish**
*slices of lemon, sprigs of parsley*

Put the milk, onion and bay leaf into a saucepan and bring the milk to the boil. Then remove from the heat, cover and leave for 10-15 minutes, for the flavors to infuse. Remove the onion and bay leaf. Bring the milk back to the boil, then sprinkle the semolina or cream of wheat over the top, stirring all the time. Let the mixture simmer for about 5 minutes, to cook the semolina or cream of wheat. Remove from the heat and beat in the cheese, mustard and seasoning to taste. Spread the mixture out on an oiled plate or baking sheet to a depth of about ½ inch. Smooth the top, then leave until completely cold. With a wet knife, cut into thick, finger-length pieces; dip each in beaten egg and then in the dry crumbs. Shallow fry in hot oil until crisp on both sides, drain well on paper towels. Garnish with lemon and parsley, and serve with Parsley Sauce.

**Protein** ▲▲▲ **Iron** ▲
**Fiber** ▲▲ **Calcium** ▲▲▲

## PARSLEY SAUCE

**Ingredients**
*1 tablespoon butter or margarine*
*1 heaped tablespoon all-purpose flour*
*1¼ cup milk*
*2 tablespoons chopped parsley*
*salt and freshly ground black pepper*

Melt the butter or margarine in a medium-sized saucepan over a gentle heat, then stir in the flour. Let the flour cook for a few seconds, then turn up the heat and pour in about a third of the milk. Stir vigorously to make a thick, smooth mixture, then add the rest of the milk, in two more batches, stirring hard. Then stir in the parsley and salt and pepper to taste.

**Protein** ▲ **Iron** ▲
**Fiber** ▲ **Calcium** ▲

## FRUIT SALAD

**Ingredients**
*2 oranges*
*6 ounces strawberries, hulled and washed*
*½ pound black grapes, halved and seeded*
*2 kiwi fruit, peeled and sliced*
*2 apples, cored and sliced (unpeeled if skins are good)*
*⅔ cup orange juice*

Holding the oranges over a bowl and using a sharp knife, cut away the peel and white pith, using a sawing action and cutting round the fruit as if peeling an apple to produce a long piece of peel. Then cut the segments away from the white inner skin. Put the oranges into the bowl and add the rest of the fruit and the orange juice. Serve on its own, or with thick yogurt.

**Protein** ▲ **Iron** ▲
**Fiber** ▲▲ **Calcium** ▲

TWO
*Cheese-topped Bell Peppers*

*Honeyed Pears*

## CHEESE-TOPPED BELL PEPPERS

**Ingredients**
*4 green bell peppers*
**For the filling**
*1 large onion, peeled and finely chopped*
*2 tablespoons olive oil*
*½ pound mushrooms, wiped and chopped*
*1 cup mixed nuts, grated*

*¼ pound tomatoes, peeled and chopped*
*1 tablespoon chopped mixed herbs*
*1-2 teaspoons yeast extract*
*salt and freshly ground black pepper*
*¼ cup Mozzarella cheese, cut into four*
**To serve**
*Fresh Tomato Sauce (see page 49)*

Cut the tops off the green bell peppers and scoop out the seeds. Boil in 1 inch water for 5 minutes, until they begin to soften. Drain, then dry on paper towels. Place in a greased casserole. Preheat the oven to 350°. Fry the onion in the oil for 10 minutes. Add the mushrooms and cook for a further 2-3 minutes. Stir in the nuts, tomatoes, herbs, yeast extract and salt and pepper to taste. Spoon into the bell peppers. Place a piece of Mozzarella cheese on top of each pepper. Bake for 25-30 minutes.

**Protein** ▲▲▲ **Iron** ▲▲▲
**Fiber** ▲▲▲ **Calcium** ▲▲

## HONEYED PEARS

**Ingredients**
*4 large ripe sweet pears, peeled, cored and sliced*
*2 tablespoons honey*
*2 tablespoons boiling water*
*4 tablespoons chopped walnuts*
**To serve**
*thick plain yogurt*

Put the pears into a bowl. Mix the honey and water, then spoon this over the fruit. Leave to marinate for about 30 minutes, turning the slices gently once or twice, to distribute the honey. Divide the pears between four individual bowls and sprinkle with the chopped walnuts.

**Protein** ▲ **Iron** ▲
**Fiber** ▲ **Calcium** ▲

**THREE**

*Whole Wheat Cheese and Onion Pie*

*Peas with mint*

*Water cress sprigs*

*Little Honey Egg Custards
(recipe page 81), or
Banana and Almond Crumble*

## WHOLE WHEAT CHEESE AND ONION PIE

**Ingredients**
*2 cup 85 or 100 per cent
whole wheat flour
½ teaspoon salt
1 stick butter or margarine
3 tablespoons cold water*
**For the filling**
*3 large onions, peeled and sliced
1½ cup grated cheese
salt, freshly ground black pepper
freshly grated nutmeg*

Preheat the oven to 425°. Cook the onions in 1 inch boiling salted water for 5 minutes, to soften slightly. Drain and cool. Meanwhile, make the pastry. Sift the flour into a large bowl, adding the residue of bran from

*Dishes to please young and old. Clockwise from the top: Cheese-topped Bell Peppers; Cheese Fritters with Parsley Sauce and oven French fries; Fruit Salad; Honeyed Pears with thick plain yogurt (recipes on pages 68-69).*

the sieve if you're using 100 per cent whole wheat flour. Add the salt, then rub in the butter with your fingertips until the mixture looks like fine bread crumbs. Mix to a dough with the water, then roll out half the pastry to fit an 8-9 inch pie pan. Mix the cheese with the onions, season to taste and sprinkle with nutmeg. Spoon the mixture on top of the pastry. Roll out the remaining pastry to fit the top; trim and press edges together. Bake for 30 minutes.

*Variation:* for Onion and Sour Cream Pie, use a small carton of sour cream and 2 teaspoons wholegrain or Dijon mustard instead of the grated cheese. For Onion Pie with a Cheesy Crust, sprinkle the pastry with 1 tablespoon grated Parmesan cheese, and reduce the quantity of cheese in the pie to ½ cup.

*Protein* ▲ ▲ ▲     *Iron* ▲
*Fiber* ▲ ▲     *Calcium* ▲ ▲ ▲

## BANANA AND ALMOND CRUMBLE

**Ingredients**
*4 bananas, peeled and sliced
1 cup 100 per cent whole wheat flour
¾ cup ground almonds
2½ tablespoons butter or margarine
⅓ cup dark brown moist sugar
3 tablespoons sliced almonds, crushed*

Preheat the broiler. Put the bananas into a lightly greased, shallow casserole. Mix together the flour, ground almonds and butter or margarine. Add the sugar and sliced almonds, then put this mixture over the bananas in an even layer. Place under the broiler for about 15 minutes, until the crumble is crisp and lightly browned.

*Protein* ▲ ▲ ▲     *Iron* ▲ ▲
*Fiber* ▲ ▲ ▲     *Calcium* ▲

<table><tr><td>

### BEAN FEAST
*Serves 4*

*Kidney Bean Stew with Millet Pilaff*

*Blackberry Fool*

</td><td>

tomatoes to the vegetables and season to taste. Cook over a low heat for 5-10 minutes, until heated through, adding a little of the reserved liquid if necessary. Serve the millet with the stew; sprinkle with chopped parsley.

**Protein** ▲▲▲   **Iron** ▲▲▲
**Fiber** ▲▲▲   **Calcium** ▲

</td><td>

### SIMPLE SPECIAL LUNCH
*Serves 4*

*Lentil Roast*

*Honey-baked Apples*

</td></tr></table>

## KIDNEY BEAN STEW WITH MILLET PILAFF

**Ingredients**
*1½ cup millet (see page 132)*
*2½ cup water*
*½ teaspoon salt*
**For the stew**
*2 tablespoons olive oil*
*2 large onions, peeled and chopped*
*4 carrots, scraped and sliced*
*1 red bell pepper, seeded and chopped*
*1 green bell pepper, seeded and chopped*
*1 cup dry kidney beans, soaked
and cooked (see page 131), or 2 cans
(about 3 cup) kidney beans*
*2 cup canned tomatoes*
*salt and freshly ground black pepper*
**To garnish**
*chopped parsley*

Put the millet into a dry saucepan and toast over a medium heat for about 5 minutes, stirring all the time. The grains will brown lightly and some will start to 'pop'. Add the water and salt and bring to the boil. Cover the saucepan, turn down the heat and leave to cook for 15-20 minutes, until the millet is fluffy and has absorbed all the water. Meanwhile prepare the stew. Heat the oil in a large saucepan and fry the onions, carrots and bell peppers gently, cover the saucepan, for 15-20 minutes, until tender. Stir from time to time. Drain the beans, keeping the liquid. Add the beans and

## BLACKBERRY FOOL

This simple, creamy fool can be made with other fruits instead of blackberries. Red-currants are delicious; cook these as described and sieve them to remove stems and seeds. Strawberries and raspberries do not need to be cooked. For a lower fat version, use a carton of thick Greek yogurt instead of the cream.

This mixture can also be served like ice cream. Freeze the chilled mixture until firm. Place in the refrigerator for 10-15 minutes before required.

**Ingredients**
*1 pound fresh or frozen blackberriess*
*½ cup smooth low-fat white cheese*
*honey, sugar or fruit sugar to taste*
*⅔ cup whipping cream, whipped*

Put the blackberries into a dry saucepan and heat gently until the juices run and the blackberries are tender. Remove from the heat and leave to cool. Drain and reserve the juice from the blackberries and either purée and sieve the fruit for a smooth texture, or mash them. Stir in the low-fat white cheese and enough of the reserved blackberry juice to make a creamy consistency. Sweeten as necessary with sugar, honey or fruit sugar, then fold in the whipped cream. Serve chilled.

**Protein** ▲   **Iron** ▲
**Fiber** ▲   **Calcium** ▲▲

## LENTIL ROAST

Mint sauce goes well with this lentil roast, which makes a pleasant alternative to the nut roast for a special lunch, and is also good cold, served in slices, with pickles.

**Ingredients**
*butter or margarine and dry bread crumbs
for coating the pan*
*1 cup split red lentils*
*generous 1 cup water*
*1 bay leaf*
*1 cup grated cheese*
*1 onion, peeled and finely chopped*
*1 cup button mushrooms, wiped and
finely chopped*
*scant 1 cup soft whole wheat bread crumbs*
*1 tablespoon chopped parsley*
*1 tablespoon lemon juice*
*1 egg*
*salt and freshly ground black pepper*

Prepare a 8×5×3½ inch bread pan by putting a long narrow strip of greased wax paper on the base and up the narrow sides. Grease the pan well with butter or margarine and sprinkle generously with dry crumbs. Put the lentils, water and bay leaf into a medium-sized saucepan and simmer very gently, uncovered, for about 20 minutes, until the lentils are tender and all the liquid absorbed. Remove the bay leaf. Preheat the oven to 375°. Add the grated cheese to the lentils, together with the onion, mushrooms, bread crumbs, chopped parsley, lemon juice and egg. Mix well and season with salt and pepper. Spoon the mixture into the pan and level the top. Bake, uncovered, for 45-60 minutes, until firm and golden brown on top. Slip a knife around the edges of the loaf to loosen, then turn out on to a warmed serving plate.

Serve in slices, with gravy (recipe page 116), mint sauce, roast potatoes and vegetables.

**Protein** ▲▲▲   **Iron** ▲▲▲
**Fiber** ▲▲   **Calcium** ▲▲▲

## HONEY-BAKED APPLES

**Ingredients**
*4 medium-sized tart apples*
*¾ cup raisins or cooking dates*
*1 tablespoon honey*
*6 tablespoons hot water*

Preheat the oven to 375°. Core the apples, then, using a sharp knife, score the skin around the middle of the apples. Stuff the centers with raisins or dates, then put the apples in a lightly-greased shallow casserole. Dissolve the honey in the water and spoon over and round the apples. Bake for about 40 minutes, until the apples are soft but still whole.

*Variation:* for a special treat, make apple snowballs. Prepare the apples as described, but peel before baking. Bake until just tender, then drain off the liquid and allow the apples to cool. Beat 4 egg whites until stiff, then beat in scant ½ cup sugar. Spread the mixture all over the apples, then bake at 225° for 3 hours, until the meringue is crisp and golden.

**Protein** ▲   **Iron** ▲
**Fiber** ▲▲   **Calcium** ▲

---

## A FLAVOR OF INDIA
### Serves 4

*Potato and Pea Curry*
*with Turmeric Rice*

*Fresh Onion Chutney*

*Spiced Okra*

*Poppadums*

*Dhal Curry*
*Apple, Tomato and Leek Salad*
*Samosas*

*Sliced bananas or fresh mango*

---

## POTATO AND PEA CURRY

**Ingredients**
*2 tablespoons butter or margarine*
*1 onion, peeled and chopped*
*2 teaspoons each turmeric, ground cumin and ground coriander*
*¼ teaspoon chili powder*
*2 bay leaves*
*1 cup canned tomatoes*
*1 pound potatoes, peeled and quartered*
*1¼ cup water*
*salt and freshly ground black pepper*
*¾ pound frozen peas*

Melt the butter or margarine in a large saucepan and fry the onion until soft. Stir in the spices and bay leaves. Add the remaining ingredients. Bring to the boil, then cover and simmer for 10-15 minutes.

**Protein** ▲▲   **Iron** ▲▲▲
**Fiber** ▲▲▲   **Calcium** ▲

---

## TURMERIC RICE

**Ingredients**
*1⅓ cup brown rice*
*1½ tablespoons oil*
*¾ teaspoon turmeric*
*3 cloves*
*1 bay leaf*
*2½ cup water*
*salt and freshly ground black pepper*

Wash the rice and drain well. Heat the oil in a medium-sized saucepan, add the rice, and fry for 3-4 minutes without browning. Stir in the turmeric, cloves and bay leaf. Cook for a few seconds longer, then add the water and seasoning. Bring to the boil, cover and turn the heat down as low as possible. Cook for 40-45 minutes, until tender and all the water has been absorbed. Stir with a fork before serving.

**Protein** ▲▲   **Iron** ▲
**Fiber** ▲   **Calcium** ▲

---

## FRESH ONION CHUTNEY

This chutney is simple to make, tasty and colorful. It makes a delicious sambal.

**Ingredients**
*1 onion, peeled and sliced*
*salt and freshly ground black pepper*
*2 tablespoons lemon juice*
*1 teaspoon paprika*

Sprinkle the onion with salt then leave on one side for 30 minutes to soften. Rinse and drain. Mix with the lemon juice, paprika and salt and pepper to taste. Serve in a small bowl.

**Protein** ▲   **Iron** ▲
**Fiber** ▲   **Calcium** ▲

## · QUICK MAIN MEALS ·

## SPICED OKRA

**Ingredients**
*1 onion, peeled and chopped*
*2 tablespoons oil*
*1 garlic clove, crushed*
*1 teaspoon ground cumin*
*1 teaspoon ground coriander*
*2 tomatoes, peeled and chopped, or*
*1 cup canned tomatoes*
*½ pound okra, washed and trimmed*
*4 tablespoons water*
*1 tablespoon tomato paste*
*salt, sugar and freshly ground black pepper*

Fry the onion in the oil for 5 minutes without browning, then add the garlic, cumin and coriander. Stir for a couple of minutes, then put in the tomatoes and okra. Add the water and tomato paste. Cover the pan and leave to cook for 20 minutes, until the okra is tender, stirring from time to time. Season with salt, a dash of sugar, and freshly ground black pepper.

*Protein* ▲          *Iron* ▲
*Fiber* ▲          *Calcium* ▲

## APPLE, TOMATO AND LEEK SALAD

**Ingredients**
*3 sweet apples, cored and diced*
*3 tomatoes, diced*
*1 large leek, washed, trimmed and sliced into thin rings*
*2 tablespoons lemon juice or 2 tablespoons lime juice*
*salt and freshly ground black pepper*

**Clockwise from top left: Spiced Okra; fresh mango; Potato and Pea Curry with Turmeric Rice; sliced bananas; Fresh Onion Chutney (recipes on pages 73-75).**

Put the apples into a bowl with the tomatoes, leek and lemon juice. Mix well; season with salt and pepper.

*Protein* ▲          *Iron* ▲
*Fiber* ▲          *Calcium* ▲

## POPPADUMS

Thin, crisp, golden poppadums make the perfect accompaniment to curries and the poppadum wafers are now available at most supermarkets. They can be prepared under the broiler or by shallow-frying, but I prefer to hold the poppadums with a pair of tongs and plunge them into a deep fryer for just a few seconds, until puffed up.

## DHAL CURRY

**Ingredients**
*1 tablespoon butter or margarine*
*1 onion, peeled and chopped*
*1 garlic clove, crushed*
*generous 1½ cup split red lentils*
*½ teaspoon chili powder*
*1 teaspoon each ground cumin, turmeric, salt*
*3½ cup water*
*¼ cup creamed coconut*

Melt the butter or margarine in a large saucepan. Add the onion and fry gently for 10 minutes, until soft but not browned, then stir in the garlic and fry for a further 1-2 minutes. Add the lentils, chili powder, cumin, turmeric, salt and water. Bring to the boil, then cover and leave to simmer gently for 25-30 minutes. Add the creamed coconut and stir until dissolved. Check seasoning and serve.

*Protein* ▲▲▲          *Iron* ▲▲▲
*Fiber* ▲▲▲          *Calcium* ▲

## SAMOSAS

**Ingredients**
**For the filling**
*1 large onion, peeled and chopped*
*2 tablespoons olive oil*
*1 large garlic clove, crushed*
*1 teaspoon mustard seed*
*1 teaspoon grated fresh ginger*
*1 teaspoon ground cumin*
*1 teaspoon ground coriander*
*1½ pounds potatoes, cooked and diced*
*½ pound frozen peas, defrosted*
*salt and freshly ground black pepper*
**For the pastry**
*2 cup whole wheat flour*
*½ teaspoon salt*
*½ teaspoon baking powder*
*½ stick butter or margarine, melted*
*6-7 tablespoons cold water*
*oil for deep frying*

Fry the onion in the oil for 8 minutes, until soft but not browned. Add the garlic, mustard seed, ginger, cumin and coriander and cook for a further 2 minutes. Remove from the heat and add the potato and peas. Mix well; season. Cool.

For the pastry, put the flour, salt and baking powder into a bowl, make a well in the center and add the melted butter or margarine and water. Mix to a dough; it should be soft but not sticky. Knead the dough for 5 minutes, then divide into 16 pieces. Roll each piece into a circle about 6 inches in diameter, then cut the circles in half to make 32 half-circles. Put a heaped teaspoonful of the filling on top of each half-circle of pastry, brush the edges with water and press them together to form a triangular-shaped packet. Heat the oil to 350° then fry the samosas in batches. Drain well.

*Protein* ▲          *Iron* ▲
*Fiber* ▲          *Calcium* ▲

· QUICK MAIN MEALS ·

## CHINESE STYLE
### Serves 4

*Savory Fried Rice*

*Mushrooms in Soy Sauce*

*Bean Curd with Bamboo Shoots and Carrots*

*Lychees, kiwi fruits or tangerines*

## SAVORY FRIED RICE

**Ingredients**
*1 teaspoon salt*
*1¼ cup brown rice*
*1 tablespoon olive oil*
*⅔ cup frozen corn kernals*
*6 scallions, chopped*
*1 tablespoon soy sauce*

Fill a large saucepan two-thirds full of water, add a teaspoon of salt and bring to the boil. Add the rice, bring back to the boil and cook for about 20 minutes until the grains are tender, then drain. Heat the olive oil in another saucepan and add the rice, corn and scallions, stirring all the time. Continue to stir-fry for 3-4 minutes, until all the ingredients are heated through. Add the soy sauce, and check seasoning before serving.

*Variation:* stir in ¾ cup bean sprouts just before serving.

**Protein** ▲▲        **Iron** ▲▲
**Fiber** ▲▲          **Calcium** ▲

## MUSHROOMS IN SOY SAUCE

**Ingredients**
*1 tablespoon olive oil*
*½ pound button mushrooms, wiped*
*1 teaspoon cornstarch*
*3 tablespoons soy sauce*

Heat the oil in a saucepan, then put in the mushrooms and fry them quickly over a high heat for about 2 minutes, until beginning to soften. Quickly mix the cornstarch with the soy sauce and add this to the mushrooms in the saucepan. Stir for about 2 minutes, until thickened. Serve at once.

**Protein** ▲        **Iron** ▲
**Fiber** ▲          **Calcium** ▲

## BEAN CURD WITH BAMBOO SHOOTS AND CARROTS

**Ingredients**
*2 tablespoons olive oil*
*½ pound firm bean curd (tofu), diced*
*1 teaspoon grated fresh ginger*
*generous 1½ cup grated carrot*
*½ pound canned bamboo shoots, drained*
*1 tablespoon soy sauce*
*½ teaspoon sugar*

Heat the olive oil in a skillet, add the bean curd and fry, turning the pieces so that they become crisp and golden on all sides. Add the remaining ingredients and stir-fry for about 2 minutes.

**Protein** ▲▲        **Iron** ▲
**Fiber** ▲           **Calcium** ▲

*Clockwise from top left: Mushrooms in Soy Sauce; Savory Fried Rice; Bean Curd with Bamboo Shoots and Carrots; soy sauce; fresh lychees, kiwi fruits and tangerines*

# COOKING FOR CHILDREN

O nce children are past the weaning stage (described on page 15), there is no reason why they should not share meals with the rest of the family. However, there are often times when they need to eat earlier, or occasions when the family doesn't eat together. So in this chapter I've gathered together menus and recipes for the kind of meals which, in my experience, children like, and which are healthy and fairly quick and easy to prepare. All recipes are single servings, unless stated otherwise. Some of them, such as the Little Nut Roast and Frozen Bananas, will store well in the freezer. So, if these prove popular, they can be made in larger batches for use as required. I've also included some ideas for health drinks and snacks, and, if you're brave enough to undertake it, there's also a children's party menu – and the very best of luck!

*Left: Irresistible eats for the very young. Clockwise from top left: Strawberry Milk shake; Pretty Platter; Fresh Orange Jelly (recipes on page 80).*

## PRETTY PLATTER

This is a plate containing small amounts of different foods, attractively arranged. There's plenty of scope for variety; choose your child's favorite foods – older children will have plenty of ideas and enjoy helping you to fill the plate, but some extra suggestions are matchsticks of celery, a few crisp lettuce leaves, or sprigs of fresh cauliflower or broccoli. Small bunches of seedless grapes, and whole nuts such as almonds and peanuts are also suitable for children over 6 years.

**Ingredients**
*1 small tomato, sliced*
*scant ½ cup vegetarian Cheddar-type cheese, cut into small cubes*
*½ sweet apple, cored and sliced*
*1 small carrot, scraped and cut into matchsticks*
*a few thin slices of cucumber*
*a few raisins*
*a few sunflower seeds*
*pitted dates filled with a mixture of ground almonds and honey*

Arrange all the ingredients attractively on a plate or in a shallow basket.

**Protein** ▲ ▲          **Iron** ▲
**Fiber** ▲               **Calcium** ▲ ▲

## STRAWBERRY MILK SHAKE

This frothy pink drink is popular, especially if it's served with one of those extra-wide drinking straws.

**Ingredients**
*1-2 tablespoons strawberry yogurt made with live yogurt, real fruit and dark brown moist sugar*
*small glass of milk*

Put the yogurt and milk into a blender or food processor and blend until smooth and frothy, or beat well. Pour into a glass.

**Protein** ▲ ▲          **Iron** ▲
**Fiber** △               **Calcium** ▲ ▲ ▲

## FRESH ORANGE JELLY

**Ingredients**
*¼ teaspoon vegetarian gelatine (see page 139)*
*generous ¼ cup orange juice*
*1 small orange, peel and pith removed, flesh chopped*
**To decorate**
*orange segments and pieces of orange*

Put the gelatine into a small saucepan and gradually add the orange juice, mixing until smooth. Heat gently to boiling point, stirring; boil for 1 minute, then remove from the heat. Put the diced orange flesh into a small serving bowl; pour the orange juice mixture over; cool. Chill until set. Turn out and decorate with orange.

*Variation:* other fruits and fruit juices can be used instead of orange. Try pineapple juice and cubed apple.

**Protein** ▲          **Iron** ▲
**Fiber** ▲            **Calcium** ▲

## FUNNY FACE OPEN SANDWICHES

These are great fun to make and a marvellous way of tempting reluctant eaters! If you do the basic preparation of the bread and ingredients, the children might like to decorate the face themselves (my young daughter does!).

**Ingredients**
*1-2 slices whole wheat bread*
*sesame seed spread or peanut butter*
*1 small carrot, grated, or some cress*
*a small piece of tomato*
*2 raisins*
*a few sunflower seeds*
*a small piece of date*
*some little seedless green grapes, or triangles of cucumber, carrot or cooked beet*

Using a sharp knife, trim off the corners of the bread to make a roughly circular shape. Spread the bread all over with the sesame seed spread or peanut butter. Press grated carrot or cress around the top edges for hair; position the raisins for eyes, sunflower seeds for eyebrows, a slice of date for the nose and a thin piece of tomato for the mouth. Arrange some tiny grapes for beads or two triangles of cucumber, carrot or cooked beet for a bow.

**Protein** ▲ ▲ ▲          **Iron** ▲ ▲
**Fiber** ▲ ▲ ▲            **Calcium** ▲

## LITTLE HONEY EGG CUSTARD

**Ingredients**
*1 egg yolk*
*1 teaspoon honey*
*3 tablespoons light cream or milk*
*1 drop of vanilla*
*a little grated nutmeg (optional)*

This can be quickly and easily steamed. To save time, you could do this while preparing the open sandwiches. Half-fill a saucepan with water and heat. Meanwhile, put the egg yolk and honey into a small heatproof custard cup or small bowl and mix together, then add the cream or milk and vanilla and mix again until well blended. Grate a little nutmeg on top if liked (not for a child under 2 years). Cover the custard cup with a piece of aluminum foil then put it in the steamer, cover and steam for 15-20 minutes, until the custard is set in the center.

Cool slightly before serving, or chill the custard, which will make it firmer and creamier-tasting. Serve in the custard cup or bowl.

| | | | |
|---|---|---|---|
| *Protein* ▲▲ | | *Iron* ▲▲ | |
| *Fiber* △ | | *Calcium* ▲ | |

## FLIPS AND FIZZES
Real orange or apple juice: apple juice can be made up from concentrate which you can buy at the health store; juices can be made more interesting by adding some soda water
Tomato juice with crushed ice
Milk, made into a yogurt milk shake (recipe page 80)
Warm milk with chocolate syrup or carob
Iced mineral water (much more inviting than plain water)

## TWO

*Little Nut Roast*

*Healthy Oven Chips*

*Broccoli*

*Fruit Fingers, or Frozen Bananas*

## LITTLE NUT ROAST

A delicious bake that's popular with grown-ups too. The uncooked mixture freeezes well. Thaw before using, then cook.

**Ingredients**
*1 tablespoon grated onion*
*1 tablespoon butter or margarine*
*scant 1 cup whole wheat breadcrumbs*
*¾ cup mixed nuts, grated*
*8 tablespoons water*
*¼ teaspoon yeast extract*
*1-2 tablespoons soy sauce*

This dish can be cooked near the bottom of the oven while the Oven Chips are cooking. If you are preparing this nut roast on its own, preheat the oven to 325°. Fry the onion gently in the butter for 5 minutes, then remove from the heat and add all the other ingredients. Spoon the mixture into 2 or 3 small custard cups and bake for about 20 minutes, until heated through and slightly browned on top.
Serves 2-3

| | | | |
|---|---|---|---|
| *Protein* ▲▲ | | *Iron* ▲ | |
| *Fiber* ▲▲▲ | | *Calcium* ▲ | |

## HEALTHY OVEN CHIPS

**Ingredients**
*1 small potato (about 4 ounces), peeled and cut into ⅛ inch slices*
*olive oil*

Preheat the oven to 400°. Brush a baking sheet or roasting pan with olive oil and place the pieces of potato on this; brush with a little more olive oil. Bake for 30-45 minutes, until crisp.

| | | | |
|---|---|---|---|
| *Protein* ▲ | | *Iron* ▲ | |
| *Fiber* ▲ | | *Calcium* ▲ | |

## FRUIT FINGERS

**Ingredients**
*2 cup mixed dry fruit: dates, raisins, dry pears*
*1 cup nuts, any type, or a mixture: cashews, almonds, walnuts or hazelnuts*
*generous 2 cup unsweetened shredded coconut*
*grated peel of 1 well-scrubbed orange*
*hot water to blend*
*extra shredded coconut for coating pan*

Put the dry fruit and nuts into a blender or food processor and blend until finely chopped. Then add the coconut and grated orange peel, and blend again, adding enough hot water to make a firm paste. Sprinkle a little shredded coconut into an 8 inch square pan, press the mixture on top, then sprinkle with more coconut and press down well. Put a weight on top and place in the refridgerator to firm up. Then slice into 1 inch squares. These squares can be eaten as they are or with a little cream, for a treat.

| | | | |
|---|---|---|---|
| *Protein* ▲ | | *Iron* ▲ | |
| *Fiber* ▲ | | *Calcium* ▲ | |

## FROZEN BANANAS

This recipe is based on the 'Rocky Road Bananas' described in *Raw Energy* by Leslie Kenton. These bananas are very popular with my young daughter (and me too!) You can either prepare the pieces of banana as 'popsicles' or as a dessert.

**Ingredients**
*1 banana, peeled*
*3 or 4 popsicle sticks (optional)*
*1 tablespoon honey*
*1 tablespoon chopped nuts: almonds or walnuts*
*1 tablespoon carob powder*

Cut the banana into 3 or 4 pieces and push a popsicle stick into each, or slice the banana fairly thickly for a frozen dessert. Put the honey, nuts and carob on to separate plates or pieces of wax paper. Coat the banana pieces thoroughly, first in the honey, then in the nuts, and finally in the carob powder. If you're making popsicles, place these on a piece of aluminum foil; for a frozen dessert, spoon the coated banana pieces into a small freezer-proof bowl. Freeze for about 1 hour, until solid. If the bananas become very hard, allow them to stand at room temperature for 15 minutes or so before serving.

*Variation:* this recipe can be made with other fruits instead of bananas. Peeled ripe peach or nectarine slices are good; so too are ripe pear slices, but don't allow these to become over-hard. Peeled and diced mango is also delectable for a special treat. It makes a good dessert for grown-ups too after a spicy meal! In the summertime try strawberries, but be sure to eat them before they defrost too much and become soggy.

**Protein** ▲▲      **Iron** ▲▲
**Fiber** ▲▲▲      **Calcium** ▲

## THREE

*Cheese Dippers*

*Favorite Ice Cream with chopped fresh fruit*

## CHEESE DIPPERS

**Ingredients**
*1 teaspoon butter or margarine*
*½ cup finely grated cheese*
*2 tablespoons milk*
*1 small carrot, cut into matchsticks*
*1 small celery stick, cut into matchsticks*
*a few sprigs of raw broccoli or cauliflower*

Put the butter or margarine into a small bowl and beat until soft, then gradually beat in the cheese and milk to form a soft consistency. Spoon this cheese dip into a small container or egg cup and stand it in the center of a larger plate with the prepared vegetables round it.

**Protein** ▲▲▲      **Iron** ▲
**Fiber** ▲▲      **Calcium** ▲▲▲

## FAVORITE ICE CREAM

**Ingredients**
*4 squares semi-sweet chocolate or carob bar, broken into pieces*
*3¾ cup milk*
*1 tablespoon cornstarch*
*2 tablespoons dark brown moist sugar*
*1 can evaporated milk*

Put the chocolate or carob pieces into a saucepan with most of the milk and bring to boiling point. Blend the cornstarch and sugar to a paste in a bowl with the rest of the milk. Add a little of the boiling milk mixture, stir, then pour the cornstarch mixture into the saucepan. Stir over a moderate heat for 2-3 minutes, until slightly thickened. Remove from the heat. Cool slightly, then add the evaporated milk and blend to a smooth consistency. Pour the mixture into a plastic container, allow to cool completely, then freeze, beating once during freezing.

This ice cream needs to be removed from the freezer about half an hour before it is required.
Serves 6

**Protein** ▲▲▲      **Iron** ▲
**Fiber** △      **Calcium** ▲▲▲

---

### BETWEEN MEALS

**Snacks** between meals may not necessarily be a bad thing if they're nutritious, in fact they can sometimes be the easiest way of getting nourishment into a fussy eater. Here are some ideas for healthy between-meal nibbles:
Sticks of raw carrot
Celery sticks, perhaps filled with grated cheese, peanut butter, sesame spread, or cottage cheese
Fingers of whole wheat toast or 'rusks'

made by drying out slices of whole wheat bread in a cool oven (these were very popular with my children long past babyhood!)
From 6 years onwards, whole almonds, Brazil nuts, pumpkin seeds and sunflower seeds (given to a young child under supervision in case of choking)
Homemade popsicles, made from real fruit juice frozen in popsicle moulds

· COOKING FOR CHILDREN ·

## BIRTHDAY PARTY
### Serves 10

*Whole Wheat Triangles*

*Egg Bites*

*Nutty Sausages*

*Chips*

*Crackers*

*Little Fruit Jellies*

*Dreamy Ice Cream*

*No-cook Chocolate Cakes*

*Baby Meringues*

*Clown Cake*

## WHOLE WHEAT TRIANGLES

You can make these and the egg sandwiches the day before required. Wrap in foil or plastic wrap and refrigerate.

**Ingredients**
*6 slices whole wheat bread from a sliced loaf*
*soft butter or margarine*
*yeast extract*

Spread the bread with butter or margarine and a little yeast extract: don't spread it too thickly. Sandwich the slices together; cut off the crusts, then cut the sandwiches diagonally across twice, so that each one makes 4 triangles. Put on a plate, cover loosely with plastic wrap and refrigerate until required.
Makes 24

**Protein** ▲          **Iron** ▲
**Fiber** ▲          **Calcium** ▲

## EGG BITES

Beat a little mayonnaise into the egg as a pleasant alternative to cream.

**Ingredients**
*6 slices whole wheat bread from a sliced loaf*
*butter or margarine*
**For the filling**
*3 hard-cooked eggs, finely chopped*
*2 tablespoons cream*
*salt and freshly ground black pepper*

First make the filling. Mix the chopped hard-cooked eggs with the cream and seasoning, mashing them so that the mixture holds together. Spread the bread thinly with butter or margarine, then spread half the slices with the egg mixture. Place the remaining slices of bread on top to make sandwiches, press down firmly, then cut off the crusts. Cut the sandwiches diagonally twice, making each into 4 triangles. Put the sandwiches on a plate; cover with plastic wrap and refrigerate until required.
Makes 24

**Protein** ▲          **Iron** ▲
**Fiber** ▲          **Calcium** ▲

## NUTTY SAUSAGES

**Ingredients**
*2 tablespoons grated onion*
*1 teaspoon mild curry powder*
*1 cup walnut pieces, grated*
*1 cup cashew nut pieces, grated*
*1 cup vegetarian Cheddar-type cheese, grate*
*salt and freshly ground black pepper*
*wheat germ for coating*
*olive oil for shallow-frying*
**To serve**
*wooden toothpicks*

Mix all the ingredients together, seasoning with salt and pepper. Press the mixture with your hands so that it clings together firmly, then divide into small pieces and roll each into a sausage about ⅓ inch wide by 1 inch long. Fry the sausages in hot, shallow olive oil for 2-3 minutes, turning them so that they brown on all sides. Drain well on paper towels. Serve the nutty sausages on toothpicks if appropriate or in small napkin-lined bowls.
Makes about 50

**Protein** ▲          **Iron** ▲
**Fiber** ▲          **Calcium** ▲

## LITTLE FRUIT JELLIES

Either follow the directions given for Fresh Orange Jelly on page 80, using 3½ cup orange juice and 3 teaspoons vegetarian gelatine, or, if you prefer, make up two of the vegetarian jellies, which you can buy at health stores, using 3½ cup water. These jellies are vegetarian but not wholefood (children love them!).

**Protein** ▲          **Iron** ▲
**Fiber** ▲          **Calcium** ▲

## CLOWN CAKE

This is an easy cake to decorate but looks most effective.

**Ingredients**
**For the cake**
*2 sticks soft butter or margarine*
*generous 1½ cup soft brown sugar*
*4 eggs, beaten*
*2 cup self-rising 85 per cent*
*whole wheat flour*
*4 heaped tablespoons raspberry jam or jelly*
*(preferably low-sugar)*
**For the frosting and decoration**
*2 cup powdered sugar*
*3-4 tablespoons water*
*chocolate sticks*
*1 packet of jelly diamond cake decorations*
*1 round red candy (or colored marzipan)*

Preheat the oven to 350°. Grease and line the bases of two deep 9 inch layer pans. Cream the butter and sugar until very light, pale and fluffy, then gradually add the beaten egg, beating well between each addition. Sift the flour into the mixture and fold in with a metal spoon. Divide the mixture between the two pans and level the tops. Bake for 20-25 minutes, until the cakes spring back if touched lightly in the center. Cool on a wire rack. Spread one of the cakes with jam or jelly and place the other on top.

   To decorate the cake, mix the powdered sugar with the water to make a pouring consistency; pour over the top of the cake, spreading gently to the edges if necessary. Arrange chocolate sticks around the top edge of the cake, for hair, jelly diamonds for eyes, eyebrows and mouth, and the candy for a nose, as shown.
Makes one 9 inch cake

*Protein* ▲▲     *Iron* ▲▲
*Fiber* ▲     *Calcium* ▲

## DREAMY ICE CREAM

This is a very simple ice cream with a deliciously creamy texture. Eat it on its own, or use in other desserts.

**Ingredients**
*½ vanilla bean, finely crushed*
*2½ cup whipping cream*
*1×14 ounce can condensed skim milk*

Put the crushed vanilla bean into a bowl with the cream and whip the cream until thick. Add the condensed milk and whip again. Pour the mixture into a plastic container and freeze until firm. This ice cream can be served in various ways: for example, try combining it with any fresh, ripe or lightly-cooked fruit. Alternatively, it can be topped with a sauce made by melting a carob bar with a little milk.

*Protein* ▲▲▲     *Iron* ▲
*Fiber* ▲     *Calcium* ▲▲▲

## NO-COOK CHOCOLATE CAKES

An ever-popular favorite that the children will enjoy helping to make!

**Ingredients**
*½ pound sweet chocolate or carob bar, melted*
*2 cup whole wheat flakes*
*24-26 paper cupcake cases*

Mix all the ingredients together. Drop spoonfuls of mixture into the cupcake cases and leave in a cool place to set.
Makes 24-26

*Variation:* other ingredients, such as finely chopped or sliced nuts, and chopped dates and raisins, can be added for extra interest and nourishment. If you can't get whole wheat flakes, cornflakes can be used.

**Protein** ▲          **Iron** ▲
**Fiber** ▲          **Calcium** ▲

## BABY MERINGUES

These baby meringues are very popular with the young (and the not-so-young!).

**Ingredients**
*2 egg whites*
*pinch of cream of tartar*
*scant 1 cup brown sugar*
**For the filling**
*1¼ cup whipping cream*
*pinch sugar*

Preheat the oven to 300°. Line a cookie sheet with a piece of greased wax paper, and sprinkle with flour. Put the egg whites into a clean, grease-free bowl with the cream of tartar and beat until stiff and dry. You should be able to turn the bowl upside down without spilling the egg white. Then beat in half the sugar. Add the remaining sugar and beat well.

Pipe 40 small mounds or drop heaped teaspoonfuls of the mixture onto the prepared cookie sheet. Place in the lowest part of the oven, then reduce the setting to 225°. Bake for 1½-2 hours, until the meringues are dried out. Turn off the heat and leave them to cool in the oven. Carefully remove the meringues from the cookie sheet with a flat knife. Whip the cream with the sugar and use this to sandwich the meringues together in pairs.

The meringues can be filled about 1 hour before serving. Keep in a cool place.
Makes 20 pairs

**Protein** ▲▲          **Iron** ▲
**Fiber** ▲          **Calcium** ▲

*Clockwise from top left: Clown Cake; Whole Wheat Triangles and Egg Bites; No-cook Chocolate Cakes; Little Fruit Jellies with Dreamy Ice Cream; Nutty Sausages; Baby Meringues; assorted chips and crackers (recipes on pages 83-85).*

# OUTSIDE EATING

Eating in the open air, whether it's a family picnic by the sea, a fancy picnic at the races, a summer lunch or evening buffet party in the backyard, or a barbecue on a warm, lazy evening, it has a charm all of its own. People often wonder what vegetarians cook on these occasions, especially where barbecues are concerned! The answer is absolutely delicious as I hope pages 93-96 will demonstrate. A vegetarian barbecue can be just as exciting and delightful as the conventional type and what an ideal way to pass an evening!

In this chapter you'll also find unusual ideas for summer picnics, campfire (or camper or boat) cooking, and for a summer lunch or dinner party in the backyard, so make sure you make the most of the good weather and enjoy some meals al fresco.

▲

*Left: A luscious spread for warm, sunny days and meals in the garden. Clockwise from top right: Red Salad; Mushroom and Sherry Pâté with Melba Toast; Creamy Onion Tart; fresh figs, Chocolate Roulade (recipes on pages 88-89).*

AL FRESCO LUNCH
*Serves 6*

*Mushroom and Sherry Pâté
with Melba Toast*


*Creamy Onion Tart*


*Red Salad*


*Chocolate Roulade or fresh figs*

This is a knife-and-fork-style meal to enjoy in the backyard. The menu starts with a tasty pâté that's easy to make and to pack. The main course is a classic, creamy tart, and the salad provides a contrast both in color and texture. Finally, luscious fresh figs or, wicked but wonderful for a special treat, serve Chocolate Roulade.

## MUSHROOM AND SHERRY PÂTÉ WITH MELBA TOAST

**Ingredients**
*½ stick butter or margarine*
*1½ pounds small firm button mushrooms, wiped and thinly sliced*
*3 tablespoons heavy cream*
*1 tablespoon dry sherry*
*salt and freshly ground black pepper*
**For the Melba toast**
*6-8 slices whole wheat bread*

Heat the butter or margarine in a large saucepan and put in the mushrooms. Keeping the heat up high, fry the mushrooms quickly for 3-4 minutes, until just tender and lightly browned. If they begin to make liquid, the butter is not hot enough; the mushrooms should be dry. Remove 6 perfect mushroom slices and reserve for the garnish. Blend the rest in a blender or food processor with the cream, sherry and seasoning to taste. Spoon the mixture into 6 individual custard cups or pâté dishes, level the tops, then press one of the reserved mushroom slices into the top of each. Cool, then chill the pâtés.

To make the Melba toast, first toast the bread on both sides as usual, then with a sharp knife cut through the bread to split each piece in half, making each into two thin pieces. Toast the uncooked sides until crisp and brown – the edges will curl up. Allow the toast to cool. Melba toast will keep for 2-3 days in an airtight container.

*Protein* ▲▲      *Iron* ▲
*Fiber* ▲      *Calcium* ▲

## CREAMY ONION TART

**Ingredients**
**For the pastry**
*1 cup self-rising 85 per cent whole wheat flour*
*¼ teaspoon salt*
*½ stick plus 1 tablespoon butter or margarine*
*1 tablespoon cold water*
**For the filling**
*1 pound onions, peeled and sliced*
*1 tablespoon butter or margarine*
*⅔ cup light cream*
*2 egg yolks*
*salt and freshly ground black pepper*
*grated nutmeg*
*chopped parsley*

Preheat the oven to 400°. Place a cookie sheet in the oven to heat up. Sift the flour and salt into a bowl, then add ½ stick of the butter or margarine; rub it into the flour with your fingertips until the mixture resembles bread crumbs. Add the water, then press the mixture together to make a dough. Roll the dough out on a lightly-floured surface, then use to line an 8 inch pie pan. Lightly prick the base of the tart. Place it on the cookie sheet and bake for 15-20 minutes, until the pastry is firm and golden brown. Just before you take the tart out of the oven, put the remaining tablespoon butter or margarine into a small saucepan and heat it without browning. When the tart case is cooked, use the hot butter to brush the inside surface. This will seal the pastry and keep it crisp. Turn the oven setting down to 350°.

For the filling fry the onions in the butter or margarine for 25-30 minutes, until very soft. Take off the heat and add the cream, egg yolks, salt, pepper and grated nutmeg. Pour into the tart case, and bake for 30-35 minutes until just set. Serve sprinkled with parsley.

*Protein* ▲▲      *Iron* ▲
*Fiber* ▲      *Calcium* ▲

## RED SALAD

**Ingredients**
*½ teaspoon mustard powder*
*2 teaspoons redcurrant jelly or honey*
*1 tablespoon red wine vinegar*
*3 tablespoons olive oil*
*salt and freshly ground black pepper*
*bunch of radishes, trimmed and sliced*
*1 radicchio (about ½ pound), washed*
*2 cup shredded red cabbage*
*1 sweet red bell pepper, seeded and diced*

Put the mustard powder, redcurrant jelly or honey, red wine vinegar, oil and a little salt and pepper into a salad bowl and mix well to make a dressing. Add the salad ingredients, and toss to coat the vegetables with the dressing. Serve at once.

*Protein* ▲      *Iron* ▲
*Fiber* ▲      *Calcium* ▲

## CHOCOLATE ROULADE

**Ingredients**
*5 eggs, separated*
*generous 1 cup soft brown sugar*
*3 tablespoons hot water*
*6 ounces semi-sweet chocolate, melted*
**For the filling**
*1¼ cup whipping cream, whipped*
**To finish**
*powdered sugar*
*a few fresh baby pink rose buds or*
*chocolate curls*

Preheat the oven to 400°. Grease a 10×14 inch jelly roll pan and line with a piece of greased wax paper. Put the egg yolks into a bowl with the sugar and beat until thick and pale. Mix the hot water with the melted chocolate then gently stir this into the egg yolk mixture. Beat the egg whites until stiff, then fold these gently into the mixture. Pour the mixture into the pan, quickly spreading it out to the edges. Bake for 15 minutes until well risen and just firm to the touch. Cool the mixture in the pan for 10 minutes, then cover with a damp cloth and leave for 10 minutes or overnight. Remove the cloth, turn the cake out on to a piece of wax paper that has been generously dusted with powdered sugar. Carefully remove the wax paper from the top of the cake, then leave to cool completely. When cold, trim the edges and spread evenly with the whipped cream, then carefully roll the cake up, using the paper to help: don't worry if it cracks! Sprinkle with more powdered sugar.

This roulade will keep well in the refrigerator for several hours, and can also be frozen successfully. Serve on a large plate decorated with the rose buds or chocolate curls.

**Protein** ▲▲▲    **Iron** ▲
**Fiber** ▲    **Calcium** ▲

## PORTABLE PICNIC
### Serves 5

*Cream of Potato Soup*

*Salad Sticks*

*Wheat-filled Pitas*

*Sticky Gingerbread*

*Fresh fruit*

Here's a picnic that's easy to pack, serve and eat, just right for a car journey or day at the beach. With the thought of cool sea breezes, I've suggested hot soup to start with, followed by stuffed French bread, gingerbread and fresh fruit.

## CREAM OF POTATO SOUP

This simple soup, a family favorite, can be varied by the addition of chopped fresh herbs, or a bunch of washed water cress, blended with the soup. This gives a pretty speckled appearance to the soup.

**Ingredients**
*1 tablespoon butter or margarine*
*1 onion, peeled and chopped, or 1 small leek*
*1 pound potatoes, peeled and diced*
*3¾ cup water*
*2 teaspoons vegetarian bouillon powder*
*salt and freshly ground black pepper*
*⅔ cup light cream, or*
*plain yogurt*

Heat the butter or margarine in a fairly large saucepan and fry the onion without browning for 5 minutes. Add the potato and fry for a further 5-10 minutes, stirring often. Mix in the water and bouillon powder, bring to the boil, then turn the heat down and let the soup simmer for about 15 minutes, until the potatoes are tender. Blend in a blender or food processor with some seasoning and the cream or yogurt.

**Protein** ▲    **Iron** ▲
**Fiber** ▲    **Calcium** ▲

## SALAD STICKS

**Ingredients**
*2 French bread*
*butter or margarine*
*Dijon or wholegrain mustard, mayonnaise or olive oil*
*1 lettuce, washed and shredded*
*1 pound tomatoes, sliced*
*1 onion, peeled and sliced*
*1 cucumber, peeled and sliced*
*salt and freshly ground black pepper*
**To garnish**
*scallion curls or*
*salad cress*

Using a sharp knife, make a slit down the side of each French bread, ease it open without breaking it apart and scoop out a little of the loose crumb (this can be used for other recipes or made into crumbs and frozen). Spread the inside of each French bread thinly with butter or margarine, mustard, mayonnaise or olive oil, then pack each with the salad, filling them up well. Press the slits together, wrap the bread tightly in aluminum foil and chill until required. Garnish with scallion curls or salad cress before serving.

**Protein** ▲▲▲    **Iron** ▲▲▲
**Fiber** ▲▲    **Calcium** ▲▲▲

## WHEAT-FILLED PITAS

These hearty, nutty sandwiches make a delicious and substantial main course and can be filled with your own choice of salad ingredients. Try endive and sliced tomatoes, cucumber and salad cress, or thinly sliced zucchini and water cress.

If whole wheat pita bread is unobtainable, split and fill large whole wheat buns. Cut them in half to serve.

### Ingredients
*½ pound whole wheat grains, covered with cold water and soaked for 6-8 hours or overnight (see page 132)*
*2 tablespoons red wine vinegar*
*2 tablespoons olive oil, optional*
*1 medium-sized onion, purple if possible, peeled and sliced*
*2 tablespoons chopped parsley or chopped fresh coriander*
*2 tomatoes, peeled and chopped*
*salt and freshly ground black pepper*
### To serve
*1 head radicchio or a small lettuce, separated into leaves*
*whole wheat pita bread*
### To garnish
*water cress sprigs, flat-leafed parsley or salad cress*

Drain the wheat, then put it into a saucepan and cover with fresh water. Bring to the boil and simmer for 1¼ hours, or 25 minutes in a pressure cooker. Drain and cool. Put the red wine vinegar into a bowl with the olive oil if you're using this and add the wheat, onion, parsley, tomatoes and a little salt and pepper to taste. Spoon the mixture with the radicchio or lettuce leaves into warm whole wheat pita bread. Garnish with water cress sprigs.

**Protein** ▲▲     **Iron** ▲▲▲
**Fiber** ▲▲▲     **Calcium** ▲▲

## STICKY GINGERBREAD

### Ingredients
*2 tablespoons honey*
*½ cup blackstrap molasses*
*1 stick butter or margarine*
*generous 1¼ cup 100 per cent whole wheat flour*
*½ teaspoon ground ginger*
*2 teaspoons baking powder*
*½ cup dark brown moist sugar*
*½ cup chopped walnuts or candied fruit*
*2 eggs, beaten*
*½ teaspoon baking soda*
*⅔ cup milk*

Preheat the oven to 325°. Grease an 8 inch square pan and line with greased wax paper. Melt the honey, molasses and butter or margarine in a saucepan over gentle heat, then cool. Sift the flour, ginger and baking powder into a bowl, adding the residue of bran from the sieve. Stir in the sugar and nuts, or candied fruit if using. Then make a well in the center and pour in the molasses mixture and the beaten eggs. Dissolve the soda in the milk, then stir this into the mixture. Pour the mixture into the pan. Bake for 1½ hours, until well risen and firm to touch. Cool the gingerbread in the pan.

*Variation:* for a richer, more festive-looking alternative, spread the top with curd cheese beaten with a little honey or soft brown sugar and sprinkle with chopped candied ginger or walnuts.

**Protein** ▲     **Iron** ▲
**Fiber** ▲     **Calcium** ▲

***Just right to pack for picnics and holidays. Clockwise from top left: Fresh fruit; Leek and Potato Soup; Wheat-filled Pitas; Salad Sticks; Sticky Gingerbread (recipes on pages 89-90).***

squash and eggplant. Stir, cover the saucepan and cook for 20-25 minutes, until all the vegetables are tender. Stir in the tomatoes and cook, uncovered, for a further 4-5 minutes, to heat the tomatoes through. Season and sprinkle with chopped parsley.

**Protein** ▲▲    **Iron** ▲▲
**Fiber** ▲▲    **Calcium** ▲

---

## SPICY LENTIL AND VEGETABLE STEW

This is a delicious stew, spicy but not 'hot'. Serve it with mango chutney and a salad made from sliced tomatoes and onion rings.

**Ingredients**
*1 large onion, peeled and chopped*
*2 tablespoons olive oil*
*½ pound leeks, trimmed and sliced*
*½ pound carrots, scraped and diced*
*2 garlic cloves, crushed*
*1 tablespoon white mustard seed*
*1 tablespoon coriander seed*
*1 teaspoon turmeric*
*small piece of fresh ginger, grated*
*1⅓ cup split red lentils*
*3¾ cup water*
*1 tablespoon lemon juice*
*salt and freshly ground black pepper*
**To garnish**
*fresh chopped coriander leaves if available, or chopped parsley*

Fry the onion in the oil for 5 minutes, then add the leeks and carrots, stir well and fry for a further 5 minutes. Add the garlic, mustard seed, coriander, turmeric, ginger and lentils and stir for 2-3 minutes. Then pour in the water. Bring to the boil, then half cover the pan, reduce the heat and leave the mixture to simmer gently for 25-30 minutes, until the lentils are tender.

Add the lemon juice and season carefully to taste. Serve sprinkled with the chopped coriander or parsley.

**Protein** ▲▲▲    **Iron** ▲▲▲
**Fiber** ▲▲▲    **Calcium** ▲▲

---

## VEGETABLE RICE

This is a very versatile recipe. Try your own combinations of vegetables to cook on top of the rice mixture. Parsnip, turnip, zucchini or rutabagas could be used to replace the carrots and string beans.

**Ingredients**
*1 onion, peeled and chopped*
*1 red bell pepper, seeded and sliced*
*1 garlic clove, crushed*
*1 tablespoon olive oil*
*½ teaspoon ground turmeric*
*1⅓ cup brown rice*
*2½ cup water*
*salt and freshly ground black pepper*
*2 carrots, scraped and diced*
*½ pound string beans, cut into 1 inch pieces*
*½ pound tomatoes, peeled and sliced*
*2 tablespoons chopped parsley*
*2 tablespoons chopped chives*

Fry the onion, bell pepper and garlic in the oil, without browning, for 10 minutes. Add the turmeric and rice and stir for 2 minutes, then pour in the water with some salt. Bring to the boil, cover and cook for 20 minutes. Uncover and carefully put the carrots and beans on top of the rice – don't stir them in. Cover and cook for a further 25 minutes, until the rice is done. Add the tomatoes, parsley and chives and gently toss the mixture, to distribute the vegetables before serving.

**Protein** ▲▲    **Iron** ▲▲▲
**Fiber** ▲▲    **Calcium** ▲▲

---

ONE-POT MEALS
*Serves 4*

*Ratatouille with crusty bread; lettuce and tomato salad*

*Spicy Lentil and Vegetable Stew*

*Vegetable Rice; bean sprout and mushroom salad*

*Potato and Onion Fry; Sliced Tomato Salad*

---

## RATATOUILLE

Serve this delicious, easy-to-make summer stew with plenty of crusty bread and a crisp salad on the side.

**Ingredients**
*2 large onions, peeled and chopped*
*1 pound sweet red bell peppers, seeded and sliced*
*3 tablespoons olive oil*
*3 garlic cloves, crushed*
*1 pound zucchini or squash, cut into even-sized pieces*
*1 pound eggplant, diced*
*1½ pounds tomatoes, peeled and chopped*
*salt and freshly ground black pepper*
**To garnish**
*chopped parsley*

Fry the onions and bell peppers gently in the oil in a large pan without browning for 5 minutes. Add the garlic, zucchini or

## POTATO AND ONION FRY

This is a simple dish, easy to make and delicious served with some grated cheese.

**Ingredients**
*2 tablespoons olive oil*
*1 large onion, peeled and sliced*
*2 pounds potatoes, peeled and diced*
*salt and freshly ground black pepper*
**To serve**
*sunflower seeds*
*grated cheese*
*chopped parsley*

Heat the oil in a large saucepan then put in the onion and fry gently for about 5 minutes. Add the potatoes, stir, then cover the saucepan and cook gently for 20-30 minutes, until the potatoes are tender and lightly browned. Stir from time to time, especially towards the end of the cooking time. Season, sprinkle with sunflower seeds, grated cheese and chopped parsley before serving.

**Protein** ▲▲▲      **Iron** ▲▲
**Fiber** ▲          **Calcium** ▲

## SLICED TOMATO SALAD

**Ingredients**
*1 tablespoon Dijon mustard*
*1 tablespoon white wine vinegar*
*3 tablespoons olive oil*
*salt and freshly ground black pepper*
*¾ pound beefsteak tomatoes, sliced*

Mix together the mustard, white wine vinegar and oil. Season. Arrange the tomatoes on a serving plate and pour over the dressing.

**Protein** ▲      **Iron** ▲
**Fiber** ▲        **Calcium** ▲

## A VEGETARIAN BARBECUE
### Serves 12

*Vegetable Kebabs*

*Special Rice*

*Nutburgers in soft buns with assorted pickles*

*Baked potatoes*

*Lettuce and mint salad*

*Tomato and Onion Salad*

*Creamy Coleslaw*

*Molasses Tart*

*Grape Cheesecake*

A barbecue can be a very tasty affair and I think you'll find this a popular menu. You'll need to light the barbecue in good time if you're planning to cook the potatoes in the fire. Cups of hot soup can be very welcome at the beginning of a barbecue to sip while the food is cooking, especially if the weather is cool. The potato soup on page 89, or the tomato soup on page 43 would be ideal: make three times the quantity for 12 people.

Alternatively, serve a warm red wine cup spiced with cloves and cinnamon.

## VEGETABLE KEBABS

**Ingredients**
*36 small button mushrooms, wiped*
*1 eggplant (about ½ pound), cut into chunks about 1 inch long, ½ inch wide and ¼ inch thick, sprinkled with salt, left for 30 minutes, then rinsed and drained*
*1 medium-sized red or green bell pepper, seeded and cut into strips about 1 inch long and ½ inch wide*
*24 baby pickling onions, peeled, or*
*2 onions, peeled and cut into chunks*
*6 small zucchini (about ¾ pound) cut into slices ½ inch thick*
**For the marinade**
*3 tablespoons Dijon mustard*
*3 garlic cloves, crushed*
*3 tablespoons dark brouwn moist sugar*
*3 tablespoons soy sauce*
*3 tablespoons olive oil*
*1½ teaspoons salt*
*freshly ground black pepper*

Thread the vegetables on to 12 skewers, putting on first a mushroom, then a piece of eggplant followed by a piece of red bell pepper, an onion and a chunk of zucchini. Continue in this way until all the skewers are full.

Next, mix together the marinade ingredients. Lay the skewers flat on a non-metal tray, plastic container, large plate or casserole. Spoon the marinade over them, turning the skewers to make sure that all the vegetables are coated with the mixture. Leave to marinate for at least 1 hour, basting occasionally.

Cook the kebabs on the grill of the barbecue or broil for 10-15 minutes, until the vegetables are tender. Serve the kebabs on the Special Rice with the remaining marinade in a small jug.

**Protein** ▲      **Iron** ▲
**Fiber** ▲        **Calcium** ▲

## SPECIAL RICE

This is 'special' because of the inclusion of some wild rice which is more expensive, but is bound to impress your guests! Its wonderful smoky flavor and delightful chewy texture make it well-worth seeking out. When you're in a less extravagant mood, leave out the wild rice and just increase the quantity of brown rice to 2 cup and stir in ¾ cup bean sprouts.

**Ingredients**
*1⅔ cup brown rice*
*⅓ cup wild rice*
*3 cup water*
*3 teaspoons vegetarian bouillon powder*
*salt and freshly ground black pepper*
*2 tablespoons butter or margarine*
*3-4 tablespoons finely chopped mixed herbs*

Put the rice into a saucepan together with the water, bouillon powder and a seasoning of salt and pepper. Bring to the boil, then cover the saucepan and turn the heat down as low as possible. Cook the rice for 40-45 minutes, until the grains are tender and all the water has been absorbed. Add the butter or margarine and herbs, stirring gently over a low heat until well coated. Check seasoning, adding more salt or pepper as necessary, and serve.

**Protein** ▲          **Iron** ▲
**Fiber** ▲          **Calcium** ▲

*A barbecue feast to feed a crowd. This delicious menu proves that a vegetarian barbecue can be just as exciting and delightful as the conventional type. Clockwise from top left: Grape Cheesecake; Lettuce and Mint Salad; Baked Potatoes; Molasses Tart; Tomato and Onion Salad; Creamy Coleslaw; Vegetable Kebabs on Special Rice; Nutburgers in soft buns; assorted pickles (recipes on pages 93-96).*

## NUTBURGERS IN SOFT BUNS

**Ingredients**
*2 onions, peeled and chopped*
*2 celery sticks, finely diced*
*1 stick butter or margarine*
*2 teaspoons mixed herbs*
*2 tablespoons whole wheat flour*
*1¼ cup water*
*2 teaspoons vegetarian bouillon powder*
*2 tablespoons soy sauce*
*2 teaspoons yeast extract*
*1 pound mixed nuts: almonds, Brazil nuts, walnuts, cashew nuts, grated*
*4 cup soft whole wheat bread crumbs*
*salt and freshly ground black pepper*
**To finish**
*dry breadcrumbs to coat*
*olive oil for shallow frying*

Fry the onions and celery in the butter or margarine for 10 minutes, browning them lightly. Add the herbs, stir for 1 minute, then mix in the flour and cook for a further 1-2 minutes. Pour in the water and stir until thickened. Add the bouillon powder, soy sauce, yeast extract, nuts, bread crumbs and salt and pepper to taste. Allow the mixture to cool, then form into 12 flat burgers about ½ inch thick, and coat with dry bread crumbs. Cook in a greased skillet over the barbecue. Serve the nutburgers in soft burger buns, with chutney and pickles as required.

**Protein** ▲▲▲          **Iron** ▲▲
**Fiber** ▲▲▲          **Calcium** ▲

## BAKED POTATOES

Scrub and prick the potatoes. Wrap each one in foil and bake in the barbecue fire, allowing 1¼-1½ hours. Top with sour cream and chives or thick Greek yogurt.

## TOMATO AND ONION SALAD

**Ingredients**
*1½ pounds tomatoes, peeled and sliced*
*2 onions, peeled and thinly sliced*
*2 tablespoons olive oil*
*salt and freshly ground black pepper*

Put the tomatoes and onions into a shallow bowl, mixing them together. Pour the oil over them, making sure it's well distributed. Season with salt and pepper. This salad is best made an hour or so in advance and stirred several times.

**Protein** ▲         **Iron** ▲
**Fiber** ▲           **Calcium** ▲

## CREAMY COLESLAW

**Ingredients**
*1 pound white cabbage, finely shredded*
*½ pound carrots, scraped and coarsely grated*
*2 onions, peeled and finely chopped*
*⅔ cup raisins*
**For the dressing**
*1 teaspoon dry mustard*
*⅔ cup sour cream*
*salt and freshly ground black pepper*

Put the cabbage, carrots, onions and raisins into a large bowl. In a small bowl, blend the mustard with the sour cream, and season with salt and pepper. Add this to the salad, mixing well. Check seasoning.

*Variation:* try a spicy yogurt dressing. In a small bowl, beat together ⅔ cup thick Greek yogurt, 1 teaspoon ground turmeric and 1 clove garlic, crushed.

**Protein** ▲         **Iron** ▲
**Fiber** ▲▲         **Calcium** ▲

## MOLASSES TART

I'm including this tart because it's a top favorite with men, and makes a pleasant treat. Use regular molasses or blackstrap molasses if you prefer. It's very good made with whole wheat flour and bread crumbs. Serve it warm, cut into wedges, with thick Greek yogurt.

**Ingredients**
*4 cup fine whole wheat flour*
*2 teaspoons salt*
*3 sticks hard butter or margarine*
*4 teaspoons lemon juice*
*about 16 tablespoons water*
**For the filling**
*6 tablespoons molasses or 4 tablespoons molasses and 2 tablespoons blackstrap molasses*
*1½ cup fine whole wheat bread crumbs*
*1 teaspoon lemon juice*

First make the pastry. Mix the flour and salt in a large bowl and grate in the butter. Add the lemon juice and water, then mix quickly to a fairly soft dough. Gather this into a ball, wrap in plastic wrap and chill for at least 1 hour. Preheat the oven to 400°. Roll out the pastry and line an 8 inch pie pan. Trim the edges, roll the trimmings into strips to make a lattice for the top of the tart and set aside.

Chill the pastry case and strips while you make the filling. Put the molasses into a saucepan and heat gently to melt, then remove from the heat and add the crumbs and lemon juice. Spoon this mixture into the pastry case, level the surface, arrange the pastry strips in a lattice on top. Bake for 25 minutes, until the pastry is crisp and lightly browned. Serve the molasses tart warm with thick Greek yogurt.

**Protein** ▲▲         **Iron** ▲
**Fiber** ▲▲           **Calcium** ▲

## GRAPE CHEESECAKE

**Ingredients**
*2 cup finely crushed semi-sweet whole wheat cookies*
*⅔ stick butter or margarine, melted*
*2 cup curd or cream cheese*
*2 cup plain thick yogurt*
*4 tablespoons honey*
*⅓ cup brown sugar*
*4 eggs*
*2 tablespoons ground almonds*
*1 teaspoon vanilla*
**For the topping**
*⅔ cup sour cream*
*¼ pound black grapes, halved and seeded*
*¼ pound green grapes, halved and seeded*
*3 tablespoons honey*

Preheat the oven to 325°. First make the crust. Mix together the cookie crumbs and melted butter or margarine. Spoon this mixture into the bottom of an 8 inch loose-bottom pan or spring mould. Press down firmly. Next, make the filling. Put all the ingredients into a bowl and beat together until smooth and creamy. Pour this mixture on to the cookie crust and spread evenly. Bake the cheesecake for 1-1¼ hours until firm in the center. Remove the cheesecake from the oven and carefully spoon the sour cream on top, gently levelling it with a knife. Turn off the heat but put the cheesecake back in the still-warm oven for 15-20 minutes. Then cool.

When completely cold, gently release the sides of the mould and lift the cheesecake onto a serving plate. Arrange the grapes on top in circles of alternating colors. Put the honey into a small saucepan and heat, to make it more liquid, then spoon or brush this over the grapes. Allow the honey glaze to cool before serving.

**Protein** ▲▲▲         **Iron** ▲
**Fiber** ▲               **Calcium** ▲

## SUMMER BUFFET
*Serves 20*

*Tomato and Avocado Salad*

*Tsatsiki*

*Corn and Radish Salad*

*Two-Bean Salad in Radicchio*

*Potato Mayonnaise*

*Flaky Mushroom Roll with Sour Cream and Fresh Herb Sauce*

*Strawberry Pavlova*

*Chocolate Chestnut Gâteau*

When the weather is warm, a buffet is a pleasant way to entertain a group of friends, either for lunch or dinner. This menu is based around a delicious, flaky mushroom roll which is served with a creamy, fresh herb sauce, a variety of colorful salads and a choice of delectable desserts! Much of the preparation can be done in advance. All the salads, except the tomato and avocado salad, can be made ahead, covered and stored in the refrigerator until required. Make the pastry and the filling for the mushroom roll, ready to assemble before cooking. The Pavlova base and the gâteau can also be made well ahead.

## TOMATO AND AVOCADO SALAD

**Ingredients**
*1½ pounds tomatoes, peeled and sliced*
*2 avocados, peeled, halved, and pits removed*
*2 tablespoons lemon juice*
*2 tablespoons olive oil*
*salt and freshly ground black pepper*
**To garnish**
*dill or fennel tops*

Put the tomato slices into a shallow bowl. Cut the avocados into thick slices, sprinkle with the lemon juice (to preserve the color) and arrange neatly with the tomatoes. Sprinkle with olive oil and season. Garnish with dill or fennel.

*Protein* ▲    *Iron* ▲
*Fiber* ▲    *Calcium* ▲

## TSATSIKI

**Ingredients**
*1 large cucumber, peeled and diced*
*salt and freshly ground black pepper*
*generous 1 cup thick Greek yogurt*
*4 tablespoons chopped mint*
*2 garlic cloves, crushed*
**To garnish**
*mint leaves*

Put the cucumber into a strainer or colander and sprinkle with salt. Set a weight on top and leave for 30 minutes. Rinse and pat dry on paper towels. Put into a bowl with the yogurt, mint, garlic and pepper. Stir well, and season. Put into a shallow serving bowl and garnish with mint leaves.

*Protein* ▲    *Iron* ▲
*Fiber* ▲    *Calcium* ▲

## CORN AND RADISH SALAD

**Ingredients**
*1 pound frozen corn kernals*
*1 teaspoon mustard powder*
*1 teaspoon honey*
*1 tablespoon red wine vinegar*
*3 tablespoons olive oil*
*salt and freshly ground black pepper*
*1 small bunch or packet of radishes, washed, trimmed and sliced*

Cook the corn in a little boiling water for about 5 minutes, until tender. Drain well. Mix the mustard, honey and vinegar in a large bowl, then gradually add the oil, stirring well. Season the mixture with some salt and pepper. Put the hot corn into the bowl, mix well, add the radishes and mix again to make sure that the vegetables are thoroughly coated. Cool, cover and chill the salad before serving.

*Protein* ▲    *Iron* ▲
*Fiber* ▲    *Calcium* ▲

## POTATO MAYONNAISE

**Ingredients**
*1½ pounds small young potatoes, cooked, drained and cut into even-sized pieces*
*4 tablespoons mayonnaise*
*2 tablespoons thick plain yogurt*
*salt and freshly ground black pepper*
*chopped chives*

Put the potatoes into a bowl and add the mayonnaise and yogurt. Stir gently to distribute all the ingredients. Season with salt and pepper. Spoon the mixture into a serving bowl and sprinkle with chives.

*Protein* ▲    *Iron* ▲
*Fiber* ▲    *Calcium* ▲

· OUTSIDE EATING ·

## TWO-BEAN SALAD IN RADICCHIO

**Ingredients**
*½ pound packet frozen lima beans*
*½ pound fresh or frozen string beans*
*1 tablespoon red wine vinegar*
*3 tablespoons olive oil*
*salt and freshly ground black pepper*
*2 tablespoons chopped summer savory*
*2 medium-sized radicchio*

Cook the beans together in a little boiling water for 5-10 minutes. Drain well. Put the vinegar and oil into a bowl and mix together, then add the hot beans, some salt and pepper and the chopped herbs. Mix well, then leave until cool. Arrange the radicchio leaves along a shallow serving plate and spoon over the bean mixture.

| | |
|---|---|
| **Protein** ▲ | **Iron** ▲ |
| **Fiber** ▲ | **Calcium** ▲ |

## FLAKY MUSHROOM ROLL

You'll need to make two of these for 20 servings so make up the whole quantity of puff pastry on page 125.

**Ingredients**
*½ quantity of puff pastry (see page 125)*
**For the filling**
*1 tablespoon butter or margarine*
*1 onion, peeled and chopped*
*½ pound mushrooms, wiped and chopped*
*2 tablespoons chopped parsley*
*⅔ cup brown rice, cooked*
*salt and freshly ground black pepper*
*a little raw egg yolk*

Preheat the oven to 425°. Heat the butter or margarine in a large saucepan and fry the onion and mushrooms quickly over a high

heat for 2-3 minutes. Remove from the heat, add the parsley, rice and seasoning and cool.

Divide the pastry in half, roll each piece into a rectangle 12×10 inches. Place one of these rectangles on a cookie sheet, spoon the mushroom mixture on top, brush the edges with cold water. Put the second piece of pastry on top and press the edges together; trim. Make a few holes for the steam to escape, decorate with pastry trimmings and brush with egg yolk. Bake for 30 minutes. Serve with sour cream and fresh herb sauce.

| | |
|---|---|
| **Protein** ▲ | **Iron** ▲ |
| **Fiber** ▲ | **Calcium** ▲ |

## SOUR CREAM AND FRESH HERB SAUCE

**Ingredients**
*1¼ cup sour cream*
*3 tablespoons chopped mixed herbs such as parsley, tarragon, chives and thyme*
*salt and freshly ground black pepper*

Put the sour cream into a bowl, add the herbs and seasoning and mix together. Chill in the refrigerator for 15 minutes.

| | |
|---|---|
| **Protein** ▲ | **Iron** ▲ |
| **Fiber** △ | **Calcium** ▲ |

## STRAWBERRY PAVLOVA

**Ingredients**
*4 egg whites*
*pinch of cream of tartar*
*1 ½ cup brown sugar*
*2 teaspoons vinegar*
*4 teaspoons cornstarch*
*½ teaspoon vanilla*
**For the filling**
*1 ¼ cup whipping cream, whipped*
*2 peaches, peeled, halved and cut into thin slices*
*2 kiwi fruit, peeled and cut into thin slices*
*¼ pound strawberries, hulled and halved*

Preheat the oven to 275°. Line a cookie sheet with a piece of wax paper and brush with oil. Beat the egg whites and cream of tartar until the egg whites are so stiff that you can turn the bowl upside down without spilling them. Then beat in a quarter of the sugar. When this has been absorbed, beat in another quarter, and so on, until all the sugar has been added. Add the vinegar, cornstarch and vanilla; mix until combined. Pile the meringue mixture on to the prepared cookie sheet, spreading it out into a large circle. Bake the Pavlova at the bottom of the oven for 1¼-1½ hours, until crisp. Remove from the oven, carefully peel off the wax paper and cool on a wire rack. Just before serving, place the Pavlova on a serving plate and spread the cream all over the top. Arrange the peach slices around the edge, like spokes of a wheel, then add a circle of kiwi fruit and finally put the strawberries in the center; or have an outer ring of strawberries and an inner ring of peaches.

Protein ▲          Iron ▲
Fiber ▲            Calcium ▲

## CHOCOLATE CHESTNUT GÂTEAU

**Ingredients**
*1 ½ sticks sweet butter or margarine*
*1 ¼ cup dark brown moist sugar*
*8 ounce can unsweetened chestnut purée*
*9 squares semi-sweet chocolate, melted*
*½ cup walnuts, roughly chopped*
*⅔ cup whipping cream, whipped*

Grease and line an 8×5×3½ inch bread pan with wax paper. Beat the butter or margarine and sugar together until light and fluffy. Mix together the chestnut purée and melted chocolate until well blended. Add to the butter and sugar, beating all the time. Mix in all but 1 tablespoon of walnuts. Spoon the mixture into the prepared pan, cover and chill for at least 3 hours, until the mixture is firm.

To finish the gâteau, turn it out on to a plate and strip off the paper. Pipe or spoon the cream on top, then decorate with the reserved walnuts.

Protein ▲          Iron ▲
Fiber ▲            Calcium ▲

*Fork food for easy summer eating. From the left: Flaky Mushroom Roll with Sour Cream and Fresh Herb Sauce; Tomato and Avocado Salad; Corn and Radish Salad; Potato Mayonnaise; Tsatsiki; Chocolate Chestnut Gâteau; Strawberry Pavlova (recipes on pages 97-99).*

# ENTERTAINING

▲

Newly converted vegetarians often ask whether they should cook meat and fish for their family and friends. There is absolutely no need to do this because there are so many delicious vegetarian dishes to make that there's bound to be something to please even fussy eaters! In fact, I look upon entertaining as an excellent opportunity to show just how good vegetarian food can be.

This section contains menu suggestions and recipes for various occasions. I'm not keen on spending too much time in the kitchen while everyone else is enjoying themselves, so you'll find that most of the menus can be largely prepared ahead. Also, they're all straightforward to cook and very good to eat. They should win you plenty of compliments and even one or two conversions to vegetarian cookery!

▲

*Left: A beautiful presentation for more formal occasions. Clockwise from the left: Stripy Vegetable Pâté with Bell Pepper Sauce; Pears Poached in Honey with Brandysnaps; Wild Mushroom Feuilleté (recipes on pages 102-103).*

## ELEGANT ENTERTAINING
### Serves 6

*Stripy Vegetable Pâté with
Bell Pepper Sauce*

*Wild Mushroom Feuilleté*

*Pears Poached in Honey with
Brandysnaps*

This is an impressive dinner party menu that's decorative and quite easy to prepare, because both the pretty pâté and the pudding can be made in advance. This just leaves the main course – creamy mushrooms with puff pastry served with an attractive garnish of fresh vegetables – needing last-minute attention.

## STRIPY VEGETABLE PÂTÉ WITH BELL PEPPER SAUCE

This pâté is easy to make, yet looks most effective with its contrasting stripes.

**Ingredients**
*½ pound carrots, scraped and cut into even-sized pieces*
*½ pound frozen or fresh lima beans, shelled*
*½ pound frozen spinach, defrosted*
*3 egg yolks*
*3 tablespoons heavy cream*
*salt and freshly ground black pepper*
*freshly grated nutmeg*
**For the sauce**
*1 red bell pepper, about 6 ounces*
**To garnish**
*sprigs of dill*
*twists of lemon*

Preheat the oven to 325°. Grease an 8×5×3½ inch bread pan with butter and line with a strip of greased wax paper to cover the bottom of the pan and extend up the short sides. Cook the carrots and lima beans in separate saucepans in ½ inch boiling water until tender. Cook the spinach in a dry saucepan for 3-4 minutes. Drain the vegetables thoroughly, saving the water (for the sauce), then blend separately, adding one of the egg yolks to each mixture. Add the cream to the puréed lima beans. Season the mixtures with salt and freshly ground black pepper, and add a little grated nutmeg to the spinach purée. Spoon the spinach into the bottom of the prepared pan, levelling to make a smooth layer. Then carefully spoon the lima bean purée in an even layer on top, and finally add the carrot purée. Cover with a piece of aluminum foil and bake for 1 hour, removing the foil after 45 minutes. The pâté should be firm in the center when touched lightly; leave it to cool in the pan. (The pâté can be completed to this stage the day before. When cold, cover with plastic wrap and store in the refrigerator).

To make the sauce, put the bell pepper under a hot broiler until the skin is blackened and blistered all over. Then place in cold water and peel off the outer skin, which should come away easily. Remove the stalk and rinse away the seeds. Purée the pepper in a blender with a generous ¾ cup of the reserved cooking water; season to taste and chill.

When you're ready to serve the pâté, spoon a pool of sauce onto the center of six small flat plates. Slip a knife round the sides of the pâté to loosen it then turn it out of the pan and strip off the wax paper. Cut the pâté into ¾ inch wide slices and place one on each plate on top of the sauce. Garnish with sprigs of dill and lemon twists before serving.

**Protein** ▲ ▲          **Iron** ▲ ▲
**Fiber** ▲ ▲          **Calcium** ▲

## WILD MUSHROOM FEUILLETÉ

Wild oyster mushrooms give a touch of luxury, and a delicious flavor and texture, to this dish, but if you can't obtain them, simply use cultivated mushrooms.

**Ingredients**
**For the pastry**
*1½ cup fine whole wheat flour*
*½ teaspoon salt*
*1 stick hard butter or margarine*
*1 teaspoon lemon juice*
*about 6 tablespoons water*
**For the filling**
*1 tablespoon butter or margarine*
*1 pound white button mushrooms, wiped and sliced*
*¾ pound oyster mushrooms (pleurotes), wiped and sliced, or a 6½ ounce jar, drained*
*1¼ cup sour cream*
*1¼ cup light cream*
*1 garlic clove, crushed*
*salt and freshly ground black pepper*
**To serve**
*¾ pound small young potatoes, scraped*
*¾ pound broccoli*
*¾ pound carrots, scraped and cut into matchsticks*
*½ pound snow peas, topped and tailed*
*lemon twists*

Make the puff pastry according to the directions on page 125. Preheat the oven to 450°. Roll the pastry out to a depth of about ⅛ inch and cut out 6×3 inch circles and 6×2 inch ones. Put the circles on a baking sheet and bake for 10-12 minutes, until puffed up and golden brown. Meanwhile melt the butter or margarine and fry the white mushrooms and oyster mushrooms (if you're using fresh ones) for 5 minutes, until tender.

Remove the mushrooms with a slotted spoon and boil the remaining liquid rapidly until reduced to 1 tablespoon. Add the mushrooms and bottled mushrooms (if using), sour and light cream, garlic and seasoning. Cook the vegetables separately until they are just tender – the potatoes will go in the bottom of a steamer with the carrots and broccoli on top. The peas should be cooked separately for about 3 minutes in a little boiling water. Drain the vegetables well.

To serve, reheat the mushroom mixture by stirring over a gentle heat. Place a large pastry circle on a warm plate, with a serving of the mushroom mixture and liquid on top. Cover with one of the smaller pastry circles. Arrange the vegetables in piles round the pastry. Garnish with a twist of lemon. Repeat with the remaining plates and serve at once.

*Protein* ▲▲      *Iron* ▲▲
*Fiber* ▲▲▲      *Calcium* ▲▲

## PEARS POACHED IN HONEY WITH BRANDYSNAPS

The brandysnaps can be made a day or two in advance and stored in an airtight container until needed. You can either fill them with the cream, or serve them as they are and hand round the cream separately.

**Ingredients**
*6 ripe pears*
*¾ cup honey*
*2 cup water*
**For the brandysnaps**
*½ stick butter or margarine*
*scant ½ cup dark brown moist sugar*
*⅓ cup light molasses*
*½ cup 85 per cent whole wheat flour*
*½ teaspoon ground ginger, or ground mixed spice*
*a little grated lemon peel*
**To serve**
*⅔ cup heavy cream, whipped*

Peel the pears, keeping them whole and leaving on the stalks. Put the honey and water in a fairly large saucepan and bring to the boil; boil for 2 minutes, then put in the pears. Bring back to the boil, then cover the saucepan and leave the pears to simmer gently for 30-40 minutes. They should feel soft right through to the center; if they are undercooked, the centers may go brown, so cook them thoroughly. When they're ready, take the pears out of the saucepan using a slotted spoon and put them on a serving plate. Boil the honey and water mixture rapidly until it has reduced to about 3 tablespoons of glossy-looking syrup. Spoon this syrup over the pears then leave them to cool.

To make the brandysnaps, first preheat the oven to 325°and grease one or two large cookie sheets. Next stir the butter, sugar and molasses together in a pan over a gentle heat until melted. Remove from the heat and sift in the flour and ground ginger, and grate in a little lemon peel to taste. Drop teaspoonfuls of the mixture onto the cookie sheet, leaving plenty of room for the brandysnaps to spread; flatten lightly with a flat knife. Bake for 8-10 minutes, until evenly browned.

Remove the brandysnaps from the oven and cool on the sheet for 1-2 minutes, until just firm enough to handle. Loosen with a knife and quickly roll the brandysnaps round the greased handle of a wooden spoon, then slide them off and leave to cool. This process has to be done quickly or the brandysnaps will harden. If this happens, pop them back into the oven for a few minutes to soften and start again!

Serve the brandysnaps with the pears, either as they are, accompanied by a bowl of whipped cream, or, just before serving, use a pastry bag with a star tip (or a teaspoon) to fill the brandysnaps with whipped cream.

*Protein* ▲      *Iron* ▲
*Fiber* ▲      *Calcium* ▲

---

### TWO'S COMPANY
*Serves 2*

*Asparagus with Butter and Lemon*

*Cheese Fondue*

*Rainbow Flower Salad*

*Melba Peaches*

---

Try this stylish dinner with a luxurious first course of tender asparagus followed by a pot of bubbling fondue, with crusty bread and a very pretty salad.

## ASPARAGUS WITH BUTTER AND LEMON

**Ingredients**
*½ bunch asparagus – about 12 pieces*
*½ stick butter*
*1 tablespoon fresh lemon juice*
*salt and freshly ground black pepper*
**To serve**
*lemon wedges*

Wash and trim the asparagus, removing the tough stalk ends. Cook in ½ inch boiling water or steam for 10-15 minutes or until the spears feel tender when pierced with the point of a knife. Drain the asparagus then heat the butter and lemon juice in a small saucepan and season with salt and pepper. Serve the asparagus spears immediately with the butter and lemon sauce and lemon wedges.

*Protein* ▲      *Iron* ▲
*Fiber* ▲      *Calcium* ▲

ENTERTAINING

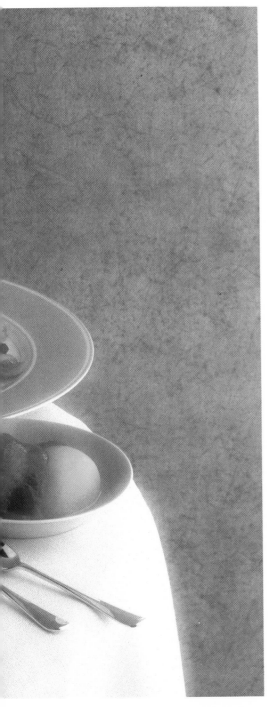

## CHEESE FONDUE

**Ingredients**
*1 small garlic clove, halved*
*6 tablespoons dry white wine*
*½ pound Edam cheese, grated*
*1 teaspoon cornstarch*
*1 tablespoon Kirsch or gin*
*a few drops of lemon juice*
*freshly ground black pepper*
*freshly grated nutmeg*
**To serve**
*1 French bread, cut into bite-sized pieces*
*and warmed in the oven, or*
*1 crusty whole wheat loaf, cut into similar*
*sized pieces and warmed in the oven*

Rub the garlic clove around the inside of a small saucepan then discard. Put the wine into the pan and bring nearly to the boil. Add the grated cheese, stirring over a low heat until the cheese has melted. Blend the cornstarch with the Kirsch or gin to form a smooth paste. Add to the wine and melted cheese, still stirring, until the mixture has thickened slightly. Remove from the heat, add a few drops of lemon juice and season with pepper and nutmeg. Set the pan over a candle burner or fondue burner and serve immediately with the bread.

To eat, spear pieces of bread with long forks (or fondue forks, if you have them) then dip the bread into the fondue and eat it. The Rainbow Flower Salad makes a crisp and refreshing contrast to the rich fondue and the chunky pieces of vegetable can be used for dipping, too.

**Protein** ▲▲▲       **Iron** ▲▲▲
**Fiber** ▲▲▲        **Calcium** ▲▲▲

*Simple but impressive for a romantic supper.*
*Clockwise from top left: Cheese Fondue with*
*crusty bread; Rainbow Flower Salad; Melba*
*Peaches; Asparagus with Butter and Lemon*
*(recipes on pages 103-105).*

## RAINBOW FLOWER SALAD

**Ingredients**
*4 leaves of curly endive, broken into even-sized pieces*
*1 small head of radicchio, broken into even-sized pieces*
*2 medium-sized cooked beets, cut into bite-sized chunks*
*6 scallions, trimmed*
*8 radishes, cut into roses (see page 137)*
*4 cherry tomatoes (if available), peeled*
*1 large carrot, scraped and chopped*
*4 inch piece of daikon, scraped and cut into several chrysanthemums (see page 137)*

Arrange all the ingredients attractively on one or two large plates.

**Protein** ▲▲       **Iron** ▲▲
**Fiber** ▲▲▲        **Calcium** ▲▲

## MELBA PEACHES

**Ingredients**
*2 ripe peaches*
*½ pound fresh or frozen raspberries*
*1 tablespoon fruit sugar*
**To decorate**
*mint sprigs*

Put the peaches into a bowl, cover with boiling water and leave for 2 minutes. Drain and peel. Cut the peaches in half and remove the pits. Purée the raspberries with the fruit sugar in a blender or food processor. Sieve into a bowl. Put two peach halves, cavity side down, on each plate. Spoon the raspberry mixture over the peach halves and decorate with mint.

**Protein** ▲        **Iron** ▲
**Fiber** ▲▲▲        **Calcium** ▲

· ENTERTAINING ·

## SOMETHING SPECIAL
### Serves 8

*Chilled Two-color Melon Soup*

*Hot Stuffed Avocados*

*Buttered Broccoli*

*Broiled tomatoes*

*Raspberry and Pistachio Ice Cream*

Here is a special dinner which will bring you plenty of compliments because it is impressive but is quite easy to prepare. The watch-point is the avocados – put them into the oven just before serving the soup – they should be ready by the time you've cleared away the plates and finished cooking the other vegetables. Take the ice cream out of the freezer just before the meal begins to allow it to soften.

## CHILLED TWO-COLOR MELON SOUP

This soup is made from melons with contrasting flesh – orange and pale green. It's very easy to prepare and makes a stunning first course.

**Ingredients**
*1-2 honeydew melons, about 3 pounds*
*1-2 cantaloupe melons, about 3 pounds*
*2 tablespoons superfine sugar*
**To decorate**
*sprigs of fresh mint*

Halve the melons and remove the seeds. Then scoop out the flesh, keeping the two colors separate. Purée each batch in a blender and sweeten with the sugar. Put the puréed melon into two separate jugs and chill. To serve the soup, pour into bowls holding one jug at each side of the bowl, and pouring from both at the same time, so that each half of the bowl is a different color as in the picture. Place a small sprig of mint in the center.

**Protein** ▲          **Iron** ▲
**Fiber** ▲          **Calcium** ▲

## HOT STUFFED AVOCADOS

**Ingredients**
*4 large ripe avocados*
*peel and juice of 1 well-scrubbed lemon*
*1 bunch of scallions, trimmed and chopped*
*1⅔ cup peeled hazelnuts*
*1½ cup grated vegetarian Cheddar-type cheese*
*4 tablespoons chopped parsley*
*4 tablespoons dry sherry or wine*
*salt and freshly ground black pepper*
**To garnish**
*lemon twists*

Preheat the oven to 400°. Cut the avocados in half and remove the pits. Put the avocado halves, cavity side up, in a shallow casserole, then brush the cut surfaces with a little of the lemon juice. Mix together the scallions, hazelnuts, cheese, parsley and sherry or wine. Add 2 teaspoons lemon juice and the peel and mix thoroughly so that all the ingredients are well blended. Season to taste. Divide this mixture between the avocado halves, and bake for 15-20 minutes, until golden brown.

**Protein** ▲▲▲          **Iron** ▲▲
**Fiber** ▲▲▲          **Calcium** ▲▲▲

## RASPBERRY AND PISTACHIO ICE CREAM

**Ingredients**
*¾ pound fresh raspberries, washed*
*scant 1 cup sugar or honey*
*2 cup whipping cream*
*1 cup pistachio nuts, chopped*

Blend then sieve the raspberries to remove the pips and make a smooth purée. Add the sugar or honey. Whip the cream until it is thick, then fold in the raspberry purée. Pour the mixture into a plastic container and freeze until half-frozen, then stir well and add most of the pistachio nuts, reserving a few for decoration. Return to the freezer and freeze until solid. Remove the ice cream from the freezer for 30 minutes before serving. Spoon into individual bowls and sprinkle with pistachio nuts.

**Protein** ▲▲          **Iron** ▲▲▲
**Fiber** ▲          **Calcium** ▲

## BUTTERED BROCCOLI

**Ingredients**
*3 pounds broccoli, trimmed*
*½ stick butter*
*salt and freshly ground black pepper*

Place the broccoli in a steamer and steam for 15-20 minutes until just cooked. Toss in the butter and season, and serve with the Hot Stuffed Avocados.

**Protein** ▲          **Iron** ▲
**Fiber** ▲▲          **Calcium** ▲▲

***Clockwise from the top: Hot Stuffed Avocados with broiled tomatoes and Buttered Broccoli; Raspberry and Pistachio Ice Cream; Chilled Two-color Melon Soup.***

## CARROT AND CORIANDER SOUP

**Ingredients**
*1 tablespoon butter or margarine*
*1 pound carrots, scraped and sliced*
*¾ pound leeks, washed and sliced*
*1 tablespoon coriander seeds, lightly crushed*
*pared peel of ½ lemon*
*2 teaspoons vegetarian bouillon powder*
*3¾ cup water*
*1 tablespoon lemon juice*
*⅔ cup light cream*
*salt and freshly ground black pepper*

Melt the butter or margarine in a large saucepan, add the carrots and leeks and fry gently, covered, for 15 minutes, until the vegetables are almost soft. Stir in the coriander, lemon peel and bouillon powder and fry for a further 2-3 minutes. Add the water, and simmer for about 10 minutes. Add the lemon juice, cream and seasoning then blend. Reheat and serve.

**Protein** ▲     **Iron** ▲
**Fiber** ▲▲     **Calcium** ▲▲

## INDIVIDUAL ASPARAGUS TARTS

**Ingredients**
**For the pastry**
*3 cup all-purpose 85 per cent whole wheat flour*
*½ teaspoon salt*
*1¾ sticks butter or margarine*
*4-5 tablespoons cold water*
**For the filling**
*1 bunch asparagus, trimmed and cooked as described on page 136*
*1¼ cup light cream*
*2 egg yolks*
*salt and freshly ground black pepper*
*freshly grated nutmeg*

Preheat the oven to 400°. Sift the flour and salt into a bowl, add 1½ sticks of the butter or margarine, then rub it into the flour with your fingertips. Add the water, and bind to a dough. Roll the dough out on a lightly-floured surface, then use to line 6×4 inch tart pans. Prick the pastry bases and place in the oven on a baking sheet. Bake for 15-20 minutes, until golden brown. Turn the oven down to 350°.

Trim the asparagus spears and divide between the tarts. Beat the cream and egg yolks together; season with salt, pepper and nutmeg. Pour a little of this mixture into each tart, on top of the asparagus. Return the tarts to the oven and bake for about 15 minutes, until the filling has set. Don't allow them to overcook: they should be just firm to the touch and no more.

**Protein** ▲▲▲     **Iron** ▲▲▲
**Fiber** ▲     **Calcium** ▲

*Clockwise from top right: Carrot and Coriander Soup; Individual Asparagus Tarts with Red Salad (recipe on page 88); Hazelnut Meringues with Chocolate Sauce (recipes on pages 108-111).*

## HAZELNUT MERINGUES WITH CHOCOLATE SAUCE

These meringues conveniently use up the egg whites left over from the tarts.

**Ingredients**
*2 egg whites*
*pinch of cream of tartar*
*scant 1 cup brown sugar*
*½ cup hazelnuts, roasted and grated*
**For the filling and sauce**
*½ pound sweet chocolate*
*⅔ cup milk*
*1¼ cup whipping cream*

Preheat the oven to 300°. Line a cookie sheet with a piece of wax paper, grease with butter or oil and sprinkle with flour. Put the egg whites into a clean, grease-free bowl with the cream of tartar and beat until stiff and dry. You should be able to turn the bowl upside down without spilling the egg white. Then beat in half the sugar. Add the remaining sugar and hazelnuts and beat well. Drop spoonfuls of the mixture on to the prepared cookie sheet, making 12 meringues.

Put the meringues into the oven, then reduce the setting to 225°. Bake for 1½-2 hours, until they are crisp. Turn off the heat and leave the meringues to cool in the oven. Remove them from the cookie sheet with a flat knife.

While the meringues are cooking, make the filling. Put the chocolate into a small saucepan with the milk and heat gently until the chocolate has melted. Remove from the heat, pour into a serving jug, and cool. Whip the cream and use this to sandwich the meringues together in pairs. Serve with the sauce.
Makes 6 pairs

**Protein** ▲▲        **Iron** ▲
**Fiber** ▲           **Calcium** ▲

---

**INFORMAL DINNER**
*Serves 6*

*Vegetables à la Grecque*

*Pancakes with Red Bell Pepper and Tomato Filling*

*Buttered spinach or Swiss chard*

*Baby potatoes*

*Vanilla Ice Cream with Kumquats in Brandy and Orange Sauce*

---

This is another menu with minimum work at the last minute. All the courses can be prepared in advance, leaving only the baking of the pancake dish and the cooking of the spinach (or Swiss chard) to be done after your guests have arrived. Put the pancake dish into the oven 15 minutes before you start your first course. Remember to take the ice cream out of the freezer just before you sit down to the meal, to give it time to soften a little.

**Protein** ▲         **Iron** ▲
**Fiber** ▲           **Calcium** ▲

## VEGETABLES À LA GRECQUE

This delicious, lightly spiced mixture can be made with other vegetables in season. Try replacing the cauliflower with baby Brussels sprouts, quartered, and the string beans with sliced leeks. Carrots would also make a colorful addition.

---

Vegetables prepared in this way can also be served as a light midday meal or dinner with some grated cheese sprinkled on top. Serve with a tasty bread such as the Warm Herb Bread on page 55.

**Ingredients**
*2 tablespoons olive oil*
*1 large onion, peeled and chopped*
*3 garlic cloves, crushed*
*1 small medium-sized cauliflower, trimmed, washed and broken into florets*
*¾ pound string beans, trimmed and cut into 1 inch pieces*
*6 ounces button mushrooms, wiped and cut into even-sized pieces*
*1 tablespoon coriander seeds, crushed*
*6 teaspoons lemon juice*
*2 teaspoons salt*
*freshly ground black pepper*
**To decorate**
*chopped parsley or a few black olives*
**To serve**
*Soft warm rolls or French bread*

Heat the oil in a large saucepan, then fry the onion for 5 minutes, without letting it brown. Add the garlic, cauliflower and beans and stir-fry for a further 2-3 minutes, then put in the mushrooms and coriander seeds and continue to fry for about 2 minutes, until the mushrooms are beginning to soften. Remove from the heat, add the lemon juice, salt and black pepper. Cool, then chill. Serve on individual plates, sprinkled with chopped parsley and garnished with black olives.

**Protein** ▲▲▲       **Iron** ▲▲
**Fiber** ▲▲▲         **Calcium** ▲

*Left: This is a make-ahead meal involving the minimum of last-minute attention. From the top: Vegetables à la Grecque; Pancakes with Red Bell Pepper and Tomato Filling, buttered spinach and baby potatoes; Vanilla Ice Cream with Kumquats in Brandy and Orange Sauce (recipes on pages 111-112).*

## PANCAKES WITH RED BELL PEPPER AND TOMATO FILLING

Stuffed pancakes are a versatile and popular vegetarian dish. They're also a very practical one, because both the pancakes and the filling can be made in advance and frozen. To freeze the pancakes, simply stack them up on top of each other with a layer of wax paper between each one. Allow to cool, then pack in a plastic bag. Different fillings can be used instead of the red bell pepper mixture; the Ratatouille on page 92 is delicious, as is the wild mushroom mixture on page 102. Another favorite that's beautifully easy to do is simply sliced ripe avocado tossed in a little lemon juice. Spoon a little avocado on each pancake and roll up as directed. Bake the pancakes for about 10-15 minutes until hot through.

**Ingredients**
**For the pancakes**
*1 cup 85 or 100 per cent whole wheat flour*
*½ teaspoon salt*
*1 large egg*
*1 egg yolk*
*⅔ cup milk*
*⅔ cup water*
*2 tablespoons melted butter or oil*
*extra butter or oil for frying*
**For the filling**
*1½ pounds red bell peppers*
*2 tablespoons olive oil*
*1 onion, peeled and chopped*
*3 pounds tomatoes, peeled, seeded and chopped*
*2 tablespoons chopped parsley (optional)*
*salt and freshly ground black pepper*
**To finish**
*1¼ cup sour cream or thick Greek yogurt*
*paprika*

First make the filling. Heat the red bell peppers under a hot broiler until they're browned all over, and the outer skins will come off easily. Put the peppers into cold water and peel off the skins. Remove the stalk ends and seeds and cut into small pieces. Heat the oil in a large saucepan and fry the onion for 10 minutes, then put in the peppers and tomatoes and cook, uncovered, for about 30 minutes, until the mixture is fairly thick and dry. Stir frequently towards the end of the cooking time to prevent burning. Season to taste.

To make the pancakes, put all the ingredients into a food processor or blender and blend until smooth. Alternatively, put the flour and salt into a bowl, mix in the eggs, then gradually add the milk, water and butter or oil to make a smooth, fairly thin batter.

Heat a little butter or oil in a small skillet; when it sizzles, pour off excess butter or oil, so that the skillet is just glistening. Keeping the skillet over a high heat, give the pancake batter a quick stir, then put two tablespoons into the pan. Tip it to make the batter run all over the bottom. Cook the pancake for about 30 seconds, until the top is set and the underside is tinged golden brown. Flip the pancake over and cook the other side. Remove the pancake with a flat knife and put it on to a plate. Make about a dozen more pancakes in the same way, piling them up on top of each other.

To assemble the dish, put a spoonful of the pepper and tomato mixture on each pancake and roll up neatly. Place the pancakes side by side in a shallow casserole. Give the cream a quick stir, then spoon this over the top of the pancakes. Sprinkle with paprika and cover with aluminum foil. To finish the dish, heat the oven to 375° and bake the pancakes for about 20 minutes, until heated through. Serve at once with the spinach or Swiss chard, and potatoes.

**Protein** ▲▲▲      **Iron** ▲▲▲
**Fiber** ▲▲          **Calcium** ▲▲▲

## VANILLA ICE CREAM WITH KUMQUATS IN BRANDY AND ORANGE SAUCE

**Ingredients**
*1 quantity vanilla ice cream (recipe page 84)*
**For the Kumquats in Brandy and Orange Sauce**
*1 pound kumquats, washed*
*1¼ cup orange juice*
*1¼ cup water*
*6 tablespoons fruit sugar, or soft brown sugar to taste*
*2 tablespoons brandy*
*pared peel of 1 large well-scrubbed orange*

Make and freeze the ice cream as described on page 84. To prepare the kumquats, prick them in two or three places, then put them into a saucepan with the orange juice, water and fruit sugar or brown sugar. Bring to the boil, then turn the heat down low and leave them to simmer gently for about 20 minutes; the fruit should feel tender when pierced with a knife and the liquid will have reduced to a syrupy consistency. Remove from the heat and add the brandy and pared orange peel. Cool, then chill the kumquats. Put scoops of ice cream into individual bowls, and top each with two or three kumquats, spooning over some syrup.

*Variation:* use a little white wine or Kirsch instead of brandy for an equally delicious sauce.

**Protein** ▲▲▲      **Iron** ▲
**Fiber** ▲          **Calcium** ▲▲▲

*A casual evening with friends demands an easy menu such as this. Clockwise from top left: Spinach Lasagne; Lettuce and Fresh Herb Salad (recipe on page 66); Garlic Mushrooms with French Bread; Lucky Dip Basket (recipes on page 114).*

## A RELAXED MEAL
### Serves 6

*Garlic Mushrooms
with French Bread*

*Spinach Lasagne*

*Lettuce and Fresh Herb Salad
(recipe page 66)*

*Lucky Dip Basket*

This meal is perfect for a day when you have been out with friends and want to continue to enjoy their company in the evening without having to spend most of the time in the kitchen! Lay the table and have all the preparations done in advance, so that you've only got to switch on the oven to cook the lasagne, and warm up the bread. Swiftly fry the mushrooms at the last minute to make sure that they're piping hot when you sit down.

## GARLIC MUSHROOMS WITH FRENCH BREAD

This is a first course which can be ready in moments.

**Ingredients**
*1 stick butter
4 garlic cloves, crushed
1½ pounds button mushrooms, wiped and quartered
salt and freshly ground black pepper*
**To serve**
*1 French bread warmed*

Melt the butter in a large saucepan and add the garlic. When the butter is really hot (but not brown), put in the mushrooms. Fry these quickly for 2-3 minutes, so that they become tender but slightly crisp on the outside. Divide the mushrooms between six hot, deep bowls (soup bowls are ideal), pour the butter over, and serve at once, with the warm French bread.

*Protein* ▲      *Iron* ▲
*Fiber* ▲      *Calcium* ▲

## SPINACH LASAGNE

A big dish of lasagne makes a very welcoming meal and can be prepared well in advance. This version can be varied by the addition of more cheeses: ½ cup grated Parmesan can be added to the spinach mixture, and 1½-2 cup Mozzarella can be sliced and layered with the lasagne, spinach mixture and sauce, for a richer (more fattening!) version.

The whole dish (with or without the extra cheese) can be frozen before cooking, if more convenient, and is always a useful item to have in your freezer. Allow to defrost completely before use, then cook as described in the recipe.

**Ingredients**
*2 large onions, peeled and chopped
1 tablespoon olive oil
2 garlic cloves, crushed
3¾ cup canned tomatoes
salt and freshly ground black pepper
1 pound packet frozen leaf spinach, defrosted, or 2 pounds fresh spinach, cooked, drained and chopped
¾ pound cream cheese
¼ pound quick-cook lasagne*
**For the topping**
*soft whole wheat bread crumbs
a little butter or margarine*

Preheat the oven to 375°. Fry the onions in the oil for 5 minutes, then add the garlic and fry for a further 5 minutes, without browning. Purée 3 tablespoons of this onion mixture in a blender with the tomatoes and some salt and pepper to make a sauce. Add the rest of the onion to the spinach, together with the cream cheese and seasoning to taste. Put a layer of spinach mixture into the bottom of a shallow casserole and cover with a layer of lasagne, then half the tomato sauce. Repeat the layers, ending with the sauce.

To finish the dish, sprinkle crumbs all over the top of the lasagne and dot with butter or margarine. Bake, uncovered, for 50-60 minutes. If more convenient, this can cook for 1½-2 hours at a lower temperature, 300°.

*Protein* ▲▲▲      *Iron* ▲▲
*Fiber* ▲▲      *Calcium* ▲▲▲

## LUCKY DIP BASKET

This is a pretty and popular dessert which can be prepared in advance, and the individual ingredients can be varied according to your own taste. All you do is line a shallow basket or tray with fresh leaves, then on top of this you arrange all kinds of nuts, fresh and dry fruits, candied ginger, banana chips, candied paw-paw, little cheese crackers, small cheeses, candies and chocolates, making the selection as colorful and varied as you can.

For a more personal touch, some of these ingredients can be homemade, if you've got time, such as dates pitted and stuffed with cream cheese or marzipan, dry apricots plumped in sweet wine or sherry then stuffed with a piece of marzipan or a shelled almond, or homemade marzipan candies or carob or chocolate truffles (page 121). Guests simply keep on helping themselves to whatever they want!

## TRADITIONAL CHRISTMAS DINNER
### Serves 8

*Water Cress and Stilton Soup*

*Chestnut, Walnut and Red Wine Loaf*

*Horseradish Sauce*

*Gravy with Sherry*

*Brussels sprouts*

*Diced carrots and rutabagas in butter*

*Traditional English Christmas Pudding with Brandy Butter*

*Frozen Christmas Pudding*

*Extra Moist Christmas Cake*

*Vegetarian Mince Pies*

*Chocolate Rum Truffles*

The centerpiece of this menu is a moist and tasty chestnut, walnut and red wine loaf which looks mouthwatering when brought to the table garnished with parsley and tomato and surrounded by golden roast potatoes. Non-vegetarians say that it tastes rather like a good, rich turkey stuffing; it certainly combines well with the other traditional flavors of an old-fashioned Christmas: the sprouts, gravy and cranberry or horseradish sauce. The loaf can be made up to 4 weeks in advance and frozen.

## WATER CRESS AND STILTON SOUP

The combination of water cress and Stilton gives this soup a pleasant tang. The cheese can be coarsely grated and offered separately in a small bowl if you prefer.

**Ingredients**
*1 pound leeks, trimmed, washed and sliced*
*2 bunches of water cress, washed*
*1 tablespoon butter or margarine*
*2 teaspoons vegetarian bouillon powder*
*3¾ cup water*
*1 teaspoon cornstarch*
*⅔ cup light cream*
*¼ pound Stilton cheese, grated*
*salt and freshly ground black pepper*

Fry the leeks and water cress in the butter or margarine in a large saucepan over a low heat for 15 minutes. Keep covered, but stir the mixture from time to time, and don't allow it to brown. Add the bouillon powder, cover and fry for a further 3-4 minutes. Pour in the water, bring to the boil, and simmer for about 10 minutes. Blend the cornstarch with the cream and add to the soup, together with the Stilton, then blend in a blender until smooth. Season, reheat and serve.

*Variation:* sour cream and vegetarian Cheddar-type cheese can be used to replace the cream and Stilton. This gives a slightly mellower flavor to the soup. Sprinkle a few chopped walnuts on top just before serving.

**Protein** ▲▲    **Iron** ▲
**Fiber** ▲    **Calcium** ▲▲

## CHESTNUT, WALNUT AND RED WINE LOAF

**Ingredients**
*1 onion, peeled and chopped*
*1 celery stick, finely chopped*
*1 tablespoon butter or margarine*
*4 garlic cloves, crushed*
*¾ pound cooked fresh or canned chestnuts, roughly mashed*
*¾ pound cashew nuts, grated*
*1 cup walnuts, grated*
*1 cup grated Cheddar cheese*
*⅔ cup red wine*
*3 tablespoons chopped parsley*
*1 tablespoon brandy*
*½ teaspoon paprika*
*½ teaspoon dry thyme and basil*
*2 eggs*
*salt and freshly ground black pepper*
**To garnish**
*sprigs of parsley, tomato and lemon slices*

Preheat the oven to 375°. Grease and line a 2 pound bread pan with a long strip of greased wax paper to cover the base and the short sides of the pan. Fry the onion and celery in the butter or margarine for 7 minutes, then add the garlic and cook for a further 2-3 minutes. Remove from the heat and add the remaining ingredients, seasoning well with salt and pepper. Spoon the mixture into the prepared pan. Cover with a piece of aluminum foil and bake for 1 hour, then remove the aluminum foil and continue cooking for a further 15 minutes, until firm in the center.

Remove the loaf from the oven and allow to stand for 4-5 minutes, then loosen the edges by slipping a knife between the loaf and the pan. Turn the loaf out on to a warmed serving plate. Garnish with parsley, tomato and lemon slices.

**Protein** ▲▲▲    **Iron** ▲
**Fiber** ▲▲    **Calcium** ▲▲

## HORSERADISH SAUCE

**Ingredients**
*2 tablespoons horseradish*
*⅔ cup sour cream*
*salt and freshly ground black pepper*

Mix all the ingredients together, seasoning to taste. Serve in a small bowl.

## GRAVY WITH SHERRY

People often wonder how you make vegetarian gravy – well, here is one way! And this is the simplest version, but it is also very good. This particular gravy is a thin one (that's how I prefer it!), but it can easily be made thicker by simply increasing the amount of cornstarch until the gravy is the right consistency for you. The bouillon powder and soy sauce are essential for the flavor and color.

**Ingredients**
*2½ cup water*
*3 teaspoons vegetarian bouillon powder*
*3 tablespoons soy sauce*
*1½ tablespoons redcurrant jelly*
*3 teaspoons cornstarch*
*1½ tablespoons orange juice*
*1½ tablespoons sherry*
*salt and freshly ground black pepper.*

Put the water, bouillon powder, soy sauce and redcurrant jelly into a saucepan and bring to the boil. Blend the cornstarch with the orange juice and sherry. Stir a little of the hot liquid into the cornstarch mixture, then tip this into the saucepan. Stir well, then simmer over a gentle heat until slightly thickened.

**Protein** ▲          **Iron** ▲
**Fiber** △          **Calcium** ▲

## FROZEN CHRISTMAS PUDDING

This makes a very pleasant and refreshing alternative to the traditional Christmas pudding and looks just as festive.

**Ingredients**
*generous 1 cup mixed dry fruit*
*½ cup candied cherries, halved*
*2 tablespoons brandy (optional)*
*1¼ cup whipping cream*
*4 pieces of preserved ginger in syrup, drained and chopped*
*2 sweet apples, cored and finely grated*
*½ cup sliced almonds*
*grated peel of 1 well-scrubbed orange*

Put the dry fruit and cherries into a bowl and sprinkle with the brandy. Leave for 30 minutes, stirring from time to time. Whip the cream, then fold in all the other ingredients, mixing well. Spoon the mixture into a 2½ pint ceramic bowl. Freeze until firm. To serve, loosen the ice cream around the edges with a knife. Invert the bowl over a plate, hold briefly under the hot faucet, then dry excess water and give the bowl and the plate a sharp shake. The pudding should unmold onto the plate. (Repeat this process if the pudding is sticking). This pudding can be decorated with a sprig of holly, like a traditional Christmas pudding.

**Protein** ▲          **Iron** ▲
**Fiber** ▲          **Calcium** ▲

*The chestnut loaf combines well with other traditional Christmas flavors. Clockwise from top left: Water Cress and Stilton Soup; Horseradish Sauce; diced carrots and rutabagas; Frozen Christmas Pudding; Brandy Butter; Traditional English Christmas Pudding; Chestnut, Walnut and Red Wine Loaf (recipes on pages 115-119).*

## TRADITIONAL ENGLISH CHRISTMAS PUDDING WITH BRANDY BUTTER

In this pudding, butter or a hard white vegetable suet (see page 139) replace the traditional suet. The pudding tastes just as good, and has a deliciously spicy flavor. It can be made up to two months in advance and will keep well (and mature) in a cool, dry place.

**Ingredients**
*1½ cup currants*
*¾ cup white raisins*
*¾ cup raisins*
*¾ cup chopped candied fruit*
*¼ cup almonds, peeled and chopped*
*1 cup 85 or 100 per cent whole wheat flour*
*½ teaspoon salt*
*½ teaspoon grated nutmeg*
*½ teaspoon ground ginger*
*1½ teaspoons mixed spice*
*1½ cup dark brown moist sugar*
*2 cup fresh whole wheat bread crumbs*
*2 sticks hard butter or ½ pound vegetable suet, coarsely grated*
*peel and juice of 1 lemon*
*2 eggs*
*1 tablespoon blackstrap molasses*
*about 4 tablespoons milk or milk and rum mixed*

Grease a 2½ pint ceramic bowl and have ready a saucepan which is large enough to hold the bowl. Wash the currants and raisins in warm water, then pat dry on paper towels. Put the fruit into a large bowl with the candied fruit and almonds. Sift the flour, salt and spices into the bowl on top of the fruit, then add the sugar, bread crumbs and butter or vegetable suet. Mix well, then stir in the lemon peel and juice, eggs, molasses and enough of the milk or milk and rum to make a soft mixture which will fall heavily from the spoon when you shake it.

## ENTERTAINING

Spoon the mixture into the bowl, cover with a piece of wax paper and then aluminum foil, and secure.

Put the bowl into the saucepan and pour in enough water to come half-way up the bowl. Bring to the boil, then cover the saucepan and leave the pudding to steam gently for 4 hours. Watch the water-level in the saucepan and top up with some boiling water from time to time if necessary. Cool, then store the pudding in a cool dry place. Steam the pudding again for 3 hours before eating, then turn it out on to a warm serving plate and flame with brandy. To do this, put 4 tablespoons of brandy into a metal soup ladle and warm by holding over a gas flame or electric element, then quickly ignite the brandy and pour over and round the pudding.

*Optional Extras:* Insert some small silver coins into the pudding before serving: sterilize them by boiling them in the water while the pudding steams, wrap well in wax paper then insert them into the pudding with the point of a knife, covering the damage with a sprinkling of superfine sugar! Make sure the children are careful to search their helping of pudding well for coins before eating it to avoid any swallowed coins!

This pudding is delicious with whipped cream, light cream or a brandy or rum butter made by beating ¾ cup light brown sugar and enough rum or brandy to flavor into 1 stick soft sweet butter. This can be made well in advance, and frozen.

If you find cream or brandy or rum butter too rich with Christmas pudding, custard or a thin white sauce, sweetened and flavored with a little rum or brandy, are other possibilities.

**Protein** ▲▲     **Iron** ▲▲▲
**Fiber** ▲     **Calcium** ▲

*Christmas coffee: Left to right: Vegetarian Mince Pies; Extra Moist Christmas Cake (recipes on page 120).*

## EXTRA MOIST CHRISTMAS CAKE

I love to see a traditional Christmas cake, with snowy-white frosting and festive decorations, and my family certainly wouldn't think it were Christmas without it! But if you don't like to use frosting, you can make a very pretty decoration by brushing the cake with warmed honey then arranging a selection of colorful fruits and nuts on top: candied cherries, Brazil nuts, blanched almonds, candied pineapple, for instance. Brush with more honey for a final glaze. A red ribbon round the cake completes the festive look!

**Ingredients**
*1½ pounds mixed dry fruit (including mixed candied fruit), washed and dried on paper towels*
*generous ½ cup candied cherries, rinsed under hot water and halved*
*grated peel and juice of 1 orange*
*6 tablespoons brandy, whisky or rum*
*1½ sticks soft butter or margarine*
*1½ cup dark brown moist sugar*
*3 eggs, beaten*
*1½ cup 85 or 100 per cent whole wheat flour*
*1 teaspoon mixed spice*
*1 tablespoon blackstrap molasses*
*2 tablespoons ground almonds*
*½ cup sliced almonds*
**For the almond paste**
*1 pound ground almonds*
*1 pound soft brown sugar*
*1 teaspoon lemon juice*
*a few drops of almond flavoring*
*2 eggs, beaten*
*3 tablespoons redcurrant jelly, melted*
**For the frosting**
*4 egg whites*
*2 pounds powdered sugar, sifted*
*1 tablespoon lemon juice*
*2 teaspoons glycerine*

**To decorate**
*red ribbon, candle, decorations, etc.*

Put the dry fruit and cherries into a large bowl and add the orange peel and juice and the spirit. Stir, then cover the mixture and leave for 48 hours, stirring from time to time. Preheat oven to 300°. Grease an 8 inch round pan and line with a double layer of greased wax paper. Cream the butter or margarine and sugar, then add the eggs a little at a time, beating well between each addition. Sift the flour and mixed spice, then fold this in. Finally stir in the fruit, molasses and the ground and sliced almonds. Spoon the mixture into the prepared pan, hollowing out the center slightly. Bake for 3½-4 hours, until a toothpick or cake tester inserted into the center comes out clean. Cool in the pan, then remove the wax paper. Wrap in fresh wax paper and store in an airtight container.

One week before Christmas, make up the almond paste by mixing together all the ingredients except the redcurrant jelly. Trim the cake if necessary to make it level, then brush with the melted redcurrant jelly. Roll out two-thirds of the almond paste and cut into two pieces to cover the sides of the cake; press them into position. Roll the remainder into a circle to cover the top; press down and trim. Leave the cake in a dry, airy place for 3-7 days.

To make up the frosting, beat the egg whites until they're frothy, then gradually beat in all the other ingredients. Spoon all the frosting on top of the cake and roll it backwards and forwards a few times with a flat knife to remove air bubbles. Spread the frosting over the top and sides of the cake. Finally use the blade of the flat knife to flick the frosting up into peaks. Decorate the cake and tie a ribbon round it when the frosting has set.

**Protein** ▲▲▲        **Iron** ▲▲
**Fiber** ▲▲             **Calcium** ▲▲

## VEGETARIAN MINCE PIES

This mincemeat relies on the fruit for sweetness, without added sugar, and it doesn't contain any fat. It tastes excellent and can be stored for a week in a covered bowl in the refrigerator, but doesn't keep in the same way as ordinary mincemeat because of the lack of sugar.

Before serving, warm the mince pies in the oven, and serve them sprinkled with sugar. This quantity of mincemeat will make 36 mince pies.

**Ingredients**
**For the mincemeat**
*¾ cup currants*
*¾ cup raisins*
*¾ cup white raisins*
*generous ¼ cup cooking dates*
*½ cup candied fruit*
*generous ¼ cup candied cherries*
*½ cup sliced almonds*
*1 ripe banana, peeled*
*4 tablespoons brandy or whisky*
*½ teaspoon each ground ginger, grated nutmeg, mixed spice*
**For the pastry**
*2 cup 85 per cent whole wheat flour*
*1 stick butter or margarine*
*6 teaspoons cold water*
**To serve**
*a little superfine sugar*

To make the mincemeat, simply mix everything together. You can do this in a food processor (which will chop the fruit, making a smoother texture), or by hand.

When you're ready to make the mince pies, preheat the oven to 400°. Lightly grease a shallow muffin pan. Sift the flour and salt into a bowl, add the butter or margarine, and rub into the flour with your fingertips until the mixture resembles bread crumbs. Add the water, then press the mixture together to make a dough. Roll the

dough out on a lightly floured surface, then cut out 4¾ inch circles and 4 inch circles using round cookie cutters. Press one of the larger circles gently into each section of the muffin pan, then put a heaped teaspoon of mincemeat into each and cover with the smaller pastry circles. Press down firmly at the edges, make a hole in the top for steam to escape, then bake for about 10 minutes, until the pastry is lightly browned. Cool in the pan.
Makes 36

**Protein** ▲      **Iron** ▲
**Fiber** ▲      **Calcium** ▲▲

## CHOCOLATE RUM TRUFFLES

**Ingredients**
*¼ pound good quality semi-sweet chocolate*
*⅔ cup heavy cream*
*1 tablespoon rum*
**To finish**
*cocoa for coating*
*small paper candy cases, if available*

Break the chocolate into pieces and put into a small saucepan with the heavy cream. Heat very gently until the chocolate has melted, then remove from the heat, scrape into a bowl and cool. Then add the rum to the cream and chocolate mixture and beat thoroughly until paler in color and fluffy. Place in the refrigerator until firm enough to handle.

Sprinkle some cocoa over a plate, then place heaped teaspoons of the chocolate mixture on this, and sprinkle with more cocoa. Quickly roll each piece of mixture in cocoa to make a truffle and place in a candy case or on a small serving plate. Chill until ready to serve.
Makes 18

**Protein** ▲      **Iron** ▲
**Fiber** △      **Calcium** ▲

### DRINKS PARTY
*Serves 30*

*Stuffed Dates*

*Avocado Dip with Chips*

*Cream Cheese Toasts*

*Asparagus Rolls*

*Vegetable Pâté Pinwheels*

These tasty nibbles made with vegetables, fruits and cheese are ideal accompaniments for drinks – all these recipes can be prepared in advance. The choice of drink is up to you; a simple solution is to offer 2 types of medium-dry wine, a white and a rosé or red. As a rough guide to quantities, allow 6 bottles of white and 4 of the rosé or red, plus some non-alcoholic alternatives. Remember to allow plenty of time for the white wine to chill or the red wine to breath. Stock up too on soft drinks and mineral waters and remember to make extra ice cubes for these.

## STUFFED DATES

**Ingredients**
*24 fresh dates, with pits removed*
*¾ cup cream cheese*

Stuff each date with a little of the cream cheese and arrange on a serving plate.

**Protein** ▲      **Iron** ▲
**Fiber** ▲      **Calcium** ▲

## AVOCADO DIP WITH CHIPS

**Ingredients**
*Avocado Cream (recipe page 123)*
*bag of potato chips*

Make the Avocado Cream as described and serve in a small bowl. Serve the chips separately, for guests to use to scoop up the dip. Alternatively serve a selection of crisp vegetables (see page 32).

**Protein** ▲      **Iron** ▲
**Fiber** ▲      **Calcium** ▲

## CREAM CHEESE TOASTS

**Ingredients**
*¾ cup cream cheese*
*1 small beet, cooked or uncooked*
*1 tablespoon finely-chopped parsley*
*2 hard-cooked egg yolks*
*pinch of turmeric*
*1 packet of Melba toasts (about 30 pieces)*
**To garnish**
*shelled pistachio nuts, salted cashew nuts, mashed hard-cooked egg yolk, little sprigs of parsley, tiny pieces of beet, green or black olives*

Divide the cream cheese into three equal portions and put into separate bowls. Add a very little mashed or finely-grated beet to one bowl; then beat the chopped parsley into another portion and finally mash the egg yolk until it is smooth and stir this into the third portion of cream cheese, together with the turmeric. Pipe or spread these mixtures on the Melba toasts. Top each with a pistachio nut, cashew nut or other garnish as desired.

**Protein** ▲      **Iron** ▲
**Fiber** ▲      **Calcium** ▲

## ASPARAGUS ROLLS

**Ingredients**
½ whole wheat bread, sliced
butter or margarine
¾ pound canned asparagus tips, drained

Cut the crusts off the bread, then flatten each slice with a rolling pin. Thinly spread the bread with butter or margarine, then roll a piece of bread round each piece of asparagus. Cut each roll into 2 or 3 pieces so that they are a manageable size for eating. Keep in a cool place, covered with plastic wrap, until needed.
Makes about 40

**Protein** ▲          **Iron** ▲
**Fiber** ▲          **Calcium** ▲

## VEGETABLE PÂTÉ PINWHEELS

**Ingredients**
½ large whole wheat bread, sliced
1 × 4½ ounce can vegetarian pâté (see page 139)

Cut the crusts off the bread and flatten each slice with a rolling pin. Spread each slice generously with the vegetarian pâté, then roll the slices up like miniature jelly rolls. Chill for an hour or so. Cut each roll into slices about ⅓ inch wide. Place on a plate and cover with plastic wrap until required.
Makes about 50

**Protein** ▲          **Iron** ▲
**Fiber** ▲          **Calcium** ▲

**Clockwise from the top: Vegetable Pâté Pinwheels and Asparagus Rolls; Stuffed Dates; Cream Cheese Toasts; Avocado Dip with Chips (recipes on pages 121-123).**

## WEDDING RECEPTION
### Serves 50

*Avocado Cream*

*Confetti Salad*

*Hot Nut Rissoles with
Two Dipping Sauces*

*Brie Fritters with Apricot Conserve*

*Cherry Tomato Cups*

*Mushroom Tartlets*

*Stuffed Baby Mushrooms*

*Asparagus Loaf*

*Little Brown Sugar Meringues*

*Flower Cakes*

*Fresh Raspberries and Cream*

*Amaretti Trifle*

If you've got the space, the time and the stamina, nothing is more satisfying than catering for a wedding reception yourself. But do make sure you have enough back-up help, both beforehand and during the reception. In particular you'll need people to clear tables and look after guests as the reception progresses, and to see to the last-minute preparation of the hot food. The food should be arranged buffet-style, for guests to help themselves, but it's a good idea to have some helpers ready to assist in the serving.

## AVOCADO CREAM

This is a delicious, pale green, creamy dip. It can also be used, by the way, as a wonderful dressing for a salad (instead of mayonnaise!) or as a first course, spooned onto crisp lettuce leaves, garnished with a sprinkling of paprika pepper and slices of lemon and tomatoes and served with hot Melba toast. Do make sure that the avocado is really ripe – it should 'give' easily when pressed at the stalk end, and feel generally soft (but not 'soggy' when cradled in your hand). Make double this quantity for 50 people.

**Ingredients**
1 ripe avocado, halved, peeled and pit removed
1 tablespoon lemon juice
1 cup curd or cream cheese
1 garlic clove, crushed
dash of red wine vinegar
a few drops of Tabasco
salt and freshly ground black pepper
mild paprika

Mash the avocado flesh with the lemon juice, then gradually mix in the curd or cream cheese to make a smooth, creamy consistency. Add the garlic, a few drops of wine vinegar, Tabasco and season to taste. Spoon into a small bowl, smooth the top and sprinkle with some paprika. Guests can take a spoonful of this and eat it with the salad and other dishes.

**Protein** ▲          **Iron** ▲
**Fiber** ▲          **Calcium** ▲

## CONFETTI SALAD

This is a particularly pretty salad, with crisp textures which contrast well with the other dishes. It is a particularly good choice when entertaining on a grand scale as it can be made well in advance. Cover with plastic wrap and store in the refrigerator until required.

**Ingredients**
*2 tablespoons Dijon mustard*
*2 tablespoons wine vinegar*
*8 tablespoons olive oil*
*salt and freshly ground black pepper*
*4 large carrots, scraped and coarsely grated*
*1 pound white cabbage, finely shredded*
*1 pound red cabbage, finely shredded*
*tender sticks from 1 head of celery, sliced*
*1 red bell pepper, seeded and finely chopped*
*1 green bell pepper, seeded and finely chopped*

Put the mustard into a large bowl and stir in the vinegar, oil and some salt and pepper, to make a dressing. Add all the prepared vegetables, mix well. This can be made several hours in advance.

**Protein** ▲       **Iron** ▲
**Fiber** ▲         **Calcium** ▲

## HOT NUT RISSOLES WITH TWO DIPPING SAUCES

Use double the quantity of Nutty Sausage mixture given on page 83. It's a good idea to make these rissoles in advance. Place in a single layer on cookie sheets and open freeze until solid. Pack into plastic containers. To use, return to the cookie sheets, cover loosely with plastic wrap and defrost overnight at cool, room temperature. Fry the rissoles as directed.

**Ingredients**
**For the Yogurt and Mint sauce**
*generous 1 cup thick Greek yogurt*
*1 small garlic clove, crushed (optional)*
*2 tablespoons finely chopped mint*
**For the Mango Chutney Dip**
*6 rounded tablespoons mango chutney, with large pieces finely chopped*
*1-2 tablespoons warm water*

Press the Nutty Sausage mixture with your hands so that it clings together firmly, then divide into small pieces and roll each into a sausage about ⅓ inch wide by 1 inch long. You should be able to make about 100 with this quantity of mixture. Fry the sausages in hot, shallow olive oil for 2-3 minutes, turning them so that they brown on all sides. Drain well on paper towels. Serve with the dipping sauces. To make these, simply mix together the ingredients for each, season the yogurt dip well, then serve them in small bowls; offer tooth-picks for guests to use to 'spear' the sausages if they wish.
Makes about 100

**Protein** ▲       **Iron** ▲ ▲
**Fiber** ▲         **Calcium** ▲ ▲

## BRIE FRITTERS WITH APRICOT CONSERVE

**Ingredients**
*2 pounds Brie cheese*
*4 large eggs, beaten*
*wheat germ to coat*
*sunflower oil for deep frying or olive oil for shallow frying*
*apricot conserve or jelly for serving*

Cut the cheese (including the skin) into bite-sized pieces. Dip each first into beaten egg, then into wheat germ. Either deep-fry in oil heated to 350-375° (or when a cube of bread browns in 30 seconds), or shallow-fry in hot olive oil, turning the fritters frequently to brown them all over. Drain fritters well on paper towels and serve immediately with the apricot conserve or jelly. (These fritters can also be cooked from frozen.)
Makes about 100

**Protein** ▲ ▲     **Iron** ▲
**Fiber** ▲         **Calcium** ▲

## CHERRY TOMATO CUPS

The tomatoes can be trimmed and scooped out well in advance of filling. Place the hollowed out and seasoned tomato shells upside down on cookie sheets or baking trays. Cover loosely with plastic wrap and keep in a cool place until needed, then fill the tomato cups as described below.

**Ingredients**
*¾ cup curd cheese*
*a little milk*
*50 cherry tomatoes*
*salt and freshly ground black pepper*
*6 ounces vegetarian pâté (see page 139)*
**To serve**
*parsley or dill sprigs*

Put the curd cheese into a bowl and beat well until smooth, adding a little milk if needed to make a consistency which can be piped. Cut the tops off the tomatoes and slice small pieces off the bases, if necessary, so that the tomatoes will stand level. Using a teaspoon, scoop out the seeds; sprinkle the insides with a little salt and pepper. Using a pastry bag fitted with a shell tip, pipe the curd cheese into half the tomatoes; fill the remainder with the pâté. Garnish each with a tiny sprig of parsley or dill, and arrange on a plate.

**Protein** ▲       **Iron** ▲
**Fiber** ▲         **Calcium** ▲

## MUSHROOM TARTLETS

**Ingredients**
**For the puff pastry**
*4 cup fine whole wheat flour*
*2 teaspoons salt*
*3 sticks hard butter or margarine, from the refrigerator*
*4 teaspoons lemon juice*
*about 16 tablespoons cold water*
**For the mushroom filling**
*2 pounds baby white button mushrooms, wiped and sliced*
*½ stick butter or margarine*
*4 teaspoons cornstarch*
*2½ cup light cream*
*salt and freshly ground black pepper*
*freshly grated nutmeg*

First make the pastry. Mix the flour and salt in a large bowl and grate in the butter. Add the lemon juice and water, then mix quickly to a fairly soft dough. Gather this into a ball, wrap in plastic wrap and chill for at least 1 hour. Roll the dough into an oblong. Mark this lightly into 3 equal sections, then fold the bottom third up and the top third down, to make 3 layers. Seal the edges by pressing them lightly with your rolling pin (to trap the air), then give the pastry a quarter turn. Repeat the rolling, folding and turning 4 times.

Preheat the oven to 425°. Lightly grease a shallow muffin pan. Roll the dough out about ¼ inch thick and cut out rounds using a 3 inch cookie cutter. Put 12 of these into the muffin pan, pressing them down gently. Bake for about 10 minutes, until crisp and browned. Cool for a few minutes in the pan, then carefully remove the tartlets and bake another 12. Re-roll the trimmings and cut these into 60 tiny hearts, using a cookie cutter. Put these on a cookie sheet and bake until brown.

To make the mushroom filling, fry the mushrooms in all but 2 teaspoons of the butter or margarine. Fry them quickly for about 2 minutes, until just tender. Drain off any liquid. Melt the remaining butter in another saucepan, stir in the cornstarch and cook for 2 minutes, then add the cream and stir over the heat for a further 2 minutes until thickened. Remove from the heat, stir in the mushrooms and season with salt, pepper and nutmeg. Spoon this mixture into the tartlet cases and top each one with a pastry heart.

**Protein** ▲         **Iron** ▲
**Fiber** ▲         **Calcium** ▲

## STUFFED BABY MUSHROOMS

**Ingredients**
*50 open baby mushrooms, wiped*
*¼ pound Camembert cheese, diced*
*½ stick butter*
*1 cup walnut pieces, finely chopped*
*2 garlic cloves, crushed*
*2 tablespoons parsley, chopped*
*milk*

Remove the stalks from the mushrooms. Chop the stalks and put into a bowl with the Camembert (including the skin), butter, nuts, garlic, parsley and a little milk. Beat all the ingredients together until well mixed but firm.

Place the mushrooms, stalk side up, in a large shallow casserole or pizza pan. Preheat the oven to 400°. Put a spoonful of the walnut mixture on top of each mushroom, dividing it between them. Bake for about 15 minutes. If the mushrooms produce some liquid, strain this off before serving.

*Variation:* any soft cheese such as Brie or Cambozola may be substituted here.

**Protein** ▲         **Iron** ▲
**Fiber** ▲         **Calcium** ▲

## ASPARAGUS LOAF

It's well worth taking the time to arrange the asparagus neatly into the bread pan. Season carefully as the Parmesan tends to be salty. Make double this amount to serve 50 people, along with other buffet dishes. This loaf also makes a lovely summer dinner party dish, served with mayonnaise, snow peas and some crisp lettuce.

**Ingredients**
*1 small onion, peeled and grated*
*1 cup grated Parmesan*
*generous 1 cup ground almonds*
*2 eggs*
*⅔ cup light cream*
*salt and freshly ground black pepper*
*freshly grated nutmeg*
*1 pound cooked, trimmed green asparagus (make sure that all the tough part has been removed)*
**To garnish**
*sprigs of parsley or water cress*

Preheat the oven to 375°. Grease an 8×5×3½ inch bread pan and line with a long strip of greased wax paper to cover the base and the short sides. Mix together the onion, cheese, almonds, eggs and cream. Season with salt, pepper and grated nutmeg. Put a layer of this mixture in the bottom of the bread pan, then arrange a layer of asparagus spears on top. Continue in layers like this until all the ingredients are used up, ending with the nut mixture. Bake for 45-60 minutes, until risen and firm in the center. Cool in the pan, then slip a knife round the sides and carefully turn out on to a plate. Strip off the paper. Cut into slices, then cut in half again. Arrange the slices on a plate and garnish with parsley or water cress.

**Protein** ▲         **Iron** ▲
**Fiber** ▲         **Calcium** ▲

## LITTLE BROWN SUGAR MERINGUES

Use the recipe for Baby Meringues on page 85, making three times the quantity, to make about 60. Make in advance and store in airtight containers.

## FLOWER CAKES

Buy the biggest and prettiest sugar flower decorations you can find; or, better still, if you've the time and skill, make your own in soft pastel colors.

**Ingredients**
*1 quantity cake mixture (see page 84)*
*about 50 paper cupcake cases*
**To decorate**
*5 cup sifted powdered sugar*
*7-8 tablespoons water*
*cake colorings to tone with sugar flowers*
*about 50 sugar flower cake decorations*
*extra powdered sugar for dusting*

Preheat the oven to 375°. Make the cake mixture as described on page 84. Put heaped teaspoonfuls into the paper cupcake cases and place on a cookie sheet. Bake for 10-15 minutes, until the cakes spring back when touched lightly in the center. Cool on a wire rack.

Make the frosting by mixing the powdered sugar with the water; divide the mixture into 3 or 4 portions and color each portion delicately to tone with the flowers. Pour a little frosting on to the top of each cake, spread lightly to the edges with a knife. Place a sugar flower in the center of each cake. Dust lightly with powdered sugar. Makes about 50

*Protein* ▲        *Iron* ▲
*Fiber* ▲          *Calcium* ▲

Tableware courtesy of Wedgwood at Oxford Circus, London W1

## FRESH RASPBERRIES AND CREAM

This is a simple but delicious dessert. For 50 portions, allow 11-12 pounds fresh raspberries, 3¾ cup whipping cream, whipped, and 2½ cup superfine sugar. Put the raspberries into small individual bowls and serve the cream and sugar separately.

**Protein** ▲          **Iron** ▲
**Fiber** ▲          **Calcium** ▲

## AMARETTI TRIFLE

**Ingredients**
*3 cup lightly crushed Amaretti cookies*
*(or lady fingers)*
*2 tablespoons raspberry jam or jelly*
*6 tablespoons sweet white wine*
*4 white peaches, peeled and chopped*
*1¼ cup whipping cream*
*2-3 tablespoons superfine sugar*
*¼ cup blanched slivered almonds*

Mix the crushed cookies with the jam or jelly and 4 tablespoons of the white wine. Divide between 6-8 individual serving bowls, then add the peaches. Whip the cream with the sugar and the remaining white wine then spoon this on top of the peaches. Decorate with almonds and chill. Serves 6-8. For 50, make 6 or 7 times the recipe.

**Protein** ▲▲          **Iron** ▲
**Fiber** ▲          **Calcium** ▲

*Clockwise from top left: Stuffed Baby Mushrooms; Cherry Tomato Cups; Mushroom Tartlets; Asparagus Loaf; Confetti Salad; Flower Cakes; Little Brown Sugar Meringues; Fresh Raspberries and Cream; Brie Fritters; Hot Nut Rissoles with Two Dipping Sauces (on pages 123-127).*

# THE VEGETARIAN PANTRY

The colors and aromas of all the vegetarian ingredients – dry beans and grains, nuts, seeds, fresh fruits, vegetables, herbs, spices, honey and natural sugars – will enhance any kitchen. Although some of these ingredients are quite expensive, many others are cheap to buy and easy to keep, and you can gradually build up a supply by getting perhaps one or two new ingredients each week. Cereals, whole wheat bread, pulses, potatoes, peanuts, cheese, milk and eggs, also vegetables and fresh fruit in season, are quite reasonable. The nuts and seeds are more expensive, but these are used in relatively small quantities and, remember, if you're vegetarian, you're saving money by not buying meat and fish.
This list contains notes on all the major ingredients used in this book, with tips on which are the important foods to buy, and why, what to look for, how to keep and how to use the ingredients

▲

*Left: The abundance of natural ingredients used in vegetarian cooking – fresh fruit and vegetables, pulses, pastas, seeds, grains and nuts – provide color, flavor and texture with all the essentials for good health.*

· THE VEGETARIAN PANTRY ·

## Protein Foods

### Nuts and Seeds

Nuts and seeds are concentrated sources of vitamins and minerals in addition to protein. They may appear expensive, but if you look at the recipes you'll see that a little goes a long way; main course dishes made from nuts and seeds often work out cheaper than meat or fish. Buy small quantities of nuts as you need them and use them up quickly, as they tend to go stale. For this reason, too, it is best to store nuts in the refrigerator, if there is space!

Grated nuts are often called for in vegetarian recipes. To grate nuts, either put them into the food processor or blender and blend until powdered. You can also use a hand or electric grater.

**Almonds** These are among the most useful nuts and also some of the richest in iron and protein. Available whole (with the brown skin still on), blanched, sliced, slivered, chopped or ground.

**Brazil Nuts** These large brown nuts are the richest in Vitamin B1 (thiamin) and have a rich, creamy flavor. They combine well with other nuts and are especially good in a nut roast. Try them as a filling for dates to make a sweet snack for older children (or grownups!).

**Cashew Nuts** Crescent-shaped and creamy white in color, cashew nuts have a slightly sweetish flavor. Their blandness makes them equally useful for both desserts and main meal recipes. They can be bought whole or broken; broken cashew nuts are cheaper than whole ones and are fine for most cooking.

**Chestnuts** These are higher in carbohydrate and lower in oil and protein than most nuts and although they're rich in vitamin B they do not provide a very concentrated source of nutrients.

Ready-peeled, dry chestnuts can be bought at health stores and make a labor-saving alternative to fresh ones but require longer cooking time. Put them into a saucepan, cover with boiling water and soak overnight. Next day simmer for 2-3 hours, until tender. Easier still, you can buy canned, whole chestnuts and chestnut purée. Buy unsweetened chestnut purée which can then be used in both desserts and main courses.

**Coconut** Fresh coconut, removed from the hard shell and chopped or coarsely grated, makes a pleasant addition to fruit salads and lightly spiced vegetable dishes. Shredded coconut is useful for sprinkling over vegetable and fruit salads and also makes a crisp, tasty coating for burgers. Buy unsweetened coconut in small quantities.

**Hazelnuts** You can buy these with or without their dark brown outer skins. If you buy them still in their skins, you can improve the flavor by roasting them. Place the nuts on a dry cookie sheet and bake at 375°, for 15-20 minutes, or until the nuts underneath the skins are golden brown. Cool, then rub off the skins in a soft cloth, or leave them on if preferred.

**Peanuts** Botanically, these are a pulse rather than a nut, though they behave like a nut from the cook's point of view! They're rich in protein and one of the very best sources of the B vitamin, nicotinic acid. Unroasted peanuts can be bought from health stores and roasted like hazelnuts (see above); you can also buy roasted unsalted peanuts. Peanut butter is made from roasted, peeled peanuts and is a useful addition to the pantry. Buy a make which does not contain stabilizers and other additives. This may mean that the oil separates from the solid part in the jar, but all you need to do is to give the peanut butter a good stir before you use it.

**Pecans** These look rather like walnuts, but they're darker in color and longer and slimmer in shape. They have a delicious slightly sweet flavor and oily texture.

**Pine Nuts** These little soft white nuts have a delicate 'pine' flavor. They're expensive but delicious for a special treat.

**Pistachios** Useful as a garnish, because of their pretty green color, pistachios also have a delicious flavor. Buy them in their pale brown husks and remove these with your fingers. Chop the nuts to reveal the green coloring.

**Walnuts** Rich in B vitamins, walnuts have a slightly bitter flavor which makes them a useful addition to many appetizing dishes. But they should on no account be really bitter; if they are, this means that they are stale. Check and buy carefully. Walnuts can be bought in halves, or, more cheaply, in pieces.

**Pumpkin Seeds** These are large, flat green seeds. They're very nutritious, being rich in iron and zinc as well as protein. Pumpkin seeds make an excellent nibble or can be added to breakfast cereals or rice dishes.

**Sesame Seeds** One of the best non-dairy sources of calcium, sesame seeds make a delicious, crunchy coating for burgers or topping for a variety of dishes. You can buy sesame paste, sometimes called tahini, also sesame spread. These are similar to peanut butter, with the intense, slightly bitter flavor of sesame seeds.

**Sunflower Seeds** These chewy little grey seeds are a useful source of many nutrients, in particular nicotinic acid. They make a tasty nibble and can be added, whole or grated, to nut mixtures, salads and mueslis (for extra flavor toast the seeds lightly under the broiler).

## Pulses

Dry peas, beans and lentils, known as pulses, are rich in protein, minerals, B vitamins and natural fiber. They're a particularly useful addition to the vegetarian pantry because of their excellent keeping qualities. Store them in jars, ready to sprout (see page 30) or cook as required.

Most pulses need soaking before cooking. To do this, simply put them into a deep bowl or saucepan and cover with their height again in cold water. Leave for 6-8 hours. Alternatively, boil the pulses for 2 minutes, then cover and leave to soak in the water for 1 hour. Whichever method you use, drain and rinse the pulses after soaking, cover them with fresh water and boil rapidly for 10 minutes; this destroys any enzymes which could cause stomach upsets. Let the pulses simmer gently until they're tender and use as required. Cooked pulses can be frozen – drain and freeze in suitable portions.

**Alfalfa** This looks like a tiny golden brown seed, but it's really a pulse. It can be bought at health stores and makes some of the most delicious salad sprouts (see page 30). You can also sometimes buy sprouted alfalfa, which looks rather like cress, in supermarkets and vegetable stores.

**Baked Beans** One of the healthiest convenience foods, these are a useful item to have in the vegetarian kitchen for emergency snacks, especially if there are children around! Most makes do contain some sugar, but nevertheless they're still an excellent food.

**Chick Peas** A very tasty pulse, delicious both cooked and sprouted. Chick peas should be soaked before cooking, then simmered for about 1½ hours until tender. They combine well with vegetables in stews and casseroles and can be made into hummus, a delicious creamy dip from the Middle East (see page 42). They can also be bought in cans, which make a useful stand-by for the pantry.

**Kidney Beans** One of the tastiest and most colorful of the pulses, kidney beans can be added to any vegetable stew or casserole. Try them, too, in the Chili Vegetarian-Style (see page 63). They need careful preparation. The 10 minutes of cooking in fast-boiling water is essential, and as long as you do this, they are perfectly safe. They can of course also be bought in cans, and these make a time-saving addition to the kitchen, vegetarian or not!

**Lentils** Various types of lentil are available and, of these, two are particularly useful and delicious. These are the big continental lentils, sometimes called "whole green" lentils, which you can buy at health stores, and the little split orange lentils, which are available at any supermarket, and are, in fact, small whole lentils which have had their outer skin removed. Both these types of lentil cook quickly and do not need soaking beforehand. The whole green lentils take about 45 minutes and the split red ones about 20 minutes. Whole brown lentils are also available but I do not like these so much (although their flavor is excellent) because of the number of pebbles and other foreign bodies I find among them.

**Mung Beans** These little round green beans produce the bean sprouts which you can buy. They can be cooked (without soaking, like lentils) but I find them most useful for sprouting to use in salads, stir-fries etc., as described on page 30.

**Soybeans** These are hard, round and pale yellow. They take the longest of all the beans to cook (about 3 hours, after soaking) and need careful flavoring to make them taste good. I prefer them sprouted, when they make a delicious, crunchy and nutritious addition to salads and stir-fries. They are high in protein, B vitamins, iron and calcium.

**Soy Flour,** which is made from soy beans, is also nutritious, and can be a useful ingredient if you want to increase the food-value of dishes. Soy flour can be stirred into gravies and sauces or added to many tasty dishes. You can also use it to replace some of the flour (one part of soy flour to seven of whole wheat flour) in pastry, homemade bread and cakes.

**Soy Milk** is another useful product made from the versatile soybean. Some excellent soy milks are now available. If you are using a soy milk instead of dairy milk, be sure to buy one which has been fortified with riboflavin, B12, calcium and zinc, so that its food value is comparable to that of ordinary milk.

**Tofu,** or bean curd, is another product made from the soybean. It is high in protein, low in calories, and contains useful amounts of both iron and calcium. You can buy a soft tofu in a sealed pack and a firmer one, which is ideal for slicing, both at health stores.

## Dairy Produce

Most vegetarians include dairy produce in their meals, though vegans do not. For vegetarians, milk and milk products, cheese and eggs provide a useful source of nutrients as well as adding interest to meals.

**Cheese** Most hard cheeses contain a small quantity of rennet (1 part rennet to 5,000 parts milk). Rennet is a digestive juice taken from the stomachs of calves. This means that most cheeses are not 100 per cent vegetarian. Before the arrival of vegetarian rennet, using a cheese made with ordinary rennet used to be a compromise which most vegetarians decided to make. Now it is possible to buy excellent vegetarian cheeses; most supermarkets stock Cheddar and a wider range is available from health stores. In actual fact, I believe that some 'normal' cheeses are made with vegetarian rennet, because of the more uniform results which it gives. However, at present, there is no way of knowing. Personally, I do use ordinary cheeses sometimes and you will find some of these featured in the recipes in this

· THE VEGETARIAN PANTRY ·

book. You can substitute vegetarian Cheddar or another variety of vegetarian cheese if you prefer.

When it comes to soft white cheeses, which are a useful ingredient in a variety of recipes, some include rennet and some do not. Ask for information when you buy, or contact the manufacturers. Cottage cheese, low-fat or skim milk white cheese, curd cheese (or medium-fat white cheese) and cream cheese are all used in recipes in this book. Quark is a smooth white cheese and is available in skim milk and medium-fat versions.

**Eggs** Most vegetarians prefer to use farm produced eggs from hens not kept in cages. It's encouraging to find farm eggs becoming more and more widely available.

**Milk and Milk Products** If you wish to cut down on your fat intake, liquid skim milk and semi-skim milk are now widely available. Check whether the brand you are using contains vitamins A and D and boost your vitamins if necessary. This is especially important for growing children. A can of powdered skim milk is a useful item to have in the vegetarian pantry. Canned evaporated milk is also useful and is used in one of the ice cream recipes, while skim condensed milk is used for a marvellously quick and smooth special occasion vanilla ice cream.

**Yogurt** Traditionally, yogurt is made from milk and a culture of special bacteria. These bacteria remain in the yogurt so that when you eat it, they have a beneficial effect on the bacteria in your gut, encouraging the growth of health-giving ones. Many of the yogurts which you can buy in supermarkets do not have this effect because although they may have been made in the traditional manner they are then pasteurized to improve their keeping qualities and this effectively destroys the beneficial bacteria! So read the labels carefully; for maximum health-giving properties, yogurt should be 'live', unpasteurized and preferably made from goat's milk. The health store is a good

place to find this, and should also stock fruit yogurts made from 'live' yogurt and real fruit. They are absolutely delicious, but the fruit tends to sink, so give them a stir before eating.

Another healthy yogurt, and my favorite, is the Greek ewe's milk yogurt which you can get at some health stores and supermarkets. This comes in two varieties, a normal one and a 'strained' one. They're both deliciously thick and creamy, but the 'strained' one is especially so! They make a wonderful, and very healthy, replacement for heavy cream.

## Grains and Cereals

**Barley** This is a useful grain for adding flavor and texture to casseroles. 'Pot' barley (from health stores) is the most wholefood version and this is the one to buy if you want to sprout barley or if you want an extremely chewy casserole. Personally I prefer ordinary pearled barley, which you can buy anywhere and which is in fact higher in fiber than brown rice! Add a little to vegetable stews and casseroles to make them more nourishing and substantial.

**Brown Rice** Now very popular, brown rice makes ordinary polished rice seem dull and flavorless in comparison once you get used to the taste. There are two ways of cooking brown rice. 1. Bring a large saucepan of water to the boil, put in the rice and boil for 20 minutes, or until the grains are tender, then drain. 2. Put the rice into a saucepan with double its volume in water (1 cup of rice to 2 cups of water), bring to the boil, then cover and cook over a very low heat for 45 minutes, when the rice should be tender and all the water absorbed.

The second method takes longer but is better because it conserves more of the iron and B vitamins.

Brown rice can also be cooked in a pressure cooker, and this takes about 15 minutes from start to finish. Put 1 cup of rice to 2 cups water into the pressure cooker. Bring up to pressure and cook for

10 minutes at full pressure. Then allow the pressure to reduce naturally. After that, the rice should be perfectly cooked.

**Bulgur Wheat** This is sometimes called burghul wheat, or referred to as 'cracked wheat' in Middle Eastern recipes; it is wheat which has been cracked and steamed. It consists of little golden-brown grains which look a bit like brown sugar in the packet.

Bulgar wheat can be used in place of rice, for a change, with stews and vegetable dishes. It makes the popular Middle-Eastern Cracked-Wheat Salad (see page 33). To use bulgur wheat, cover it with water and leave to soak for 15-20 minutes, then drain (if necessary) and add chopped herbs and salad ingredients. You can cook it like rice, using the second method as described opposite, except that the bulgur wheat will cook much more quickly – in only 15-20 minutes.

**Couscous** This is another pre-cooked grain, made from semolina, which looks golden and granular in the packet, similar to bulgur wheat. It has a delicious flavor. To use couscous, first cover it with cold water and leave to soak for 10-15 minutes, then heat it through in a steamer, or colander over a saucepan of water. This is usually done above the stew which you're going to serve with the couscous (see page 54), so the whole dish can be cooked together.

**Millet** Small, round pale golden grains, millet is familiar to most people as 'bird' food, but delicious food for people too! It contains the most iron and protein of all the grains, and cooks quickly, in 15-20 minutes, using the second method given for brown rice. It can be served with dishes normally accompanied by rice, to make a pleasant change, and can also be made into tasty pilaff.

You can also buy flaked millet and this is useful for adding to breakfast muesli in place of some of the oats normally included, especially if you want to increase your iron intake.

**Oats** Oats in their most 'whole' form look like whole wheat grains, with a hard brown outer husk. They taste good sprouted and can also be cooked, but take 1¼-1½ hours after an overnight soak. I find them too coarse and chewy and prefer them in the form of rolled oats, which are the flaky, oatmeal oats you can get at any supermarket. Use them to make your own breakfast muesli or oatmeal, or for flapjacks. Medium oatmeal is also useful for making delicious home-made oatcakes, and to make oatmeal, though it takes longer to cook than rolled oats.

**Wheat** Whole wheat grains can be bought from health stores for sprouting or cooking. Again, the result is chewy, but cooked and cooled whole wheat grains can make the basis of a pleasant salad, with a vinaigrette dressing (see page 90). I also like it in the deep-dish salad (see page 32) as a change from potato. Cook as described for whole oat grains, above.

**Wheat Germ,** which is removed from wheat during the milling of white flour (along with the bran), is another useful product because it is a concentrated source of iron, zinc and B vitamins. Buy an unstabilized wheat germ if possible and store in the refrigerator. Sprinkle some over breakfast cereals and mueslis, eat it with plain yogurt with some honey and raisins, or make it into muffins (see page 25). I often use wheat germ as a coating for burgers instead of bread crumbs.

**Wild Rice** This is the seed of a type of grass which grows here in the USA; it is long and slim in shape and very dark brown in color. It has a wonderful, slightly smoky flavor and chewy texture. One way of trying it relatively cheaply is to buy a packet of Uncle Ben's wild rice, which is actually a mixture of white rice and a little wild rice. If you like it, try adding it to brown rice for a special meal (see page 95).

### Flours

**Cornstarch** Not a 'wholefood', but useful to have in the pantry for thickening small quantities of liquid. The wholefood alternatives are arrowroot or potato flour.

**Semolina** This is made from hard wheat. You can buy ordinary semolina at some supermarkets and 'brown' semolina (including bran) at health stores. Cream of wheat may be substituted.

**Whole Wheat Flour** '100 per cent whole wheat flour' means flour which is milled from the whole wheat grain, with nothing taken away. It therefore contains wheat germ and bran and is the most nutritious flour to use. It is excellent for making bread, pastry and dark, 'heavy' cakes like fruit cake and gingerbread. A 'strong' whole wheat flour is best for bread (because this is made from wheat with a high gluten content which makes the bread rise well). For other baking, cakes, scones, muffins etc., I prefer to use all-purpose 100 per cent whole wheat flour, as finely milled as I can find – ask at the health store. Once you're used to whole wheat flour, you'll probably want to use it for most baking, but there is a lighter whole wheat flour, containing 85 per cent of the wheat (with the coarsest bran removed) which is useful for a change or for when you want a particularly light result. I like to keep a bag of all-purpose and of self-rising 85 per cent whole wheat flour in my pantry for occasional use.

**Pasta** A favorite convenience food, pasta is even more delicious when served with vegetarian sauces instead of those made with meat or fish. Any type of pasta is good from the health point of view; the brown pastas which you can get at health stores are particularly so, since they contain more fiber. But I have to admit that, with the exception of brown pasta rings, I tend to prefer 'white pasta', especially in a lasagne. There are many wholefood cooks who would disagree with me, so do give whole wheat pasta a try.

The types of pasta used in this book are lasagne (the kind that does not require precooking), spaghetti, tagliatelle and pasta shells. Whole wheat and white pastas are interchangeable in the recipes, so choose whichever you prefer.

### Breads and Biscuits

**Bread** Real whole wheat bread is now easy to buy almost anywhere, although I often find that health stores still seem to stock some of the best. One of the biggest single improvements which anyone can make to their diet is to replace white bread with 100 per cent whole wheat. Several slices of this each day, plus fresh fruit and vegetables, should take care of your fiber requirements without any need for extra bran (which should really only be taken on medical advice). Do try the various different kinds of whole wheat breads which are available; whole wheat pita bread, rolls, buns, French bread and sliced whole wheat for sandwiches. I think you should have plenty of variety with bread and occasionally, too, I like a crusty white French bread. The only time when you need to be careful with whole wheat bread is when you're giving it to a young baby. For babies under 2 years old, a wheat meal or wheat germ bread may be better than 100 per cent whole wheat, as I've explained on page 15. Crisp whole wheat breadcrumbs, useful for coating burgers, can be bought at some health stores and are a time-saving addition to the pantry.

**Cookies** The range of whole wheat cookies available in health stores and supermarkets seems to be increasing almost every week. If you're buying cookies in the supermarket, read the labels, looking not only for additives, but also 'animal fat', which means the cookies may contain ingredients such as lard or animal oils. For the 'semi-sweet whole wheat cookies' called for in the cheesecake recipe on page 96, I suggest a whole wheat Graham Cracker-type cookie obtainable from health stores.

**Crackers** There are plenty of whole wheat and rye crackers to add further variety to meals. As with cookies (see above), read the labels. Tortilla chips are also useful for serving with dips, and whole wheat 'twigs' as a children's treat.

**Breakfast Cereals** Again, the whole wheat cereals are best from the health point of view, and there are several to choose from. If you prefer a muesli mix, choose one without added sugar and sweeten it yourself by adding chopped dates, apricots, figs or raisins. Crunchy granola is another popular breakfast cereal, but watch out for 'hidden' sugar and fat.

You can, of course, always make your own breakfast cereals: see the recipes for banana and fruit muesli on pages 20 and 23.

## Sweetenings

**Fruit Sugar** This has the same calorie value as ordinary sugar, and is just as refined as white sugar. The difference is that it is twice as sweet (it's also more expensive), so you do not need to use so much. I find it useful, for sweetening small quantities of food where honey or brown sugar would spoil the flavor.

**Honey** Honey is an essential item in my pantry (I even use it for healing cuts and burns). I like to keep jars of both clear and set honey. Try to buy pure unprocessed 'organic' honey. The clear honey is most useful in cooking, and is also my favorite for spreading on whole wheat bread or toast or for stirring into a bowl of yogurt.

**Jam and Jelly** Most jams and jellies contain a high proportion of sugar and some manufactured ones contain many other undesirable additives as well. But 'reduced sugar' or 'no-added-sugar' jams, and brown sugar marmalade which you can buy at health stores and some supermarkets, are delicious, and you will soon prefer their fresher, more 'tart' flavor.

**Maple Syrup** Real maple syrup (not 'maple-flavor' syrup) has a wonderful, slightly smoky flavor and is delicious as a topping for oatmeal, yogurt or pancakes. It's expensive but keeps well in the refrigerator.

**Molasses** Molasses is the sticky brown syrup that's left after cane sugar has been refined and contains many valuable nutrients, in particular iron and calcium. Blackstrap molasses is a less refined version of molasses; both kinds are equally high in nutrients and are an excellent food. Molasses can be taken as a food supplement (see page 9) and either type of molasses can be used in bakes such as gingerbread.

**Sugar** White sugar is a source of energy (and calories) but contains no nutrients, so it is not a good ingredient to use in any quantity, though I do use powdered sugar for frosting Christmas and birthday cakes. Dark brown moist sugar contains useful amounts of iron and other trace elements, and I see no harm in using this to make the occasional cake or dessert. Light brown sugar and granulated brown sugar (make sure it's the real thing, and not white sugar which has been dyed) contain fewer nutrients than dark brown moist sugar, but are useful if you need a lighter, less sticky sugar; in any case, they are preferable to white sugar for occasional use.

## Fruits and Juices

### Fresh Fruit

Fresh fruit and vegetables figure prominently in the vegetarian diet. However, always wash all fruit thoroughly to remove any residues of insecticides or other sprays with which the fruit may have been coated. This applies particularly to the skins of citrus fruits, which should be scrubbed in hot water if they are to be used to flavor food.

Here's a basic list of fruits which are particularly useful to the vegetarian, and which are featured in recipes in this book.

**Apples** A particularly valuable source of fiber, good in salads as well as desserts. There are numerous different types of apple, each with their own special qualities. Experiment with different varieties and wash the skins well before use. Tart apples, such as Granny Smiths, are also useful, especially for baking and stewing.

**Bananas** A good source of iron, vitamin C and some of the B vitamins, bananas are particularly good in mueslis and with yogurt. Try the crumble recipe on page 71, for something a little different.

**Blackberries** These are delicious, low in calories and free, if you've the time to pick them wild! Blackberries can be made into wonderful fools and ice creams, or combined with apples in compotes and pies. Sometimes difficult to find; raspberries may be substituted.

**Cherries** Wash sweet cherries and serve them as they are, for breakfast or as a dessert. They also make a pretty addition to fruit salads.

**Dates** Fresh dates are plump, juicy and less sweet than the dry ones. They make a delicious dessert fruit on their own.

**Figs** Usually expensive, even when in season, fresh figs make a wonderful ending to a meal.

**Grapefruit** Serve grapefruit as a refreshing starter to a meal. Look out for 'pink' and 'red' varieties, which make a pleasant change.

**Grapes** Sweet seedless grapes make a marvellous 'candy' for children; pop little bunches of them into school lunch boxes. The larger grapes, both green and purple, need halving and seeding before being added to fruit salads or used as a topping to a cheesecake (see page 96).

**Kiwi Fruit** When ripe, these 'furry' brown fruits should feel slightly soft to the touch. Peel off the skin, then cut the kiwi fruit into slices. They make a good addition to fruit salads because their bright green flesh contrasts well with other ingredients.

**Kumquats** A member of the citrus family, these baby oranges are rather sharp to eat as they are, but can be made into a topping for ice cream (see page 112).

**Lemons** Indispensable for flavoring, sliced lemons make pretty garnishes for many different dishes.

**Lychees** These little fruits are round with a hard, prickly reddish-brown skin, which you have to remove before they can be eaten. Inside, the translucent white flesh is juicy, fragrant and sweet.

**Mango** These large, oval tropical fruits are green or greenish-yellow in color, with splashes of red. They should feel soft to the touch, although they can be bought when hard and ripened at room temperature in a few days. To prepare the mango, stand it on end and cut downwards about ¼ inch from the stalk at the top. You will feel the pit with the knife as you slice and the two halves will fall apart, leaving the pit, with some mango flesh around it. Cut off the skin, then dice or slice all the flesh. Mango makes a wonderful breakfast, and can be used in desserts or fruit salads.

**Melon** Different types are available throughout the year. An unusual way of serving melon is as a two-color chilled soup (see page 106). For this you need one melon with pale green flesh, such as a honey-dew, and one with orange flesh, such as a cantaloup. Small halved melons make a refreshing dessert with a scoop of home-made vanilla ice cream inside each half, and perhaps sprinkled with some chopped preserved ginger.

**Nectarines** A type of smooth-skinned peach, nectarines are sweet and juicy dessert fruits to end a meal.

**Oranges** One of the best sources of vitamin C, and a useful source of vitamin A, oranges are useful both for flavoring and for an ingredient in fruit salads where their acidity helps to preserve the color of the other fruits.

**Peaches** Peaches are delicious served on their own or peeled and added to fruit salads. Try them sliced and covered in sweet wine or halved and coated in a purée of raspberries. To peel peaches, put them into a bowl, cover with boiling water and leave for 2 minutes. Then drain and slip off the skins with a sharp knife.

**Pears** Sweet, ripe pears are easy for children to digest. Serve them sliced with some chopped walnuts, pecans or pre-served ginger. They can also be poached whole in honey syrup or made into delicious pies. I prefer to buy sweet pears rather than tart pears for poaching because these need very little sweetening.

**Pineapple** Pineapples are widely available, but make sure you buy a ripe one. It should be dark golden brown in color, have a pronounced sweet smell and feel slightly soft to the touch.

**Raspberries** Another fruit that's high in fiber and low in calories, raspberries make a delicious summer treat. They're worth freezing, as they survive the process better than most fruits and make an excellent ice cream or sauce for serving with other fruits.

**Strawberries** Rich in vitamin C, straw-berries are delicious on their own, just hulled and washed, or as a topping for a cheesecake, or part of a fruit salad. They don't freeze well, but can be made into an ice cream or purée for serving with other fruits.

**Tangerine** Another member of the orange group is the tangerine, a favorite with children and useful for lunch boxes. They make a pleasant addition to the fruit bowl in winter.

### Dry Fruit

Dry fruits are a concentrated source of many important nutrients; they also offer a natural, high-fiber form of sweetening. Add them to breakfast cereals instead of sugar. Try stewing apples with raisins, or filling the center of cored tart apples with dates before baking. Choose sun-dry fruits without preservatives or added mineral oil if possible. They may not look as brightly colored (especially the dry apricots), but you'll find them well-flavored and good to eat.

**Apricots** Dark-brown *unsulphured* dry apricots obtainable from health stores are best, and the little round Hunza apricots, still containing the pit, are the best and most delicious of all.

**Currants** Try to buy currants prepared without added mineral oil which can impair absorption of some nutrients by the body.

**Dates** Cooking dates are an excellent buy provided that you avoid those which have been 'sugar-coated'. Shiny dates in packets make a good treat at Christmas time, although these are often coated with syrup to make them look more shiny.

**Figs** These are a useful dry fruit for vegans and vegetarians who need to in-rease their calcium, as they're rich in this mineral. Chop them up and add them to muesli mixes, fruit cakes, or yogurt; or make a spread by boiling them in a little water.

**Mixed Dry Fruit** Mixed, dry cake fruit is a mixture of raisins, currants, white raisins and cut candied fruit; try to buy it from health stores and avoid the added mineral oil that's included in supermarket packets.

Mixed dry fruit is also the term used to describe a mixture of prunes, dry apricots and apple rings, for soaking and making into compotes; go to the health store to buy these and you may be able to pick your own assortment.

**Peaches** Dry peaches make a pleasant change from dry apricots and are rich in iron. Prepare these as described for apricots on page 21.

**Prunes** Again, look for prunes which have been dried without preservatives, and pre-pare them as described for dry apricots on page 21.

**Raisins** Sun-dried seedless raisins can be found easily in most supermarkets; for white raisins, you'll need to go to the health store, where you'll also find the big, juicy seeded raisins, and delicately-flavored muscatels.

**Other Dry Fruits** Two other, non-whole-food items which I keep in my pantry are real candied peel and candied cherries, because I like these in rich fruit cakes. They can be replaced with the same weight of extra raisins, currants and dates if you prefer.

### Fruit Juices

The best fruit juices are, of course, those which you squeeze yourself. But there is a wide range of natural juices available without added sugar or preservatives including apple, orange, grapefruit, grape and prune juice (prune juice is especially rich in iron). The long-life natural juices are a useful item to have in your kitchen, but cartons of fresh juice are preferable. Apple juice concentrate, looking like a dark syrup in a bottle, is useful to keep in the refrigerator for making up quickly into children's drinks. Individual cartons of juice which you can buy complete with drinking straw make a useful addition to children's lunch boxes.

### CHILDREN'S VITAMIN C

Apple juice is popular with children and if they drink this in preference to orange juice check that your brand is fortified with vitamin C. Alternatively ensure that they are getting enough daily vitamin C from other foods; a large tomato or banana, a serving of cabbage, Brussels sprouts or young potatoes or an orange or tangerine will provide the body's needs.

## Vegetables

Fresh vegetables are a cornerstone of the vegetarian diet, often providing the basis of the main course, along with concentrated sources of protein such as nuts and seeds or cheese, as well as the accompaniments. If you buy vegetables in season, or grow your own, many vegetarian main courses can cost very little to prepare. Of course you can occasionally treat yourself to a bunch of asparagus or some wild mushrooms; it's not such an extravagance when you're serving it as a main course, especially if you compare the price of these luxury vegetables with that of meat.

When you've bought your vegetables, keep them carefully; potatoes need a cool, dark place, and the rest, especially green, leafy vegetables and salad items, are best placed in the refrigerator if possible. Wash all vegetables carefully before use to remove the residue of any horticultural sprays. Trim the vegetables as little as possible, and cook them quickly in a small amount of water; the ideal method is to use just enough water to be absorbed by the end of the cooking time. If there's any water left, don't throw it away: strain this off and use it as stock or broth, because it's full of nutrients.

**Artichokes, Jerusalem** Use a vegetable parer to remove the skin, cutting off some of the knobbles if necessary. Jerusalem artichokes are very versatile: they can be steamed, boiled or sautéed. They also make a marvellous soup; follow the recipe for potato soup on page 46, using just one potato and making up the rest of the weight with artichokes.

**Asparagus** A luxurious vegetable, asparagus spears are also wonderfully nutritious. After breaking off the tough stalk ends, steam the asparagus or tie the stems in a bunch and stand it in a saucepan containing 2 inch of fast-boiling water, with a dome of aluminum foil over the top to make a cover. Use the trimmings to make a soup; follow the potato soup recipe on page 46, adding the asparagus trimmings, and straining after blending.

**Avocados** They should feel soft when pressed lightly at the stalk end. If hard when you buy them they will need to be kept at room temperature for several days to ripen. Cut in half, twist the two halves in opposite directions to separate, and remove the pit.

**Beets** Peeled and grated raw beets make a healthy and delicious addition to salads and contain a substance which many believe may help to break up fat in the body – good news for slimmers! For recipes requiring cooked beet, either buy it freshly-cooked or prepare your own by buying raw beet and simmering gently for an hour or so until tender. When cool the skin slips off easily. Avoid packaged cooked beet which is often too vinegary and may contain preservatives.

**Bell Peppers** Another useful flavoring ingredient, bell peppers are good raw in salads, or cooked in casseroles and bakes; they can also be stuffed (see page 69). Green and red bell peppers have slightly different flavors, but are the same vegetable in different stages of ripeness.

**Broccoli** Broccoli is an excellent source of vitamins and minerals, including calcium. Children love it raw, broken into florets. You can steam it or boil it in a very little water, or stir-fry.

**Brussels Sprouts** Also highly nutritious vegetables, Brussels sprouts are at their best when young and tiny. Once trimmed and washed, I like to halve them so that they cook rapidly in the minimum of water and never become waterlogged.

**Cabbage** Crisp white or green cabbage is a year-round standby for salads. Try also a pretty half-and-half mixture of red and white cabbage in a salad. For cooked cabbage, shred finely, use the very minimum of water (a bare ½ inch for a quantity to serve 4-6 people) and cook, covered, over a high heat for about 4 minutes, until just tender. Drain, saving the water and serve with a little butter or margarine, lemon juice, freshly-ground black pepper and grated nutmeg, crushed garlic or chopped herbs.

**Carrots** Another highly nutritious vegetable, carrots cut into sticks make popular snacks for children; a large carrot will take care of their vitamin A needs for the whole day. Scrub or scrape and grate for salads or cook lightly.

**Cauliflower** This, too, is an excellent source of nutrients. Break into florets and serve raw or very lightly cooked.

*Celery* Useful for flavoring many dishes, or in salads.

*Chicory (endive)* Crisp and slightly bitter, this makes a useful addition to salads.

*Chinese Cabbage* Shred and use in salad mixtures, or stir-fry rapidly in a little hot olive oil until just heated through, then serve at once.

*Cress* High in vitamin C, cress is good in sandwiches or as a topping for salads.

*Cucumber* A refreshing addition to salads, cucumber also forms the basis for a wonderful chilled soup (see page 49).

*Daikon* This is a type of white radish, sometimes called Japanese radish. Peel, dice and add it to stir-fries or salads, or make into pretty chrysanthemums and use as a garnish. To make the chrysanthemums, take a walnut-sized piece of daikon and make criss-cross cuts as close together as you can, without cutting right through to the base. Sprinkle with salt, gently easing it between the cuts. Leave for 30 minutes, then rinse and gently open up the slits to make a chrysanthemum. Carrots can also be cut in this way.

*Eggplant* Cut off the stalk end, then slice or dice the eggplant and use as required.

*Endive, Curly* Like a curly, lacy lettuce. Makes a pretty addition to salads, and a tangy change from lettuce.

*Kale* Another highly nutritious vegetable, rich in both calcium and iron, as well as B vitamins. Prepare as for cabbage, but it may need cooking for a little longer.

*Leeks* Cut off the tough green part and the root end. Slit down one side and rinse under the faucet, carefully opening up the layers to clean thoroughly. Steam whole, or slice and cook as for cabbage.

*Lettuce* There are many different varieties to choose from nowadays ranging from the crisp Iceberg to the softer Boston or butter lettuce and the decorative loose-leaf types.

*Mushrooms* An excellent flavoring ingredient in vegetarian cooking and a useful source of nutrients, including nicotinic acid. Little white button mushrooms are the most useful generally, but both large and small open mushrooms are good for stuffing. Wild mushrooms, when available, are delicious and can be mixed with button mushrooms to make them go further. One of my favorites is the oyster mushroom, or pleurote. Wash, slice and cook as for cultivated mushrooms.

*Okra* These look like ridged green pods and are prepared like string beans. They're especially good with curried dishes and are a good source of vitamin A.

*Onions* These are a popular vegetable for adding flavor to vegetarian dishes and have natural antiseptic qualities. Use raw in salads or cooked, and try the different types: the purple onions are particularly pleasant to use and the small white baby onions are good added to casseroles or kebabs.

*Parsnips* A useful addition to stews and casseroles, parsnips also make a good soup: follow the recipe on page 46, using parsnips instead of all but one of the potatoes.

*Potatoes* Another top-value vegetable nutritionally, potatoes contain many nutrients including iron, vitamin C and some good-quality protein. They are useful as a basis for a main dish, with added protein, as well as an accompaniment. Use the skins, too, whenever possible because of their nutritional value.

*Radicchio* A pretty red lettuce with a slightly bitter flavor. It makes a pleasant and colorful addition to salads and is also useful as a garnish.

*Radishes* Fresh radishes, trimmed but with their green leaves still attached, are good to eat with dips, and they make a pretty addition to salads. For an attractive garnish, make radish roses, by slicing down thinly from the top, to make petals, then covering with cold water for 30 minutes until the 'petals' open.

*Rutabagas* Like parsnips, rutabagas are a useful addition to casseroles and soups. They are also good grated and mixed with yogurt or mayonnaise in a salad.

*Scallions* These make a crunchy addition to salads and are also good served with dips.

*Snow Peas* These are delicious peas that you cook in the pod, like a green bean. Just top and tail, then cook in a little boiling water for 1-2 minutes, until just tender, or add to vegetable stir-fries.

*Spinach* Spinach makes a good basis for main dishes (like the gnocchi on page 58) as well as making a good accompaniment.

*Swiss chard,* which is like spinach but with thick white stems, is even more delicious. You can either cook the stems with the leaves, putting them into the pan in a little water 2-3 minutes before adding the leaves or cook and serve the stems separately. Tender spinach is also good raw, when finely shredded, and mixed with a tasty dressing.

*String Beans* Make sure they are crisp and fresh-looking when you buy them; top and tail, and cook quickly as for cabbage.

*Tomatoes* Choose firm, slightly under-ripe tomatoes. Look out for the little cherry tomatoes, which make a pleasant addition to salads, and the large 'beefsteak' tomatoes, which are ideal for stuffing (see page 47) or slicing.

*Turnips* See Rutabagas.

*Water cress* Add to green salads and mixed salads; water cress makes an excellent, quick salad to serve with a main course when you're pressed for time. It's also excellent in soups.

*Zucchini* These make a useful accompanying vegetable or addition to vegetable casseroles; they can also be stuffed – follow the recipe for stuffed bell peppers on page 69. Cook lightly so that they are still firm; the same applies to marrow, which can be cooked with the skin on if it's tender, otherwise peel.

### Canned and Bottled Vegetables

Canned tomatoes are very useful. I also occasionally use canned bamboo shoots in Chinese-style dishes, and bottled oyster mushrooms (pleurotes).

### Frozen Vegetables

I find it useful to keep some vegetables in the freezer, particularly peas (the best of all being the little sweet *petit pois*), corn, leaf spinach, green beans and lima beans.

### Sea Vegetables

This is an attractive term for 'seaweed', but don't be put off, because it can be delicious. Seaweed is a potent source of many minerals, and is said to be very helpful for slimmers, because of the effect on the thyroid of the iodine which it contains.

You can buy various types of seaweed at health stores. The two following kinds are my own personal favourites.

*Dulse* A deep-red, small-leaf variety. Take a couple of sprigs, wash them under the faucet, then add them to vegetable casseroles and soups, along with the water or stock. They can be removed before serving (leaving valuable trace elements in the stock), if you feel seaweed may be the last straw for family or friends who are holding out against vegetarianism! The washed dulse can also be shredded and added to salads.

*Nori* I like this one best of all because of its crisp texture. It looks like pieces of carbon paper. All you do is hold one of these over the hot ring of your stove, turning it around until it is crisp all over, then crumble it up in your hands and sprinkle it over any salad, rice or vegetable dish. A daily dose of this is said to slow up the ageing process!

## Herbs and Spices

Herbs and spices are used to add flavor to vegetarian food, and the following list is of all the ones which appear in the recipes in this book. Buy them gradually, experimenting with different dishes and so build up your own collection.

*Basil* Perhaps one of the best of the fresh herbs, basil is delicious in any salad and in pasta and tomato dishes. You can substitute dry basil but it isn't nearly as fragrant and delicate. Fresh basil is well worth growing, and will freeze. I simply chop it up and store it in the freezer in a plastic bag, taking out as much of the herb as I need and re-sealing the bag.

*Bay Leaf* Bay adds an aromatic flavor to stews and casseroles.

*Cardamom* A highly aromatic spice which is delicious in curries. In this book it's used on page 47 to make a fragrant sweet sauce. Buy whole seeds and crush or grind them when needed.

*Chili Powder* Use it to add 'bite' to vegetarian chili and curry dishes.

*Chives, Fresh* Use scissors to snip these over salads and main dishes for a delicate onion flavor and pretty color.

*Cinnamon, Ground* A very useful, warming spice. It enhances many fruit dishes, both raw and cooked, and gives a delicious flavor to the lentil sauce for serving with pasta on page 62.

*Cloves, Whole and Ground* These give a pungent flavor to apple dishes, fruit cake and the cheese fritters on page 68.

*Coriander, Whole and Ground* Adds a delicious flavor, spicy but not 'hot', to vegetable dishes and curries. I like to have both whole and ground coriander in the kitchen as the flavors are surprisingly different.

*Cumin, Ground* Like coriander, cumin gives a spicy taste to vegetable dishes. Ground cumin is the most useful, but keep a supply of the seeds, too.

*Garlic* Garlic is another flavoring that I find indispensable, and, like onions, it is a very health-giving ingredient. Buy fresh, firm bulbs and use the cloves as required, peeled and crushed or chopped.

*Ginger* You can buy ginger in various different forms. Fresh root ginger has a delicious, lemony flavor that gives a lift to any vegetable dish. The root keeps well in the refrigerator and can be grated when needed. Ground ginger is also useful, and I also like to keep some candied ginger and a jar of preserved ginger in the kitchen, for occasional use.

*Mint, Fresh* A wonderfully aromatic herb, especially useful in salads and vegetable dishes. Chopped or whole mint leaves freeze well.

*Mixed Herbs* Dry mixed herbs are useful as a quick and easy flavoring for nut and pulse dishes.

*Nutmeg* It is possible to buy ready-ground nutmeg, but for the best flavour, buy whole nutmegs and grate them as required, using the smallest side of the grater or a special nutmeg grater.

*Oregano* Sprinkle dry oregano over pizza before baking to give an 'Italian' aroma and flavor.

*Paprika Pepper, Mild* Paprika has a pleasant, sweetish flavor and makes a colorful garnish for dishes, especially pale-colored creamy ones.

*Parsley, Fresh* Probably the most useful herb of all, fresh parsley tastes marvellous in sauces and stews and makes a decorative garnish. To save time, I generally chop up a large quantity in the food processor, then store it in a plastic bag in the freezer to take out as required. You can, of course, use dry parsley, but the flavor won't be as good.

*Pepper, Whole Black* Use freshly-ground black pepper straight from the pepper mill; the flavor is far superior to ready-ground pepper.

*Summer Savory, Fresh* This is specially good with bean dishes and salads.

*Thyme* Thyme is another useful herb for flavoring a variety of soups, casseroles and egg dishes.

*Vanilla Bean* These long black beans are expensive but have a wonderful taste. I like to crush the beans and add them to ice cream for a true vanilla flavor. In addition, a bottle of real vanilla flavoring is useful to keep in the kitchen.

*Frozen Herbs* Frozen parsley and mixed herbs, which you can buy in supermarkets, are a handy standby if you do not grow your own. Usually there is no need to thaw the herbs before using them. Simply crumble them from frozen.

## Fats and Oils

**Butter** The best choice is pale, sweet butter. This is what I use (together with olive oil) for all my cooking and baking.

**Cream** I find sour cream a useful ingredient for adding richness to a dish without too much fat (it contains far less fat, for instance, than cheese). Apart from this, light cream and whipping or heavy cream are useful occasionally.

**Margarine** Choose one that states clearly that it's 'high in polyunsaturates' or 'low cholesterol' – unsalted if possible.

**Vegetable Oils** The healthiest oil, in my opinion, is good-quality, virgin olive oil, pale green in color and with a delectable flavor. I use this for all cooking except deep-frying and making mayonnaise. A cold-pressed sunflower or ground nut oil is better for mayonnaise as the flavor is more subtle than that of olive oil. For occasional deep-frying, ordinary sunflower oil is best; there's no point in getting a cold-pressed oil for cooking as the chemical structure of the oil is changed when heated.

**Vegetable Suet** This is the vegetarian equivalent to suet which you can buy at health stores.

## Flavorings

**Almond Flavor** This is used for flavoring cakes and almond paste. Buy real almond flavor from health stores.

**Bouillon Cubes and Powder** You can get some good vegetarian bouillon cubes and powder. You should be able to get these at health stores.

**Carob Powder** Made from a dry bean, this has a chocolate-like flavor and is rich in nutrients. It can be used instead of cocoa powder in any recipe. Carob bars, from health stores, are also available and useful as an alternative to chocolate.

**Cocoa Powder** Cocoa and cocoa products are a rich source of iron, but it is not known how much can actually be absorbed by the body. A disadvantage of cocoa is that it contains caffeine, though considerably less than either tea or coffee. It also contains theobromine, which is a stimulant similar to caffeine but weaker. Cocoa and chocolate products should, therefore, be used with discrimination.

**Lemon Juice** Bottled lemon juice is a useful, time-saving ingredient to keep in the kitchen.

**Mustard** Ready-made Dijon mustard makes a wonderful 'base' for a salad dressing. Also useful is whole grain mustard, which is mild and delicious, and a can of mustard powder.

**Salt** My preference is for small quantities of sea salt – try to find a make which dissolves easily and you will find that you don't need a grinder.

**Soy Sauce** Soy sauce is a very useful flavoring for vegetarian food. Read the labels and choose one without additives and coloring. The health store is a good place to go for this; look out for both a deliciously-strong soy sauce, and one which is lighter. I think the stronger is a good one to start with.

**Tabasco** A bottle of this hot, red pepper sauce keeps for a long time and is useful for adding zing to bland dishes. Be careful because just one or two drops will add a considerable amount of heat.

**Tomato Paste** Easily stored in a refrigerator, concentrated tomato paste is useful for flavoring soups and stews. It is usually available in tubes or cans.

**Vinegar** My two favorites for flavor are red wine vinegar and rice vinegar, which is light and delicate (available from Oriental supermarkets). Cider vinegar is good to use because it contains malic acid, which aids digestion.

## Pickles and Relishes

**Horseradish** Forms the basis of a useful sauce for nut roasts. Check the labels and choose one without additives.

**Mango Chutney** Like most chutneys, this is high in sugar, but I keep a jar in the kitchen because I like it occasionally as a 'dip' for nut rissoles or with curries.

**Mayonnaise** I generally find that I only use small quantities of mayonnaise at a time so, mostly, it isn't worthwhile making my own. I therefore keep a jar of additive-free, ready-prepared mayonnaise in the refrigerator.

**Olives** Big, juicy, black olives make a piquant garnish for hummus (see page 42), some salads and pizza.

## Spreads

**Vegetarian Spread or Pâté** A good vegetarian spread or pâté can also be very popular with non-vegetarians. Different flavors are available from health stores.

**Yeast Extract** The flavors of different brands of yeast extract vary, so try small jars of different types until you find your favorite. If you're relying on yeast extract as a source of B12, read the labels, because quantities differ between the various brands. You will probably find that your family become addicted to one type and nothing else will do!

## Jelling and Raising Agents

**Baking Powder, Baking Soda, Cream of Tartar** The first two appear in the cake and scone recipes; cream of tartar (a pinch of) is added to egg whites when making meringues.

**Vegetarian Gelatine** This is used instead of ordinary gelatine (which is made from animals' hooves) and is made from a seaweed called agar agar. Buy it from health stores and follow the simple instructions on the packet. Vegetarian jellies, though not a 'whole food', can be bought at health stores and are useful for a child's birthday party or easy dessert.

**Yeast** Baking yeast is different from brewer's yeast, and is needed for the bread recipe on page 20; buy dry yeast (or 'quick-acting' instant dry yeast) in small quantities as it does not keep well. If you're using ascorbic acid (vitamin C) in the bread recipe, buy this from the drug store; it keeps well.

# —EQUIPMENT A TO Z—

## A

**APPLE CORER**   Used for removing the core of apples in one piece, a useful implement if you like baked apples.

## B

**BAKING PANS AND SHEETS**   Choose the strongest you can find, then they will last a lifetime. A basic list would be: $2 \times 8 \times 5 \times 3\frac{1}{2}$ inch and $1 \times 2$ pound capacity bread pan (my preference is for the strong, deep traditional-style); an 8 inch round, deep cake pan for baking fruit cakes (if this has a loose base or is a springform type it can be used for cheesecake); a strong baking or cookie sheet, the largest that will fit in your oven; an 8 inch pie ring (this stands on a cookie sheet); a shallow muffin pan with 12 sections; an 8 inch square cake pan; 2 shallow jelly roll pans measuring $7 \times 11$ inches and $10 \times 14$ inches; 2 deep layer cake pans, measuring 7 inches and/or 9 inches. Needed for one recipe in this book and useful to have are 6 or 8 individual tart pans or rings, 4 inches across.

**BOWLS**   My preference is for clear, heatproof glass, in a range of sizes. A $2\frac{1}{2}$ pint ceramic bowl is also needed for the Christmas pudding recipe and the frozen Christmas pudding.

**BREAD CROCK**   This is the best container for storing bread.

## C

**CASSEROLES AND DISHES**   The most useful sizes and shapes for family cooking are: a round 8-9 inch pie pan; a big round white 12 inch pizza pan; a big casserole, or Dutch oven; 3 rectangular gratin dishes at least 2 inches deep and measuring $9 \times 8\frac{1}{2}$ inches, $7\frac{1}{2} \times 11\frac{1}{2}$ inches and $12\frac{1}{2} \times 9\frac{1}{2}$ inches. In addition, it's useful to have a set of little custard cups and small bowls, an oval serving plate and some small bowls for serving pâtés and dips.

**CHOPPING BOARD**   I recommend a sturdy wooden one, 1 inch thick and not less than $16 \times 12$ inches. This can double as a pastry board.

**COLANDER**   A substantial, stainless steel colander is best; it is useful for draining pasta and vegetables, and can double as a steamer if you put it above a large saucepan of boiling water and cover with a top or piece of silver foil.

## E

**EGG BEATER**   The best combination is a hand electric mixer, and a medium-sized wire whisk (I like a fairly small, light one).

## F

**FOOD PROCESSOR/BLENDER**   A food processor is a very useful piece of equipment in the vegetarian kitchen; it will save you a great deal of time and effort. I recommend getting a large one and keeping it out in the kitchen, ready for action, if space permits. A blender is a good alternative, but not as versatile. Both will grate nuts and blend soups and purées; the food processor will, however, do many other jobs and handle larger quantities at a time.

**FONDUE BURNER OR CHAFING DISH**   By no means essential, but a handy extra if you like fondue.

**FORK**   One or two old forks are useful for pricking the tops of pies and cookies and for making a neat edging on pies.

## G

**GARLIC PRESS**   Buy a good strong one with large holes.

**GRATER**   Choose a box grater which you can stand on your chopping board and which has different sizes of holes on the various sides. A small hand-held rotary grater with a set of different-sized grating drums is also a useful piece of equipment. A nutmeg grater (with a compartment for storing the nutmeg) is also useful.

## J

**JARS**   These are essential for storing dry ingredients such as pulses and cereals. Also useful for sprouting beans and seeds (see page 30).

## K

**KITCHEN SCISSORS**   Buy sharp, stainless steel scissors.

**KNIVES**   Good, sharp knives can save hours. I like traditional French knives which are expensive but last well. The most useful size is one with a 5 inch blade. Buy a knife sharpener to sharpen it with. In addition, a serrated stainless steel knife (also with a 5 inch blade) is useful for preparing avocado and delicate fruits such as peaches and mangoes. A small, sharp curved grapefruit knife is useful not only for cutting round the inside of grapefruits but also for removing the centers of tomatoes for stuffing.

# M

**MEASURING CUPS**   Usually sold individually or in a 2 cup capacity, marked in millilitres and cups.

**MEASURING SPOONS**   Buy a set of tablespoons and teaspoons.

**MICROWAVE**   Not an essential piece of equipment, but very useful in the vegetarian kitchen, as in any other. If you're buying one, I strongly recommend a model which combines a built-in browning device and conventional oven heater. This type gives the speed of microwave cooking together with the crispness and appetizing appearance of traditional cooking.

**MORTAR AND PESTLE**   Not by any means essential, but good for crushing whole spices.

# O

**ORANGE JUICER**   The type which has a container to collect the juice is useful if you squeeze oranges in any quantity.

# P

**PAPER GOODS ETC**   Wax paper, silver foil, paper cupcake cases, plastic wrap, paper towels, plastic bags, and toothpicks.

**PASTRY BAG**   Useful for putting meringue mixture on to a cookie sheet and for adding a pretty, quick garnish to cakes. Buy a large nylon one with a plain tip and a medium-sized shell tip or a selection of tips.

**PASTRY BRUSH**   I like those which have plenty of bristles and a wooden handle.

**PASTRY (OR COOKIE) CUTTERS**   Buy a set of round cutters measuring 2 inches, 2½ inches and 3 inches.

**PLASTIC CONTAINERS**   Keep several sizes, for such jobs as storing food in the refrigerator and for freezing ice cream and sherbet. Choose the varieties with good airtight covers.

**POPSICLE STICKS AND MOULDS**   Use these for making healthy treats for kids!

**POTATO PEELER OR VEGETABLE PARER**   I prefer the swivel type, with a long handle.

**PRESSURE COOKER**   This is not essential, but can be a great time-saver. Choose a stainless steel one, which is safer to use than aluminum.

# R

**ROLLING PIN**   Choose a plain wooden one without handles, at least 16 inches long.

# S

**SALAD BOWL**   A large china, glass or wooden bowl, and a pair of salad servers is essential for mixing and serving salads.

**SAUCEPANS**   My preference is for good-quality heavy stainless steel pans. Buy a range of sizes, including a large one for cooking pasta, stews and stir-fries (taking the place of a wok). If this also has a steamer basket to fit on top, you will have an extremely versatile and useful piece of equipment.

**SCALES**   I like the type with a large bowl for weighing the ingredients and a dial which you can re-set, so that you can add one ingredient after another.

**SKEWERS**   Choose thin stainless steel skewers for making kebabs and use them for testing to see if vegetables and cakes are done.

**SKILLET**   Ideally, buy one measuring 10¾ inches across, for general frying, and one measuring 8 inches for pancakes.

**SPATULA KNIFE**   Ideally, it's useful to have 2 – a long and a short one, both with fairly firm blades.

**SPOONS**   One or two metal tablespoons are useful, plus a few teaspoons, also a metal slotted spoon for draining.

**SPROUTER**   This is a useful piece of equipment if you like sprouted seeds and beans, because it's a tidy way of growing them and means you can prepare three batches at once. You can usually buy sprouters at health stores and large department stores.

**STANDING ELECTRIC MIXER**   Not as useful or as versatile for vegetarian cooking as a food processor, although I use one for beating and for making cakes. A hand electric mixer would be just as good and is more versatile.

**STRAINERS AND SIEVES**   Two are useful – a large metal one, which can double as steamer when placed over a saucepan of simmering water and covered with aluminum foil and a large nylon one for straining delicate fruit mixtures.

**WOODEN SPOONS**   It's useful to have two or three spoons of different sizes; I like the small, straight ones with shallow bowls which you can buy at stores selling kitchen equipment.

# Z

**ZESTER**   Not essential, but a handy little gadget for raking the peel off oranges and lemons (instead of using a grater).

# INDEX